No Country

No Country

Working-Class Writing in the Age of Globalization

SONALI PERERA

Columbia University Press
New York

Columbia University Press
Publishers Since 1893
New York   Chichester, West Sussex
cup.columbia.edu

Copyright © 2014 Columbia University Press
Paperback edition, 2018
All rights reserved
Parts of chapter 3 are adapted from Sonali Perera, "Rethinking Working-Class Literature: Feminism, Globalization, and Socialist Ethics," *Differences* 19.1 (2008): 1–31.
Part of the introduction is adapted from Sonali Perera, "Working-Class Writing and the Use Value of the Literary," which appeared in *PMLA* 127.4 (October 2012): 932–938. Reprinted by permission of the copyright owner, The Modern Language Association of America.

Library of Congress Cataloging-in-Publication Data
Perera, Sonali, 1971–
No Country : working-class writing in the age of globalization / Sonali Perera.
   pages cm
Includes bibliographical references and index.
ISBN 978-0-231-15194-8 (cloth)—ISBN 978-0-231-15195-5 (pbk.)
—ISBN 978-0-231-52544-2 (e-book)
1. Working class writings—History and criticism. 2. Working class in literature. I. Title.

PN56.L22P47   2013
809'.93355—dc23   2013012758

Cover design by Noah Arlow
Cover image: © Kevin Frayer/AP Photo

For my parents, Joseph and Mallika Perera

and

For my grandmother, Sheila May Edirisinghe
(1919–2002)

> And could you not make a cameo of this
> and pin it onto your aesthetic hearts?
> —Tillie Olsen

Contents

Acknowledgments   xi

Introduction: World Literature or Working-Class
Literature in the Age of Globalization?   1

1. Colonialism, Race, and Class: Mulk Raj Anand's
   Coolie as a Literary Representation of the Subaltern   27

2. Postcolonial Sri Lanka and "Black Struggles for
   Socialism": Socialist Ethics in Ambalavaner
   Sivanandan's *When Memory Dies*   47

3. Gender, Genre, and Globalization   75

4. Socialized Labor and the Critique of Identity Politics:
   Bessie Head's *A Question of Power*   122

Epilogue: Working-Class Writing and the Social
Imagination   164

Notes	173
Bibliography	205
Index	215

Acknowledgments

Even as the culture of specific institutions changes and intellectual communities disband and re-form there is a sense of security and assurance in this thought: the U.S. academy is a much bigger space—bigger, too, in the sense of "generous"—than the fiefdoms of any one university or department. The collaborative works of the communities and other collectivities that define it and supplement it are wide ranging, transnational. At the risk of sounding like a liberal humanist, I will say it: to this Sri-Lankan-by-way-of-England, postcolonial/immigrant academic, this nonplace, the U.S. academy, has always represented a hospitable "home" of sorts—a space to live, breathe, dispute, and share ideas.

At Columbia University, I was incredibly fortunate to work closely with one of the most inspiring, generous, and challenging intellectuals in the U.S. academy—Gayatri Chakravorty Spivak. I am grateful to her for giving me so much of her valuable time. I thank her for being such a supportive mentor. I can only hope that these pages do justice, in some small measure, to her teaching, activism, and theory. As a junior faculty member, I have also had other mentors and friends who have helped me find my voice and my way and have given me critical feedback during crucial stages of this project's development. Heartfelt thanks to Josie Saldaña, David Eng, and Brent Edwards for always giving me the best advice.

This book would never have seen the light of day without the love, support, intellectual generosity, and *wicked* cool of a core group of friends and interlocutors. I thank Edlie Wong, Stacy Klein, Dominic Leggett, Chris Chism, and Suzanne Daly. Stacy, Edlie, Chris, and Dominic read the manuscript in various rough draft stages and offered insightful feedback and, when needed, unsparing criticism. David Golumbia, too, read much of the manuscript in its piecemeal incarnations. I thank him for his insights. This book is so much the better for the many, many conversations I've had with these friends. Indrani Chatterjee gave me brilliant feedback and also showed me that, no matter the outcome, some institutional battles are worth fighting for. Love and respect to her.

At Columbia, Berkeley, Duke, and elsewhere there were also other teachers who gave me words and books to live by. I owe a huge debt of gratitude to Rob Nixon for introducing me to the amazing writings of Bessie Head. I also thank him for his wisdom and kindness and for making Columbia a hospitable place for graduate students working in the field of postcolonial studies. From Priscialla Wald, Rob Nixon, Gauri Viswanathan, Ann McClintock, Susan Schweik, Janet Adelman (RIP), Ojars Kratins, and David Lloyd I learned that it is not how we professionalize our graduate and undergraduate students but how we socialize them within the profession that matters. I thank Peter Hitchcock for introducing me to the right debates in British working-class studies during the preliminary stages of dissertation writing.

While this book was begun at Columbia, I firmly believe that it could only have been completed here at Hunter College of the City University of New York. I am grateful to my brilliant Hunter students for their challenging questions and their commitment to struggles for social justice. I learn from them each day. I thank these former graduate and undergraduate students at CUNY and elsewhere for their presence in my classes: Subha Dayal, Lauren Kollar, Stephanie Basile, Bretney Moore, Allison Shelton, Shakti Jaising, Anantha Sudhakhar, Sonali Barua, Nimanthi Perera-Rajasingham, Anthony Americo, Michelle Chan, Karen Gellen, Nami Shin, and Megan Paustian. But in order to thrive in this profession—not just survive it— every junior faculty member should also encounter a supportive feminist chair. I thank Cristina Alfar, my chair, for her integrity and goodness. Along with Barbara Webb, Jeremy Glick, Tanya Agathocleus, Janet Neary, Meena Alexander, Marlene Hennessy, Leigh Jones, Gavin Hollis, Ramesh Mallipeddi, Harriet Luria, Rupal Oza, Ruchi Chaturvedi, Jan Heller Levi, and Thom Taylor, she makes Hunter a joyous place to work.

A loving shout-out to my "family" in New York. During many days of writing and revising, I was sustained by sumptuous meals and political debates at the Bose-Patel household. My gratitude to Maneesha Patel, Satyajit Bose, and especially Tansen and Zaleh Bose-Patel for community and laughter.

At a crucial turning point in this book's history, I was fortunate to find it had many supporters from across disciplines: Ed Cohen, Jasbir Puar, Julie Livingston, Sumit Guha, Michael McKeon, Matt Buckley, Richard Dienst, John McClure, Harriet Davidson, Abena Busia, Elin Diamond, Ellen Rooney, David Kazanjian, Ben Baer, Shuang Shen, Mary P. Sheridan-Rabideau, Minkah Makalani, Nancy Hewitt, Ethel Brooks, Carlos Decena, Nicole Fleetwood, Jackie Miller, Sandy Flitterman-Lewis, Val Daniel, Stephan Clingman, Stephane Robolin, Evie Shockley, Cheryl Wall, Vicky Unruh, Marianne Dekoven, Ritty Lukose, Ania Loomba, Bruce Robbins, Ranji Khanna, Srinivas Aravamudan, and Chandan Reddy. I thank these scholars for their encouragement. Their support has meant the world to me. Special thanks are due to a critical mass of Sri Lankanist scholars and activists for their spirit of camaraderie and collaboration: Ahilan Kadirgamar, Vasuki Nesiah, Fara Haniffa, Kitana Anand, Cenan Pirani, and Sharika Thiranagama. Kumari Jayawardena encouraged a clueless undergraduate researcher and set her on the right course very early on. I thank her for her uncompromising integrity and her incredible warmth and generosity of spirit. I thank Qadri Ismail for helpful criticisms offered up during the early stages of writing.

I've benefited from invitations to present parts of this book at the SSA (Social Scientists Association) in Colombo, at the Franke Institute for the Humanities at the University of Chicago, at Duke University's New Beginnings Faculty Seminar, at Columbia University's South Asia Studies University Seminar, at IRW (Rutgers Institute for Research on Women) faculty seminar, and at the Five College faculty seminar in Marxist and postcolonial theory at the University of Massachusetts,

Amherst. This book has been supported by the Hunter College President's Fund for Faculty Advancement Award. At Columbia University Press, thanks to my editor, Philip Leventhal, for his perceptive suggestions during crucial phases of revision. Also at Columbia University Press, I thank Whitney Johnson, Leslie Kriesel, and Kerri Cox Sullivan for all their help. I'm deeply grateful to Kerri and Leslie for their dedication and professionalism throughout the copyediting stages of production. The entire book is better because of their thoughtful work on the manuscript.

A book such as this one, which has taken so long to research and write, also takes a toll on family. I thank my patient family in Sri Lanka and in California. Savithri and Chandra Edirisinghe hosted me during numerous research trips to Sri Lanka. My sister, Shamali, and brother-in-law, Steve, constantly divert my attention to the funnier things in life. My parents, Mallika and Joseph Perera, have always been there for me. I could not have finished this book without their love and support. This book is dedicated to them. It is also for my grandmother, Sheila May Edirisinghe (1919–2002), who was always in my corner and always maintained that I was a "clever girl."

No Country

INTRODUCTION

World Literature or Working-Class Literature in the Age of Globalization?

> Everyone reads life and the world like a book. Even the so-called "illiterate." But especially the "leaders" of our society, the most "responsible" nondreamers: the politicians, the businessmen, the ones who make plans. Without the reading of the world as a book, there is no prediction, no planning, no taxes, no laws, no welfare, no war. Yet these leaders read the world in terms of rationality and averages, as if it were a text book. The world actually writes itself with the many-leveled, unfixable intricacy and openness of a work of literature.
> —Gayatri Chakravorty Spivak, *In Other Worlds*

> Munoo read the blue Hindustani inscription on the sacks of grain. But he was too young to know the laws of political economy, especially as they govern the export of wheat from India to England.
> —Mulk Raj Anand, *Coolie*

> The question to be answered next is: "What makes a class?"
> —Karl Marx, *Capital*

Mulk Raj Anand's 1936 late colonial/depression–era proletarian novel *Coolie* represents the paradoxes of economic globalization from an obscured vantage point—the necessarily occluded perspective of a semiliterate Indian grain market "coolie"/child laborer.[1] The subaltern antihero of Anand's novel reads globalization—here the removal of trade barriers, enabling the closer integration of disparate, unequal economies—from below.[2] His instructions are to load sacks of wheat to be transported from the local merchant to the exporters, but our protagonist, Munoo, becomes caught up in rumination on the opaqueness of world-systems theory. In a paradoxical didactic intrusion that simultaneously teaches and withholds, Anand addresses the reader of working-class fiction. We are told that "Munoo read the blue Hindustani inscription on the sacks of grain. But he was too young to know the laws of political economy, especially as they govern the export of wheat from India to England" (122). "Empire is materializing before [his] very eyes." Munoo correctly reads but cannot "become conscious" of the big picture.[3] From close up the signs don't make sense. The world system does not cohere into view.

As the reader soon discovers, Anand's novel is comprised of other such instances—breaks in the story line, key moments of textual irony, speech interferences, and "interruption[s] from a source relating 'otherwise' . . . to the continuous unfolding of the main system of meaning."[4] Ultimately, the call to revolution is interrupted in *Coolie*. All sorts of impediments (some logical, some fantastical) intervene to disrupt and derail narrative momentum. An unexpected conciliatory speech delivered by a calculating trade unionist, an unsubstantiated rumor about racially motivated child abductions, factory management–instigated "communal" rioting, and finally the kidnapping of the protagonist himself all lead up to the pivotal anticlimactic moment: the striking factory workers must be made to abandon their course of action.

Anand's child-protagonist cannot know the ins and outs of trade negotiations and the geopolitics of crisis management, but his reader is supplied with clues. The strike must be disrupted and the revolution will not take place, but not for the usual reasons suggested by sociologists of culture or even labor historians: the fatalism of the Indian working class, its "relative infancy," and so on. The subtext of Anand's *Coolie*, in fact, struggles with the problem of how to narrate an inconvenient truth that remains as persistent and present for post–Bretton Woods globalization as it did for capital and class relations in 1930s late colonialism. The contrived disruption of the strike and the crisis management efforts that follow constitute the place of an ethical aporia. The predicament of short time for the workers of the global South is somehow connected with successful socialist agitation "at home," in this case, in England. (Asymmetrically related, perhaps, is the contemporary case of rising wage demands of striking workers in China prompting transnational corporations to seek out ever cheaper labor pools, currently in the free-trade-zone regions of Bangladesh.) In fact, the internationalizing of production—globalization—leads not to the internationalizing of the workforce—internationalism—but rather to its polar opposite: an exacerbation of divisions, pitting national working class against national working class, industry against industry. In one of Anand's less subtle, less imaginative incarnations of the same dilemma, we encounter a dramatization of the problem of globalization as the international division of labor in the compressed character-logic of the glaringly evil Jimmie Thomas, the Lancashire weaver-turned-abusive-foreman in the colonies.[5]

How can there be a novel of the international working class under such circumstances? The call to revolution must be interrupted. Anand's novel confronts the ethical challenge of understanding working-class writing in a comparative, not competitive, frame. His ironic staging of Munoo's inability to make meaning of what he knows—and in fact embodies—correlates with the author's representation of a failure of the social imagination.[6] But whereas Mulk Raj Anand's *Coolie* brings into focus the difference between "feeling global" and "feeling international," in her time-bending, deterritorializing, surrealist-realist *A Question of Power* (1973), written as an epilogue of sorts to Anand's earlier milieu of anticolonial progressive writers' associations, South African born refugee/stateless writer Bessie Head asks anew the question, "What makes a class?"[7] Which structures of feeling and ethical narratives give shape and meaning to class as a unity-in-dispersal? What constitutes working-class writing apart from, or in addition to, alibis of origins and identity politics? "It seemed almost incidental that he was African [begins Head's by turns introspective, by turns telescopic novel]. So vast had his inner perceptions grown over the years that he preferred an identification with mankind to an identification with a particular environment. And yet, as an African, he seemed to have made one of the most perfect statements: I am just anyone" (11). *A Question of Power* calls for a comparative, internationalist optics of class struggle that sees the world as written from locations of peripheral labor, but always in terms of shifting relationships of power. In Head's aspirational, ethical vision, internationalism is not simply an effect or corollary of globalization, but as she demonstrates, the relationship between the two is a problem of ethics—rather than one of history as a fait accompli, or of market-driven economisms—

that must be negotiated. The relationship between the capitalist use of forced accumulation and the socialist ethical use of voluntary accumulation remains to be considered, not only in the context of grand narratives of revolutionary Marxism, but also in the daily, improvisatory practices and dialogic exchanges of the everyday.

Can there be a novel of the international working class despite the conditions and constraints of economic globalization? Extending and elaborating upon the far-reaching implications of this question, we might ask: What does it mean to invoke working-class writing as a mode of internationalism in an age of comparative advantage and outsourcing? By way of answering these questions, I discuss different yet aligned writers, such as Head and Anand, and propose a more varied scope for working-class literature than has been conceived of in previous comparative studies. More precisely, I argue the point that working-class writing can only be understood in terms of its interrelationships and dialogic tensions. Bringing together classic works by writers of working-class origins with novels, short stories, and poetry by working-class, as well as politically committed, writers of proletarian fiction from the radical 1930s to the postcolonial neoliberal present, *No Country* considers the concept of working-class writing as it relates to several interconnected senses: as social formation (not institution), cultural practice, and serial interrupted form.

This involves rethinking the genre of the working-class novel itself. In the global Anglophone academy, working-class writing, even when considered in a comparative frame, has, arguably, its ideal types, its chief illustrative contexts, and its dominant narratives.[8] Its touchstones and frames of references are drawn from British working-class and socialist fiction, U.S. popular-front radicalism, and the brief proletarian moment of the 1930s. (Anticolonial proletarian fiction—a novel like Mulk Raj Anand's 1936 *Coolie*, which, as discussed, explores the predicament of unorganized child labor in colonial India—for example, fits into this schema, but only parenthetically, as an overdetermined, if "handicapped," product of its times—the literary internationalism of the radical 1930s.) Working-class literature's emblematized and celebrated narratives are tied to the time line and mindset of revolutions as well as to particular successful *national* labor struggles.

When it *has* been considered as a cross-historical and (potentially, at least) transnational genre, working-class writing is classified in the strictest sense as writing by authors of working-class origin. Documentary realism and biographical testimony are deemed its cherished forms. "It is better that the literature of labor be barely 'literature' than for it to be barely labor," established critics of working-class fiction might admonish us;[9] Peter Hitchcock, for example—while acknowledging that "class effects" of working-class writing are more heterogeneous than individual intentions of writers—would still designate working-class writing as a category separate from that of the writing of committed socialists of non-working-class backgrounds. He would define working-class writing as categorically distinct from other overlapping groupings of literary internationalism, such as proletarian writing or socialist fiction.[10] It is hard to argue with such clarity of focus and political commitment.

The argument of literary historians of a "world republic of letters," however, emerges from a very different standpoint: Pascale Casanova's global literary history of "intellectual internationalism," for example, categorically excludes a consideration of the literary internationalism of working-class literature. Her argument is secured by the assumption that only inutilitarian, "autonomous" literary "forms detached from political purpose" can be considered quintessentially literary.[11] The depoliticization of literature, then, becomes a necessary precondition for generating works of formal genius. According to Casanova, the literature of the working-class struggle could never generate its own improvisational forms of world literature. Even as the primary aim of some literary historians of world literature is to cultivate (in some cases reconstruct) an ideal of denationalized literature predicated on the currency of autonomous form, working-class writing and its multilingual, multiform literary and political practices does not enter into their thinking. This other genealogy is repressed in cartographies of a world republic of letters and in certain circumscribed maps of transnational modernism.[12]

Working against the current of prevailing orthodoxies, I argue in the pages that follow for reconceiving working-class literature based on shared sociologies of form and comparative ideologies of socialist ethics. Working-class writings from different parts of the globe share more points of connection than are acknowledged by most literary histories. In connecting traditions of literary radicalism from the 1930s to the feminist recovery projects of the 1970s, to the anticolonial and postcolonial fiction of the 1960s decolonization movements, and to contemporary counterglobalist struggles, this book makes visible textual, political, and historical—not historicist—linkages that map the discursive unity of working-class writing across the global North–South divide. In brief, my objectives are twofold: I want to create the terms of an alternative genealogy for working-class writing as world literature that move away from a literary historiography organized by national periodization to the crossings and crisscrossings of cartographies of labor; likewise, along with Terry Eagleton, I argue that working-class writing "interrogates the ruling *definitions* of literature" itself—models of individual authors and monovocal sovereign subjects among them.[13]

However, by moving beyond the interventions of British Marxism and monolingual traditions, I am proposing a broader *comparative* focus. Specific works studied include novels by Indian anticolonial writer Anand (1905–2004), U.S. proletarian writer Tillie Olsen (1912 or 1913–2007), Sri Lankan Tamil/black British writer and political journalist Ambalavaner Sivanandan (b. 1923), Indian writer and bonded labor activist Mahasweta Devi (b. 1926), and South African–born Botswanan writer Bessie Head (1937–1986), as well as the serialized fiction and poetry published under the collective signature *Dabindu* (1984–), a group of free-trade-zone garment factory workers and feminist activists in contemporary postcolonial Sri Lanka. Beginning with the period of the global trade and currency crisis of the 1930s and ending with the contemporary period of neoliberal globalization, these writers' works reflect flash points along the time line of 1929–2001.

In Bessie Head's representation of the fluid, changing calculus of the international division of labor, the unpredictable human heterodox "connections" that happen aren't simply trade-related, prescribed by left-party politics, or organized by race and class divisions. If "the social" is produced as the differánce of globalization, the tension between competing measurements—social versus global, national versus international—is given a new, discursive life and set to work in the ideology *and form* of her *A Question of Power*. A formalized pattern of interruptions at the center of the novel, which registers as an ethico-political failing or deficiency in Anand's text, both compares and contrasts with the social and political meanings of similar forms in the writing of Head and of other working-class writers that I examine in this book.

Broken lines, interrupted narratives, and the inability to formalize meaning are resignified toward a different end in the writings of Tillie Olsen, Anand's 1930s contemporary. Writing from within the U.S. proletarian tradition, Olsen issues a challenge to the reader who would too quickly, or too glibly, reify representations of working-class struggle. If in *Coolie* we encounter how the text performs an inability to fix meaning—"[child labor] is too young to know the laws of political economy"—in Olsen's writing we meet with an active resistance to attaching a fixed, dominant meaning to figures, forms, and narratives always in flux. "I will never total it all. I will never come in to say," maintains the narrator protagonist of "I Stand Here Ironing." In Olsen's deliberately unfinished novel from the 1930s, as in her short stories and poetry, the reader-critic in search of a perfect/ed aesthetic object is admonished: "And could you not make a cameo of this and pin it to your aesthetic hearts?" Here the resistance to formalization speaks to a reluctance to give a definitive shape and make a representative claim upon the genre of working-class literature. Such a principled refusal becomes connected to the question of how to represent "the social," not global. As rhetorical and political strategies, interruptions figure the changing, moving, disappearing worlds of labor. Interpolations and interferences communicate the ethical challenge of how to represent working-class internationalism as a necessarily incomplete totality whose shape must remain partial. But furthermore, delay, deferral, time lag, and interruptions are never just clever, postmodern stylistic devices for Olsen: They are the very conditions and constraints that produce the working-class writer. Olsen as well as many others of the writers considered here must wrest a vision of aesthetics and politics from the periodic breaks opened up in the working-class writer's working day.

RETHINKING WORKING-CLASS LITERATURE AS SERIAL INTERRUPTED FORM

The preceding interrelated readings of Anand and Head establish the discursive context surrounding the subject of my book. This book, however, is not just about tracking the formal and ideological connections across the texts of two writers from the global South. The attention to these ironic and deauthorizing moments in Head and Anand dramatizes how the global is incommensurable with the social and where and how and in whose interest the difference between these two categories is elided. But, most important, the preceding comparative reading also serves to illustrate a basic, but overlooked point about my object of study: the disappearing object of working-class literature itself—class. Class is a relationship, not a fixed static object, and its general concept cannot be understood in terms of an isolated frame of reference privileging the exceptionalism of this or that successful working class in history.

The method of this book, though indebted to the work of labor historians, avoids extrapolating general truths about capital logic and class relations on the basis of any particular historical event, any brief, resplendent moment of revolution. The point is not to depose the epistemological centrality of the first industrial revolution by proposing, instead, that we now turn to agrarian revolts in Naxalbari. While I do restore to view relatively obscured, devalued narrative contexts in global labor history—a coolie's view of the 1930s global trade and financial crisis, a refugee's critical perspective on 1980s sub-Saharan development projects—this "recovery" effort is not the central intervention of this book. In that sense, to say that this book *places* working-class writing in a global frame would be a misstatement. Working-class writing is antinationalist in concept and *therefore* internationalist—global in a very specific, ideological sense. Related to this point, we must see that class subjectivities are always constitutively against simple identity politics.

Instead, *No Country* reevaluates the complex period-genre category of working-class writing, moving away from ontologizing working-class origins and fêted meanings of class limited to revolutionary contexts. I propose instead that we take stock also of what are deemed nonrepresentative, even so-called *failed* examples, that we consider working-class writing's repressed antinomies, its constitutive gaps and interruptions. I argue that the concept of working-class writing as a literary tradition is predicated in suppressing (or overlooking) the meaning of working-class writing as interruption. "Proletarian revolutions," Marx writes, "constantly engage in self-criticism, and in repeated interruptions of their own course."[14] With this in mind, I read working-class writing in the light of moments in which Marx appears to be revising and redefining such seemingly self-explanatory terms as "proletarian" and "revolution." Discontinuity in its myriad signatures—no centered subject, but a parsing of changing scenes and movable parts—comprises the figural logic of working-class writing. Repeated interruptions constitute its basis. In the place of the style of the individualist utterance are elliptical marks, interruptions, speech interferences, and signs of heteroglossia. An aesthetics and politics (and ethics, as I will show) of working-class literature cannot be gauged on the basis of a direct, unbroken line of institutions and traditions extending from the Communist Internationals to the World Social Forum. It cannot be compartmentalized by histories of specific nations or industries. It cannot be apprehended in the register of global English alone. The range of experimental forms and emergent figures studied here is testimony to the fact that the conventions of working-class literature cannot be extrapolated solely from those of the Euro-US proletarian novel or postcolonial fiction.[15]

For some critics, especially those who take their bearings from arguments in British Marxism, the departure point—if not foundational basis—for defining working-class writing must firmly remain the working-class origins of the author. To begin a book on working-class literature by affirming the instability of class as a concept and by invoking a theory of reading working-class literature primarily for its ethical (as opposed to political or historical) lessons challenges the bedrock principles of historicism and humanism underlying foundational arguments.[16] The proper place to begin, such critics might argue, would be by reaffirming the unshakeable and straightforward proposition: "Working-class literature is the literature of working-class people." Realism (not surrealism) and testimony (not self-interruption) are its cherished forms. The time line and mindset of revolutions, masculinity, and the metropole are its privileged archetypes and topoi. The shift from questions of history and agency to literature and ethics—is that not a surreptitious formalism masquerading as historicism, these critics might ask?

The claim of shared aesthetic ideologies, political and textual effects, or comparative literary forms as defining criteria for working-class literature (as opposed to or in addition to class origins) might be strenuously protested, for divergent reasons, by working-class literature's strongest detractors and proponents alike. In this book, however, the center of gravity is deliberately displaced and reversed. Literature and the literariness of working-class literature assume a logical and ethical priority over historically validated narratives of working-class agency. My focus is primarily on working-class writing as literary formation and, if I might put it this way, on the use-value of the literary, and yet the burden of my argument is to convincingly demonstrate that these two *seemingly* divergent approaches are not mutually exclusive. That is to say, the emphasis on literature does not preclude us from thinking class as a historical category. Rather, as Raymond Williams teaches us, figures and forms "at the edge of semantic availability" can compel us to confront how we produce history's concept. Of what is history made as it happens? What structures of feeling and dialectical tensions are in excess of retrospectively formalized, institutionalized meanings of history?

At one point in *Marxism and Literature*, Williams, referring to the commodification and co-optation of a particular "emergent" aesthetic tradition, calls for a recognition of the fluidity and ephemerality of figures and archetypes that retroactively become reconstituted as vaunted grand narratives—thereby discarding the oppositional elements that rubbed against the grain of official history in their initial conditions of emergence. In this instance, Williams is describing the complex, slippery process by which traditions of English working-class writing become incorporated into the (national) "cultural dominant." He was not thinking of the changing configurations of the international division of labor, nor of placing working-class writing in a comparative frame, yet his insight into the constitutive, albeit *precarious*, potentiality of working-class writing has bearing upon this study. His idiosyncratic line of thinking has further implications for the ethical questions at the heart of my book.

Because we cannot generalize its meaning from any particular historical moment, we must keep thinking of "class" as a relationship. In working-class writing this predicament is dramatized in plot devices, figures and forms of interruption that represent alternative traditions of internationalism, untimely narratives, the ordinary, the longue durée, and even an ethics of historical materialism. "Marxism is not a historicism" and neither are class relations—nor, by extension, is working-class literature.[17] Unless we come to terms with this structural and structuring aspect of class—"repeated interruptions" constitute its basis—we are doomed to reproduce, legitimizing by reversal, hierarchies of representation and power: now centering the periphery, now deriving our ideal types from India and China, even as previously we turned to Thompson's "freeborn Englishman" as a chief frame of reference for extrapolating general theories of class. Unless we read—"read" in the robust sense of "reading-as-interpreting"—the immanent provisionality of class as paradoxically its failing *and* its conditions of possibility, we will reproduce reified ideologies, rather than set for ourselves the challenge to imagine anew an ethics of historical materialism.[18] Our theories will be set in the service of merely the best, most successful working class in a particular moment in history.[19] The connection/disconnection figured in serial form represents both the ethical aporia and the open-ended conditions of possibility that constitute working-class literature, which must always be considered in a comparative frame. "It is hard for an Englishman to talk definitely about proletarian art, because in England it has been a genre with settled principles, and such as there is of it, that I have seen, is bad," observes William Empson.[20] This book takes up in earnest the question opened up by the latter part of Empson's haphazard subjective musings: What does it mean to consider working-class writing as a genre without settled principles—and to read this dispersal as the conditions of its possibility, rather than as a failing.

Characterized by an unfinished, and therefore *necessarily collaborative*, form, the working-class writings discussed here anticipate a new shape and ideological grounding for the concept of a collective subject—one that self-critically figures an ethics of historical materialism. By the same token, however, it becomes clear that the moments of willful deauthorization, self-criticism, altruism, effacement, anonymity, generosity, humility (in Head, Anand, and *Dabindu*, as well as in the uncompleted texts and moments of parabasis in Olsen) presume a very different meaning for collective selves and others than what has conventionally been celebrated by historians of class struggle. Such conventions are assuredly at odds with the key words and concepts of E. P. Thompson's lexicon—those of free will, aspiration, "making" (as in the self-made working-class), and "time discipline" (versus "untimely").

Other contemporary commentators on the ontology and history of global class struggles might explain these formal shifts in meaning as a casualty of our times. Hardt and Negri, for example, argue that the driving force of coalitional class politics is no longer the industrial working class, but "the multitude"—a new collective subject of resistance to changing configurations of postmodern, "postindustrial" global capital:

> Then the *national* proletariat had as a primary task destroying itself insofar as it was defined by the nation and thus bringing international solidarity out of the prison in which it had been trapped. International solidarity had to be recognized not as an act of charity or altruism for the good of others, a noble sacrifice for another national working class, but rather as proper to and inseparable from each national proletariat's own desire and struggle for liberation. (*Empire*, 49–50)

What is remarkably instructive and *revealing* about this passage is that, in addition to historicizing and theorizing the rise (and decline) of a particular phase of proletarian internationalism, Hardt and Negri are also arguing the case for a particular structure of feeling—self-interest, not altruism—that pertains to the successes of organized labor. Labor internationalism as an ideology, they suggest, must be understood as first arising from rational economic self-interest, not altruism or concern for others. A healthy sense of self-preservation—class interest as self-interest—underlies the making of the international working class in its—according to Hardt and Negri, now bygone—successful periods.

The ethical philosophy of the writers studied in this book proposes the exact inverse: self-interest as collective interest—"care of others as care of the self."[21] Never pure, sometimes ideologically compromised, the eccentric, other-centered structures of feeling they give language to map on to the challenges and tensions in imagining working-class writing in the age of globalization and outsourcing. How to think against one's own rational economic self-interest in the service of other (sometimes competing) class interests remains the basic ethical challenge of many of the improvisatory practices of working-class writing in its multilingual forms and its heterogeneous traditions. There is an epistemic and ethical gap between such competing frames of reference (between feelings of internationalism, the social imagination, and the structure of the international division of labor) for globalization that this book attempts to articulate across, turning to a political cultural imaginary of a dispersed, diffuse archive of working-class writing from across the North–South divide. While acknowledging that we owe a great deal to the aspirations and vision of *Empire* as a theoretical treatise and an activist polemic, my aim, nevertheless, is to direct attention to other texts and social meanings of "working class" and internationalism that supplement rather than supplant earlier ones.

As Raymond Williams reminds us, tradition understood in an instrumentalist sense is, in fact, properly speaking, selective and inert. Its viability is guaranteed by institutions: sometimes of education, sometimes of the state and civil society. But perversely, the durability of tradition, its stability, also proves to be a liability in a broader sense: that which reigns as dominant, hegemonic, or representative can remain so only at the cost of isolating "prominence" or representative status from the active, moving, revivifying substance of culture and practice as it is lived and reinvented in makeshift, ad hoc forms. What is constituted as tradition, then, is necessarily divorced from the dispersed assemblage of improvised practice and new experimental forms of the present. The historical and theoretical focus on solely "epochal" moments of synchronous strong will (and collectives of strong men) or on selective traditions of proletarian internationalism relegates working-class writing, a "living tradition," to the past:

> In . . . "epochal" analysis, a cultural process is seized as a cultural system, with determinate dominant features. . . . This emphasis on dominant and definitive lineaments and features is important and often, in practice, effective. But it then often happens that its methodology is preserved for the very different function of historical analysis, in which a sense of movement within what is ordinarily abstracted as a system is crucially necessary, especially if it is to connect with the future as well as with the past. (*Marxism*, 121)

Such an emphasis (on epochal analysis) prevents us from apprehending working-class writing (once again, in Williams's words) as a *formation*—that is to say, not only as an object of knowledge but as an aesthetic and political movement that is continuously supplemented. To grasp working-class writing as such a formation, a shifting set of alignments of worker-writers, labor activists, culture workers, readers, feminist activists, and translators is to rub against the institutionalized narratives of labor history and literary history. But formations by definition have tenuous links with institutions and hence are connected in looser, more creative ways to variable historical social processes. They are by nature ephemeral, provisional, anti-essentialist, and nonidentitarian in their very concept. Their provenance covers not just "the rise" but also the lateral "uneven development" of working-class culture and historical materialism.

This book will make the case that one can only properly come to terms with working-class writing by not only assessing epochal moments but also by considering its fleeting forms and sometimes devalued, discarded parts. And thus we give pride of place to the narrative of Mulk Raj Anand's *Coolie*—the other side of the industrial revolution in Britain. Alongside Tillie Olsen's classic proletarian novel from the 1930s, we read the stories of garment factory workers in Sri Lanka whose collaborative stories of self-making and self-sacrifice quickly live and die within the ephemerality of free-trade-zone periodicals. To add texture to a point made above via this excursus through Raymond Williams's observations on tradition, we might say the following: it is the case not only that globalization expands and complicates the object of working-class literature, but also that the global comparative frame for apprehending working-class literature (proposed here) also relies on questioning how the meaning of "tradition" has functioned as a regulative norm, alongside such other defining limits as origins, nation, period, and (event-based) history.

Needless to say, to frame the object of class and the problem and possibility of working-class writing in these terms is to radically depart from how working-class literature has been accommodated, or should we say provincialized, within literary history.

READING MARX RHETORICALLY: WORLD LITERATURE VERSUS WORKING-CLASS LITERATURE

This book calls upon the reader not only to imagine a new way of reading working-class literature but also to consider a new way of reading Marx as a theorist of literary internationalism.

The meanings of "the global" and globalization are hardly synonymous with those of "the social" and socialized labor. Moreover, the cosmopolitan character of world literature is very different from the immanent internationalism of working-class literature. As Perry Anderson warns us, "few political notions are at once so normative and so equivocal as internationalism. Today, the official discourse of the West resounds with appeals to a term that was long a trademark of the Left."²² In his earlier texts on class, including the 1848 *Manifesto*, Marx himself appears to be conflicted about the social significance of, on the surface, similar yet, in essence, incommensurable senses of the internationalism (of labor) versus the cosmopolitanism (of capital).²³ On the one hand, there is the famous rallying cry of the *Communist Manifesto*: "The working men [sic] have no country."²⁴ Reconstructing the slogan's ethical meaning and cultural significance in historical hindsight, Hardt and Negri remind us that the foundational premise of this internationalism is rooted in antinationalism: labor internationalism succeeded because it was opposed to national provincialism. On the other hand, elsewhere in the *Manifesto* Marx explains a process of denationalization as a felicitous result of the freedom of trade—the loosening of feudal ties and familial obligations replaced now by the global relationships of the market and capital.

While nowhere in his corpus do we find mention of working-class literature, Marx does describe world literature as the intellectual corollary to the economic processes of Marx's own global economic conjuncture:

> The need of a constantly expanding market for its products chases the bourgeoisie over the whole surface of the globe. It must nestle everywhere, settle everywhere. The bourgeoisie has through its exploitation of the world market given a cosmopolitan character to production and consumption in every country. . . . In place of the old wants, requiring for their satisfaction the products of distant climes . . . And as in material, so in intellectual production. The intellectual creations of individual nations become common property. National one-sidedness and narrow-mindedness become more and more impossible, and from the numerous national and local literatures, there arises a world literature.(39)

As a range of comparatist scholars have noticed, here in the *Manifesto* (of all unlikely places) Marx observes that world literature "arises" as a by-product of exploitative, even imperialist, relations.²⁵ By default or by design—and inasmuch as a corpus of literature has such a thing—the facilitating agent would appear to be the bourgeoisie, not the working class. In those places where, as in recent, influential reformulations of the genre, world literature is defined primarily as literature that in original or translated form circulates outside the boundaries of the author's country of origin, there its market-driven cosmopolitan character is the happy accident of capital movement guided by its cultural and economic custodians.[26] This freedom of movement is possible because of an infrastructure of publishing houses and an investment in translating marketable world literature. However, a conception of world literature based on circulation and mainly elite consumption is predicated on external validation—the strength of publishing houses, the validation of canonical critics and global literary prizes—rather than rules of genre.

Such formulations, I would argue, cannot account for a political concept of world literature that is collaborative in form and internationalist in its tropes, themes, and structural and structuring aspects. They cannot account for an "unsettled genre" whose representative forms figure a category of "the social" that is always partial, interrupted, serial—whose presence is receding. The totality of world literature as it is conceived in terms of a "world republic of letters" cannot in fact be attentive to a species of writing whose aesthetic vision aims to represent the conditions of "worlding" in the context of uneven development. The barometer of global literary prizes will be irrelevant for such a body of literature, which undermines the notion of single authorship and critiques ideologies of comparison by which select value forms are reified. In short, the concept of world literature cannot account for the forms and formations of working-class writing.

Bracketing Goethe's claim on the term ("world literature"), scholars of working-class literature would connect the formal experimentation of the 1930s proletarian novel with recognized canonical forms of world literature, such as magical realism, as well as other less marketable variants, such as realist anticolonial literature. Marking the challenge of "the attempt to represent a collective subject in a form built around the interior life of the individual," Michael Denning, for example, considers the ways in which the U.S. proletarian novel of the 1930s cracked open conventions and notations, breaking new ground in its figures and concepts for a collective protagonist for world literature.

I differ from these approaches (Denning's included) by confronting and contextualizing Marx's comments on world literature within an extended chronology of Marx's texts on class. In the *Manifesto* we encounter the instability of the category of the international as the effect of capital, on the one hand, and the result of organized labor, on the other. By contrast, in the "Critique of the Gotha Program," in which Marx sets out to clarify socialist principles that are being selectively misappropriated by his contemporaries, he reaffirms the importance of internationalism and maps the terrain of "the social" for a global and unequal world, starting from a premise of inequality, "against bourgeois conceptions of right." We all know the slogan: "From each according to his abilities, to each according to his needs!"[27] If we contextualize Marx's writings on class in a broader frame, it becomes impossible to read him as validating the capitalist premise of a utopian world literature. In Marx's later, unfinished texts on class, we find he attempts to think more broadly geographically and epistemologically than "the same in England as in France, in America as in Germany" and suggests the outlines of a labor internationalism deriving from a dispersed (rather than two-sided version of) class struggle and an abstract vision of "the social." In this book, the comparative methodology for working-class writing based on the changing cartographies of labor turns to the vexed, layered, rich imaginings of the social—not global—suggested by Marx's exergues, moments of revision, and uncompleted argument on class.

The unfinished manuscripts of the "Trinity Formula" chapter as well as the fragment headed "Classes" compiled by Engels after Marx's death into the final section of *Capital*, volume 3, comprise the beginnings of a line of questioning that could not be developed further. In these two fragments as well as the postface added to the second edition of *Capital*, volume 1, Marx begins to propose a fundamental rethinking of the bases of the narrative of the "three great social classes" (deriving from the dogmas of classical English economists). The "Trinity Formula" chapter in particular mocks the conceptual framework of bourgeois economists who take as eternal and unchanging the structures of a particular moment in industrial capitalism. The chapter on classes begins to follow through by debunking the reductivist construct of a three-class system based on forms of revenue and their sources. And here, as in the postface to *Capital* volume 1, Marx goes on to qualify his own use of the particular illustrative case of England:

> It is undeniably in England that this modern society and its economic articulation is most widely and most classically developed.

Even here though, this class articulation does not emerge in pure form. Here, too, middle and transitional levels always conceal the boundaries.[28]

Even though Marx's literary-critical turn in the *Manifesto* receives more attention, it is my claim that any theory of Marx's internationalism must also confront the implications of these interrupted texts. "What makes a class?" Marx asks. The manuscript breaks off before we receive an answer. Engel's preface to volume 3 of *Capital* describes the precarious state of these final texts: "Part Seven, finally, was complete in the manuscript but only as a first draft, and its endlessly entangled sentences had first to be broken up before it was ready for publication. For the final chapter there is only the beginning" (97). Here we have the broken outlines marking how Marx begins to think intermediary forms of wage labor, "important mixed experiences"—as well as schemes and instances of partial proletarianization that have relevance not only for nineteenth-century England, but also for thinking contemporary contexts of globalization. Even if, as it has been contended, Marx could not *formalize* a sustained theory of modes of collectivity outside the party form and trade unionist socialism, outside bourgeois, liberal traditions of democracy and equal rights, here in these precarious texts of *Capital*, volume 3, we have the material for mapping Marx's ethical imagination beyond his own particular historical limitations.

Contextualizing Marx in light of the broken outlines of a more expansive theory of social classes also requires us to confront the productive tension between Marxism, postcolonial studies, and subaltern historiography. As such, a key argument of this book also engages and addresses questions of historicism and the politics of history in Marx and Marxist studies. As Louis Althusser famously argued, "Marxism is not a historicism." In Althusser's lexicon, "historicism" refers to the dominant ideology of history, characterized by features of continuity, determinism, development, progression, and organicism. Dominant trends within postcolonial studies simply equate historicism with Eurocentrism. Among this school, there are those critics who would fixate on Marx's "Articles on India and China." These writings would seem to secure for posterity the idea of a Eurocentric Marx. They are summoned up to testify to Marx's belief in an inexorable march of progress where colonialism constitutes a necessary, unavoidable stage in the progress toward capitalism and where feudalism (and all other residual modes of collectivity) must eventually be superseded in the progress to socialism.

Against the binds of developmentalist thinking, the interventionist reading of Marx proposed here would expose the tenuousness of certain fixed ideas that have become reified tenets of classical Marxism, such as, for example, a geographically fixed, chronologically ordered mode of production narrative presupposed in the interest of the world-historical individual. In this way, the theoretical basis for conceptualizing working-class literature in a comparative (social), not world literary (global) perspective owes to Marx's uncompleted argument on class.

WORKING-CLASS WRITING AND ETHICS

The reader who peruses *Keywords*, Williams's lexicon for culture and society, finds that there is no entry in between the headings "equality" and "ethnic": "ethics" is missing.[29] And ethics are unaccounted for in revolutionary manifestos as well. As documents that communicate an experience of crisis and perform a rupture with the past, they are categorically at odds with the social text of the everyday and hence the time frame of ethico-political agendas. Nowhere in their body of writings did Marx and Engels specify a system of ethical philosophy. As Perry Anderson hypothesizes, "the reason that the founders of historical materialism were so wary of ethical discussions of socialism . . . is their tendency to become substitutes for explanatory accounts of history." But noting the limitations of reading Marx as merely an empiricist historian of the working class, we are recalled to this blind spot: "The notorious absence of anything approaching such an ethics within the accumulated corpus of historical materialism—its regular displacement by either politics or aesthetics—lends this project a peculiar force."[30]

On the other hand, ethics, like globalization, is everywhere in the contemporary academy. Jameson (allowing for certain exceptions, like Alain Badiou's version of political ethics) describes the return to ethics as one of the pernicious regressions of the current age: "Yet now we begin to witness the return of traditional philosophy all over the world, beginning with its hoariest of subfields such as ethics."[31]

Competing definitions abound. For some contemporary theorists of the ethico-political, like Alain Badiou, for example, most prevailing dominant ideologies of ethics are concerned with an investment in a type of defensive ethics that ultimately serves to shore up (the defenses of) liberal humanism and reductivist notions of human rights, shifting the focus away from an ethics implicit in Marxism. Badiou proposes not an ethico-political vision predicated in an attention to differences—which stance, to his mind, always devolves into one of special pleading for admission into a barred hegemony—but a politics that transforms the whole. For Spivak, concepts like "ethical singularity" and "responsibility-based ethics" need to supplement contemporary, individual rights-based discourses.

In the present study, the works considered actively shift the conceptual focus (for working-class literature) from the facts of history to questions of ethics, where ethics might be defined as incalculable measures, intuitions (for lack of a better word) of social justice in the absence of guarantees. Such a sense of ethics runs counter to assertions of rational economic self-interest. It is often predicated in autocritique. Its emphasis on responsibility versus rights rubs against *uniformly* progressive ideals. Ethics of this sort cannot be validated by historical precedence or secured by the provisions of labor laws, and yet such ethical practices (co-constitutive with politics) carry over the idealism of the revolutionary moment into the transformative task-oriented daily work that can only take place in the everyday.

Tillie Olsen dramatizes the difficulties of maintaining such an ethical position in relationship to how we produce the concept of literature itself when she questions the ways by which working-class writing becomes reified as a canonical object. Resolutely refusing the process for her own—not quite—book, her deliberately unfinished novel, pieced together from recovered manuscripts from the 1930s, published uncompleted in 1974, illuminates an ethical paradox. Might something be lost when Olsen's own book acquires the status of representative, canonical example? A key episode in the novel would seem to suggest as much. However, as feminist critics have pointed out, Olsen's uncompleted book offers us a model for thinking a postindividualist form for the working-class novel. "Reader, it was not to have ended here . . . " reads the epigraph. *Yonnondio* remains deliberately uncompleted, awaiting supplementation from the other, not yet come, addressing a feminist reader—necessarily collaborative and collective in its form. In the troping of working-class history as writing beyond the ending—as necessarily unfinished narrative as well as in the representation of speech interferences as the defining constitutive speech act/linguistic figure of working-class writing, Tillie Olsen's model of dialogical ethics instantiates a model of a deauthorized, collective subject of working-class writing, even as it acknowledges its aporetic terrain.

Difference without hierarchy—the vision of an impossible, undivided world striven for in internationalism and comparative literature—is also the vision and practice of "ethical singularity" elaborated by Spivak. In a specific, limited sense, ethics—specifically, "ethical singularity"—becomes the name given to the daily, task-oriented work that must take place in the aftermath of revolutions, after negotiated political and economic independence, after the communists come into power. Such ethical practices are improvised exercises in "slow, attentive mind changing (on both sides)." They are painstaking efforts at infrastructure building that will secure (but also actively revise) the fought-for ideals of the revolution.

Such ethics are not cultural relativist, particularist, or universal. They presuppose relationships of singularity, not difference—where singularity involves repeatable differences. Thus, such ethics cannot be systematized or formalized. They are defined by unverifiable outcomes and ethico-political agendas beyond statist realms or, indeed, international civil society schemes of rational planning:

> "Ethical singularity" is neither "mass contact" nor engagement with "the common sense of the people." We all know that when we engage profoundly with one person, the responses come from both sides: this is responsibility and accountability. We also know that in such engagements we want to reveal and reveal, conceal nothing. Yet on both sides there is always a sense that something has not got across. This we call the "secret," not something that one wants to conceal, but something that one wants to reveal.... In this secret singularity, the object of ethical action is not an object of benevolence, for here responses flow from both sides.... This encounter can only happen when the respondents inhabit something like normality. Most political movements fail

> in the long run because of the absence of this engagement. In fact, it is impossible for all leaders (subaltern or otherwise) to engage every subaltern in this way, especially across the gender divide. This is why ethics is the experience of the impossible. . . . For a collective struggle *supplemented* by the impossibility of full ethical engagement—not in the rationalist sense of "doing the right thing," but in this more familiar sense of the impossibility of "love" in the one-on-one way for each human being—the future is always around the corner, there is no victory, but only victories that are also warnings.[32]

In a more diffuse sense of the term, then, as not quite a worldview but a "structure of feeling," perhaps, Spivak describes ethical singularity in terms of the "experience of the impossible"—the active cultivation of the mindset of "love in the one on one way for each human being." The goal of this effortful striving can never be (completely) realized. There is no moral "payoff." Something is always lost or held back, despite the best intentions of both respondents involved.

In the present study, Mahasweta Devi's "Pterodactyl" and Head's *A Question of Power* dramatize such ethical interventions as scenes of imperfect communication. "[L]ove is two people mutually feeding each other . . ." (197): The realization slowly dawns upon Head's protagonist, the stateless refugee recovering from the psycho-social trauma of apartheid. "What do billions of people in the world need? Food. That's why I went into agriculture" (135). The second line is both a reiteration of and response to the first. As the reader discovers, it is the credo of working-class internationalism and sustainable farming voiced by a supporting actant in the novel's plot, the self-critical Peace Corps volunteer from America. His statement addresses itself as a concrete answer to Head's question of power, underwriting the economic and philosophical topography of the international division of labor. The novel reads as a strange "love" story (certainly by the standards of postcolonial orthodoxies). It captures the ethical nuances of the politics of a romantic? unclassifiable? friendship between historical enemies—a relationship more complicated than the binary of colonizer-colonized. In Mahasweta Devi's "Pterodactyl," a (possibly) prehistoric creature descends upon a famine-ravaged area of Pirtha, India—once the site of the agricultural green revolution. The pterodactyl's message on "development" addresses itself to the tribal populations of the dying countryside as well as to the quick fixes delivered by international civil society, including left-front state functionaries and NGO representatives: "To build it you must love beyond reason for a long time" (195).

Love as the common name for an ethics of historical materialism, though, is not readily reconciled with grand progress narratives of Marxism, or with the rationalism of socialism. "We claim that Empire is better in the same way that Marx insists that capitalism is better than the forms of society and modes of production that came before it," write Hardt and Negri. (The preceding section of this introduction addresses this representation of Marx, raising the question of his unfinished texts on class.) The working-class texts studied here propose a set of counter mandates to self-evident progress narratives that undoubtedly place us on uncertain ground: "Our double task is to resist 'development' actively and to learn to love" (xxii). "To build it you must love beyond reason for a long time" (195). The dialectical back and forth of ethical singularity marked by interruptions and interferences is not *always* forward moving. "Love beyond reason" is not in one's self interest. Choosing responsibility is antithetical to "Freedom." Such ethical investments may even entail confronting the residual within the emergent. They might require us to instrumentalize "feudal" patterns in the struggle against monocultures of globalization. In *When Memory Dies*, Sivanandan's protagonist recalls us to such a lost ethical way of being: "it was something else, a way of life perhaps, basic fundamental, feudal even ... something lost to his town memory, his merchant commerce memory" (335). In Sivanandan's novel as well as texts by Olsen, Head, and Devi scenes of missed communication and stagings of strange affinities figure relationships of ethical singularity in terms of love.

CHAPTERS

Each of the following chapters focuses on a different aspect of the narrative logic by which these examples of working-class and socialist fiction figure the cultural politics of labor history against and through the dilemmas of internationalism and ethical singularity. I begin with "Colonialism, Race, and Class: Mulk Raj Anand's *Coolie* as a Literary

Representation of the Subaltern," acknowledging an ideological blind spot: Marxist critics of "the radical 1930s" too often overlook the efforts of colonial writers of socialist fiction such as Mulk Raj Anand. Others who do encounter him in their projects of recovery and rediscovery read him as a *nationalist* anticolonial writer. The aesthetic and political contributions of a Marxist-oriented group of anticolonial *internationalist* writers remain largely unknown (among a global Anglophone readership, at least).

While Anand has enjoyed a recent revival in transnational modernist studies, my work demonstrates how he fits into the projects of subaltern studies and comparative literature. Anand's 1936 *Coolie* is in fact set against the backdrop of the global trade depression and currency crisis. This novel is the 1930s artist's remapping of *Kim*, Kipling's imperial adventure story, in terms of a cartography of migrant coolie labor— a child-worker's search for work. The novel plots the "adventures" of Munoo from the point at which he is sold into domestic servitude by his legal guardians, to his "escape" to the Bombay cotton mills, and then to his abduction and employment as a rickshaw puller in Simla, the summer capital of colonial India. Not incidentally, Simla, where the "Great Game" begins for Kim, is where Munoo dies, broken down by overwork and disease. His final moments are spent in the presence of an activist-intellectual who is compelled to rethink his own impatient, cynical formulations regarding the fatalism of the Indian working classes—and who is deeply affected by the child's passing. The book begins then with the attempt to restore history and theory to a tradition of literary internationalism and nonrevolutionary socialism generated as part of anticolonial labor (rather than nationalist) struggles.

Chapter 2, "Postcolonial Sri Lanka and 'Black Struggles for Socialism': Socialist Ethics in Ambalavaner Sivanandan's *When Memory Dies*," considers how Marxist thought and literary internationalism travel between the colonial periphery and the imperial metropole— in this case, between Sri Lanka and England. We encounter a divided readership with Ambalavaner Sivanandan, Sri Lankan Tamil/black British writer and founder-editor of the London journal *Race and Class*. On the one hand, recent postcolonial scholarship tends to focus exclusively on his 1997 book, *When Memory Dies*—part epic novel, part fictionalized memoir, set against the backdrop of the ongoing civil war in Sri Lanka. On the other hand, scholars of black British cultural studies tend to focus on Sivanandan's political journalism—his analyses of institutionalized racism, labor management, and immigration and asylum policies in contemporary Britain. My work, however, draws attention to the shifting frames of reference for Sivanandan's general theories of literary and labor internationalism. Moving between "the dialectic of here and there," I follow the uncanny doublings of scenes and subjects and the repetitions and revisions that occur across Sivanandan's texts. For Sivanandan, it seems that ultimately it is the turn to literature and literary thinking that enables an epistemic shift from debates in left-party politics to questions of socialist ethics.[33]

If Anand's and Sivanandan's writings expose the lacunae in both anticolonial nationalist historiography and trade unionist socialism, their narratives are focalized from the perspective of subalternized *male* workers cut off from access to collectivity. They are unable to think how women workers as subalterns *and* historical agents inhabit and transform the cultural politics of class struggle. According to standard Marxist terminology, the "proletarian" is by definition revolutionary and by implication male. But what of anomalous women's texts of "proletarian" fiction that propose a more counterintuitive model for the staging of historical agency? Chapter 3, "Gender, Genre, and Globalization," considers a juxtaposition of feminist proletarian texts from North America, India, and Sri Lanka to make visible the figure of a collective subject and the critique of individualism shared by different changing traditions of women's and feminist texts of labor. Bringing together Tillie Olsen's *Yonnondio*, Mahasweta Devi's "Pterodactyl" and "The Fairy Tale of Mohanpur," and the poetry, creative writings, and political statements of *Dabindu*—an NGO group of Sri Lankan free-trade-zone garment factory workers and feminist activists—this chapter analyzes the ethics and aesthetics of feminist "interruption." Considered together, the serialized poetics of the *Dabindu* papers, Olsen's deliberately uncompleted 1930s proletarian novel, and the "repeated interruptions" of Devi's writing animate the dynamism of an autocritical ethics of historical materialism—one that consistently undermines the fixity of simple identity politics. The feminist critique proposed here builds on the fact that Marx's texts on class remain unfinished and that it is a mistake to posit reified theories of capital and class relations or necessarily accept modes of production narratives based on a specific historical instance as determining historical topography. Such a reading practice proposes a comparative but not relativist approach to the changing object of working-class writing and suggests the ethico-political agency of a dispersed, collective subject of feminism.

Chapter 4, "Socialized Labor and the Critique of Identity Politics in Bessie Head's *A Question of Power*," completes the narrative arc of the history of ideas explored in this book. This fourth and final chapter is devoted to South African–born Botswanan writer Bessie Head. It shifts the focus to sub-Saharan Africa and narratives of voluntary cooperative labor and food production in the age of development. If the Eurocentric economic migrant represents a paradigmatic figure in the literature of labor in postcoloniality, Head's characters stand for the reversal of this particularly urbanist telos. Even as fellow political and literary exiles make the storied journey to the metropolitan centers of the world—London, Paris, New York—Head's own journey is from apartheid-era South Africa to Bechuanaland (pre-independence Botswana). Here she remains as a stateless refugee and writes her wildly imaginative and innovative mixed-genre texts while she works within the NGO circuit to develop techniques of sustainable farming.

A Question of Power (the focus of this chapter) is Head's best-known but also most challenging work. Moving us back and forth between Marx and Freud, it constantly switches registers between ghost story, self-help talk therapy, and philosophical meditation on the ontology and subjectivity of everyday work. Critics of Head's novel privilege psychoanalysis as an interpretative framework. They focus exclusively on the surreal narratives of interiority and the symbolism of the unconscious as the key to understanding Head's peculiar, paradoxical notions of universality and humanism. I dwell instead on the disruptive narratives of agricultural projects, and the detailed descriptions of crop rotation and skills-training activities that constantly interrupt the primary story line. I argue that these "outside" narratives—grounded in the social networks of everyday village life and in unlikely friendships (sometimes between historical enemies)—supply the content for Head's critique of identity politics.

In the epilogue, "Working-Class Writing and the Social Imagination," I return to a more in-depth consideration of maps and meanings of socialized labor and labor power.

Chapter 1

COLONIALISM, RACE, AND CLASS

Mulk Raj Anand's Coolie *as a Literary Representation of the Subaltern*

As far as capital invested in the colonies, etc. is concerned, however, the reason why this can yield higher rates of profit is that the profit rate is generally higher there on account of the lower degree of development and so too is the exploitation of labour, through the use of slaves and coolies.

—Karl Marx, *Capital*

O East is East and West is West, and never the twain shall meet.
—Rudyard Kipling, *Barrack-Room Ballads*

Navigating the bookstores and book parties of 1930s Bloomsbury, Mulk Raj Anand finds himself called upon to validate the genius of Kipling's novel, *Kim*.[1] The newly arrived graduate student turned native informant, however, soon discovers that his judgment is solicited and undermined in the same polite gesture. For among the literary elite that he encounters, it is a foregone conclusion that no better realist account of modern India exists. "If I may say so, Professor Dobrée [*Anand is compelled to take aboard one of his new mentors on the point*], . . . I have read *Kim* twice. It is a fairy tale glorifying a young boy. Going about with that exotic Hooi Sipi Lama, who keeps revolving the wheel of life. A little hero of the Empire—a fantasy boy" (*Conversations*, 15).[2] We learn from Anand's biographical reminisces published under the heading *Conversations in Bloomsbury* as well as from unpublished letters that Anand's 1936 novel *Coolie* is planned as a corrective "rewriting" of *Kim*, the boy's adventure story and celebration of Empire so admired, it appears, by certain gatekeepers of the modernist culture industry. Anand's statement, addressed to T.S. Eliot, rehearses the beginnings of an intention: "I am going to rewrite Kipling's *Kim* ... from the opposite point of view" (*Conversations*, 50).[3]

It is an interesting pronouncement on several different levels. In fact, the novel that Anand writes is not a *straightforward* counterargument to *Kim*. As "opposed" to the bildungsroman of the colonizer, Anand might have proffered up a story of the culture and education of the nationalist intellectual. Instead, as Anand envisions it, the antonym to *Kim* is *Coolie*—a generic, collective title that corresponds to the general story of unskilled, unorganized labor. The alternative perspective to the panoramic vision of India opened up by the adventures of Kipling's picaresque hero is that of a migrant child-worker who must travel all over India in search of work. *Coolie* is a rewriting that engages debates on style but also "moves beyond" Bloomsbury to engage—through the conventions, notations, and ideology of the 1930s proletarian novel form—the challenges of ethically translating worker biography into art. We know from Anand's *Conversations in Bloomsbury* that *Coolie* is a rewriting of *Kim*, but it is less well known that his literary text also follows as a supplement to Diwan Chaman Lall's 1932 part–activist polemic/part–sociological tract, *Coolie: The Story of Labor and Capital in India*, "an attempt to share the truth about the working classes in India."[4]

"Rewriting," then, as Anand conceptualizes it, is not only writing *against* (*Kim*) or, as in the most transparently obvious sense, writing *again* (with regard to Lall) but something of both. Anand's novel comes down to us a densely layered palimpsest of citations and omissions. It is at once a literary reimagining of subaltern labor history and an anticolonial rebuttal to Kipling's imperial fantasy. But ultimately *Coolie* is also a revision and challenging of its own form, that of the proletarian novel. It is both a comment on the paradoxes of capitalist modernity—a modernity that must rely on backward, feudal institutions of indentured labor for the efficient extraction of surplus value—*and* a meditation on the paradoxes of trade unionist socialism. In *Coolie*, organized industrial action in England means short time for coolies in colonial factories in India. Even sympathetic Marxist critics withhold comment on the consensus-breaking episodes in *Coolie* that dramatize the structural opposition between the working class in the metropole and that of the colony.

Postcolonial scholars have theorized on Kipling's strategy of delaying the colonial coming-of-age story through the use of the narrative device of the figure of imperialist-as-boy.[5] Anand's decision to record the seamy underside of the boy's adventure story, to make visible the trade-related, occluded antithesis to the moves and maneuvers of the Great Game, also requires a technique of delaying and deferring the boy-child's coming-of-age tale, but along very different lines and to very different ends. A child coolie's story is only imaginable in violation of the 1933 Children (Pledging of Labor) Act, a pre-Independence law whose provisions continue to be debated today by the government of India, transnational corporations, and human rights–watch agencies.[6] The very structure of Anand's novel unfolds as a scheme of postponements, detours, and interruptions. But furthermore, the indefinitely deferred story of *Coolie* lingers in decolonized terrain well into the time frame of contemporary globalization.

Though begun in London and written in English, *Coolie* addresses not just the cultural establishment of Bloomsbury but also the changing, moving, living tradition of working-class literature. Upon returning to India, now a recognized author of world literature in English, Anand advises aspiring critics to see his work in the broader context of proletarian literature as a social formation.[7] Since the proletarian moment of the 1930s, however, Anand's writings have been read and studied primarily as the cultural product of anticolonial *nationalism* (as opposed to class struggles). Thirties internationalism, in general, becomes absorbed into broader canons of culturally dominant fields like mainstream postcolonial studies and, now, transnational modernism.[8] In recent years we notice a specific effort at recuperating Anand as, first and foremost, a modernist among other modernists. His connections with other proletarian writers of the 1930s are left largely unexplored.

Under these circumstances, what does it mean to read Mulk Raj Anand's works as constitutive, but also critical, of proletarian writing as a practice of internationalism? By extension, perhaps, we should also ask what is at stake in the critical recovery of 1930s proletarian literature now, when everything old is new again? In 2008 the biggest international economic and financial crisis since the 1930s registered, albeit unevenly, across the globe. The specter of 1929 casts a long shadow, especially if we consider how today's overlooked global food crisis persists alongside, and arises from, similar yet different profit-maximization motives as the recent banking debacle. Leftist arts and culture movements are at the forefront of the Occupy Wall Street and other counterglobalist Occupy movements across the world. We are confronted with the long 1930s when we consider that post–World War II neoliberal practices of state-restructuring and international relations were put into effect as corrective measures to avoid a replay of the sequence of events that threatened to undermine the global capitalist order in 1930. Writing in the 1980s on the twists and turns of literary history as knowledge production, Cary Nelson makes the point forcefully and eloquently, reminding us that "what and who we are now, is already in part a result of what we no longer know we have forgotten."[9] Though Nelson, in context, is referring to how U.S. modernism as a national literary tradition is premised in an ideological blind spot—an active forgetfulness of the literature of labor—his provocation informs questions raised in this chapter as well.

During different phases of its reception and circulation, Anand's *Coolie* has been variously classified as Indo-Anglian fiction, world literature in English, anticolonial writing, postcolonial writing, modernist fiction, and—on rare occasions—socialist fiction of the 1930s. Most often, however, even the most comprehensive of judges and exacting of critics seem to discuss the sometimes intersecting, sometimes opposed, agendas of colonial counternarrative and proletarian writing as distinctly separate registers. This study follows a different route. Without summarily collapsing the distances and discontinuities between specific trajectories of historicization, through a close reading of the rhetorical conduct of *Coolie*, this chapter tracks some places where the breaks become visible and instructive—where something called proletarian writing and something called colonial counterdiscourse work to critique each other in productive ways. The final movement of this chapter pushes beyond this confrontation to suggest that rather than either proletarian writing or colonial counterdiscourse, Anand's *Coolie* might perhaps be read as a literary representation of the subaltern.

RECASTING THE 1930s NOVEL

"When the Georgians put money into an Indian business," raced on De la Havre, "when they fought like bulls and bears on the Stock Exchange and on London Wall, they didn't see the oppression of the black, brown and yellow coolies that was necessary to produce their dividends. . . ."
—Mulk Raj Anand, *Two Leaves and a Bud* (1937)

The aftermath of colonialism is not only the retrieval of the past but the putting together of the history of the present.
—Gayatri Chakravorty Spivak, "Feminism in Decolonization"

In *The Global Impact of the Great Depression*, Dietmar Rothermund evaluates "the '30s" according to a different scheme of events than the Bank of England's return to the gold standard in 1925, the New York City stock market crash of October 1929, and dilemmas over war debts and reparations.[10] His book shifts the center of gravity away from the United States and Europe, where the crisis originated, and instead begins with the history of other spaces hardest hit by the impact— spaces intimately connected with, yet continents apart from, the metropolitan financial centers of the world. He focuses instead on indices of export agriculture, overproduction of wheat, peasant indebtedness, and instances of rural insurgency in areas such as the Punjab. In addition to analyzing agrarian movements in the wheat-growing regions of South Asia, he considers specific case histories from Southeast Asia, Africa, and Latin America as he labors to demonstrate how the overproduction of wheat contributed to the final breakdown of the international credit system.[11]

Of course, these particular happenings, involving the rural workers of the colonial periphery, are not conventionally written up as being of global historical magnitude or meaning. In his beautifully heretical little book, Rothermund tries to correct a theoretical bias in economic historiography: "At most some attention has been paid to the supposedly positive effect which the depression had on the industries located in the peripheral countries which could benefit from import substitution. The peripheral peasantry which bore the brunt of the impact of the depression has remained dark, its fate has not entered into economic consciousness" (10). His rural-centered approach is particularly anomalous in relation to the resolutely urban focus of most contemporary studies of the current situation of economic globalization.[12]

A similar counterintuitive move to center the periphery is also the plan of Anand's writings of the 1930s. He imagines the spaces blocked from the view of colonial administrators and the British labor party alike—indeed, organized labor in general.[13] More specifically, he proceeds by way of a technique of reversing and displacing the recognized narrating subject's standpoint: once again, Coolie is the antonym to Kim. Anand gives us the precarious existence of the migrant child laborer as a foil to the questing mobility of Kipling's boy adventurer. Kim's schoolroom is the world. In Anand's novel the global is not mapped with the tools and measures of the schoolboy/imperial surveyor but rather measured sack by sack of wheat for export. The grain market coolies have a different understanding of space management all together. The "art and science of mensuration" is computed differently.[14] In 1937 Anand follows the publication of Coolie with Two Leaves and a Bud, staging the story of the exploited indentured laborers on the Assamese tea plantations. Of all his texts from the 1930s, his first novel, Untouchable (1935), attracts the most attention from the British liberal establishment, predictably perhaps, because there the subject of child labor is framed in terms of the racism of the Hindu caste system. Anand's later novels of the 1930s—which for better or worse garner less critical attention and validation—focus on the question of the exploitation of the working class in British colonial India. Two Leaves and a Bud was ultimately withdrawn from circulation because its caricature of the English plantation manager was deemed obscene. The president of the Indian Tea Association had the book placed on the list of "proscribed books in India"—of course, thereby guaranteeing it popularity and a new discursive life upon India's Independence, and thus unwittingly doing his part toward paving the way for Anand to be read and received as a *nationalist* writer.

In a collection of letters from Mulk Raj Anand to Saros Cowasjee published under the title Author to Critic, we are made privy to the author's own active attempt to (re)introduce his work in the context of traditions of working-class writing. The very first letter, dated 3 October 1965, proposes a set of instructions to be followed: "If you feel you would like to do a study then I think there is an angle which none of these books on my books has covered: that is the relation to the 30s movement in Western Europe (in fact all over the world)" (1). The published study, *So Many Freedoms*, does not follow up on this request—at least not in a consistent manner.[15] No sustained effort has been made to situate Anand's works in relation to the international alliance of writers, readers, activists, and workers that comprised the dynamic formation of proletarian writing.[16] And yet to ignore this collective identity—to uncritically designate Anand as a nationalist writer—is to ignore the fact that in 1936 he was a member of the Communist Party and that while he was living in London he cofounded the Marxist-oriented Progressive Writers Association.[17]

Also, to categorize Anand as a nationalist writer is to ignore his critiques of the way in which national liberation was won, as well as to discount his continuing work as an activist in post-Independence India in the wake of the failure of decolonization and the rise of the new transnational agencies. For example, in a second postscript to his *Apology for Heroism: A Brief Autobiography of Ideas*, he soberly recaps the revolutionary élan of the 1930s intellectual.[18] Commenting on the transition of power from imperial Britain to the pax Americana, he writes, "I do not want to hide any mistakes that I have made in my life or to defend them . . . [b]ut it is important to realize that the illusions of an Indian intellectual in the '30s could be based on a sincere belief in the necessity of national freedom and socialism" (189). Writing after Independence (and the new world-order of Bretton Woods), he goes on to comment on the thwarted legacy of proletarian writing as a counterglobalist movement: "[T]he construction of [a] poetic and philosophical vision by the enormous and intricate propaganda that deforms genuine ideals and puts them in the service of half lies and quarter lies has left little room for complacency. While the intelligentsia still inquires into the rights and wrongs of personal relations, international morality condones belligerency and war in the name of the United Nations" (200).[19]

Indian writers of the 1930s such as Anand (writing in English), Zaheer (writing in Urdu), and Premchand (writing in Hindi) constitute a genealogy for anticolonial fiction that has not been adequately theorized in English. Writing within a late colonial, pre-Independence milieu, the Progressive Writers sought to expand the definition of literature and the literary to engage the ideas of class as a structural and structuring aspect of reality. But in the impress of the predominant metropolitan myth that all Third World literature is national allegory or paradigmatically magical realism, the aesthetics and politics of this Marxist-oriented group of internationalist writers have been overlooked by contemporary literary critics.[20] Gustav Klaus, a scholar of British working-class and socialist fiction, represents a notable exception to dominant trends. In *The Literature of Labor* he identifies Anand first and foremost in relationship to a tradition of political fiction born of the decade of internationalism and the "radical" 1930s. But Klaus's well-intentioned argument, absolving Anand of a type of revolutionary defeatism, unfolds by way of taking stock of the irreducible determinations of history and burdens of cultural relativism that inevitably shape Anand's ideological viewpoint and aesthetic choices in a way that disconnects him from his European contemporaries. By contrast, as we shall see, Bessie Head references and reimagines the ideological scope (and compromises of) the Progressive Writers Association members' collective vision in the name of a broader, more diffuse antinationalist cultural politics—a politics that holds humanist lessons for Apartheid-era South Africa.

READING PROLETARIAN WRITING

> [A] text's unity lies not in its origin but in its destination. Yet this destination cannot any longer be personal: the reader is without history, biography, psychology; he [sic] is simply that someone who holds together in a single field all the traces by which the written text is constituted.
> —Roland Barthes

In Mulk Raj Anand's *Coolie*, the factory workers at Sir George White (Sirjabite) Cotton Mills cannot be mobilized by trade union speech makers. From out of nowhere come "the broken accents of a voice" (234). The socialists' incantatory message is interrupted by the rumor that a "Hindu child has been kidnapped" and anger against factory management is deflected into communal violence—collective "autodestruction."[21]

Most critical inquiries concerning this novel begin and end with a reading of the anticlimactic episode of a failed strike. In *Coolie*, the workers do not come together to act in their rational, economic self-interest as a class. Does this make it a failed socialist novel? What in fact constitute the failings of *Coolie* as a narrative? Accessible, "reasonable" explications have been volunteered by sympathetic critics. They attribute the failings of the narrative to the "fatalism peculiar to the Indian peasantry,"[22] the infancy of the Indian labor movement, the paradoxes of nationalist agency, and also the "technical handicap which limits the author's possibilities . . . the choice of the protagonist, a low-caste boy who is unlikely to become involved in revolutionary activities."[23]

The last observation, suggested by Klaus, is quite simply a misrepresentation of the central character's caste origins—a mistake that affects how we contextualize Anand as a 1930s writer. In fact, the central character shares the same caste origin as the writer: Kshatriya, the second caste. At one point in the text, when dismissed by a shopkeeper as low caste, we encounter Munoo adamantly correcting the misperception: "He said to himself, 'I let him put me in my place as a coolie, but I was paying for the soda water and I am not an untouchable. I am a Hindu Kshatriya, a Rajput, a warrior'" (157). In *Coolie*, the novelist underscores the contradiction that U.S.-Euro Marxists are largely incapable of thinking through: The "elite in caste [can be] subaltern in class."[24] If in Anand's first published novel, *Untouchable*, he inscribes the topos of child labor within the narrative of caste, in this, his second novel, he makes a pronounced statement against liberal critics when he renegotiates the story in terms of global capitalism and theories of class—not caste.[25] Arguably, this shift in object (from questions of caste to questions of class) has everything to do with why Anand's relationship to 1930s writing remains relatively obscured—why his works remain untouched by metropolitan Marxists on the one hand, and South Asian area studies specialists on the other. Outside the literary scene, the need to adjust the focus of the narrative of child labor continues as part of the consciousness-raising work of international human rights and metropolitan groups such as FOIL (Forum of Indian Leftists), which begins its exposition of the increase in the exploitation of child labor in India by addressing the governing misperception that child labor is primarily explicable in terms of the Hindu caste system.[26]

But what constitutes the making of class according to the narrative logic of *Coolie*? "Surely, the Coolies had no religion," it occurs to Munoo, as he watches the mix of Hindu hill coolies, Kashmiri Muhammedan laborers, and Sikh coolies sharing tobacco pipes and water. And yet, later on in the story we have the dramatization of the Hindu–Muslim communal riots that completely disrupt trade unionist efforts at working-class organization. Reversing and displacing the proposition (of *Coolie* as a failed revolutionary narrative), we might say instead that the defective parts and recalcitrant bits teach us something about how we produce the concept of class in working-class literature. As Ellen Rooney puts it, "when form is conceived as the effect of reading, the burden falls entirely on the reader/reading to produce the formal and to register its productive and contradictory relation to the social, including its relation to social thematics" (212).[27]

In an aligned movement—though speaking of literature, rather than form, specifically—Spivak outlines a practice of reading literature for its literariness that might work to supplement the evidentiary claims of sociological and historicist commentary. In context, the category that she is discussing is sociological constructions of gender, but the statement also holds for Marxism and the unfinished texts of class:[28]

> Such painstaking speculative scholarship on [Marxism], though invaluable to our collective enterprise, does, however, reason [class] into existing paradigms. By contrast, emphasizing the literariness of literature, pedagogy invites us to take a distance from the continuing project of reason. Without this supplementary distancing, a position and its counterposition both held in the discourse of reason keep legitimizing each other.
>
> (Spivak, "Breast-Giver," 89)

Such a reading practice enables us to open up the episode of the failed strike according to the (il)logic of the literary text, rather than to close it off as simply discontinuous with successful examples of working-class history. "The historian must persist in his efforts in this awareness, that the subaltern is necessarily the absolute limit of the place where history is narrativized into logic."[29] In *Coolie*, readers are apprised of successful moments in Indian working-class history. Topical allusions are made to the historic TISCO (Tata Iron and Steel Company) steelworkers' strikes—taking place elsewhere in Jamshedpur—in a textual space parallel with (although not connected to) the main storyline.[30] What, then, can be learned from the primary story of an anonymous coolie and a failed strike?

We know from unpublished records and autobiographical writings that *Coolie* (notice that even the definite article is stricken from the title) is the planned antonym to *Kim*. Just as Kipling's text is "about" the colonial subject coming of age and finally asserting (his) identity, Anand's text is "about"[31] the agent(s) of (colonial) production remaining anonymous—of not being able to "mak[e] their class interest valid in their proper name."[32] With regard to this last point, it is crucial to mark the significance of rumor—a narrative without author—that disrupts the trade unionist's speech. Ironically, it is here in this brief moment that the exorbitant story of an "abducted" child takes center stage—overwriting the message of trade union socialism in the name of exploited child labor.

In the area of anticolonial historiography, members of the Marxist Subaltern Studies collective draw upon structuralist analyses of narrative to show us how to read closely for indices such as "fatalism," "infancy," "handicap," and "caste" where they occur in examples of supposedly value-neutral historical documentation. Ranajit Guha, in "The Prose of Counter Insurgency," alerts us to the production of historical writings where insurgency is explained purely in terms of "an enumeration of causes—of, say, economic and political deprivation . . . where Cause is made to stand in as a phantom surrogate for Reason, the logic of that consciousness" [as well as, in our view, for creative un(r)eason] (47). In *Rethinking Working-Class History*, Dipesh Chakrabarty theorizes "the paradox of labor militancy without organization," giving us a narrative for reading resistance where it has not been coded as resistance—where "what has so far been viewed simply as an absence of trade union discipline or training reveals on closer inspection, the presence of alternative systems of power and authority."[33] Vinay Bahl's *The Making of the Indian Working Class*, detailing the situation of the TISCO strikes, has affiliations with the premise of *Rethinking* (although in her preface, Bahl goes to great lengths to distance herself from the project of subaltern studies, based on a general suspicion of "Postmodernists and Subalternists").[34] Certainly subaltern studies historians have consistently sought to make visible the constructedness of official historical discourse, drawing upon the resources of structuralist and poststructuralist theory in the service of those subaltern populations that fall outside established systems of representation (nationalist history, trade union socialism, and others). What is missing from Bahl's critical assessment of the general oeuvre—a critical assessment that, let us notice, confuses poststructuralist theory with postmodernism—is a consideration of the broader implications of reading failure, otherwise. To extend the critical impetus of subaltern studies into the field of literature is to recognize that the making/unmaking of class happens in counterintuitive ways—outside the speech acts of the state, oppositional nationalisms, and organized labor.

Consider, for example, this scene in *Coolie* where (writing) working-class history is staged as predicated upon the suppression of a child's testimony. In terms of the plot sequence, this scene occurs after the management-provoked "communal riots." In terms of the rhetorical conduct of the text, this space is imprinted by the calculated silence following a sequence of rhetorical questions. We might say that this scene composes the center of the book. In it, the subaltern is placed in the twisted position of eavesdropping as the official account of his story is being negotiated by the press, Congress wallahs, and community leaders:

> "Bande Mataram," Munoo heard the Congress-Wallah greet his majesty. He did not know who he was. But he was impressed and curious.
>
> "What are your leaders doing?" the dignitary exclaimed. "What are the police and the government doing? What are the newly elected members of the corporation doing? For a whole night Pathans have been murdered by Hindus and the Congress has done nothing about it. If Miss Mayo came to India and wrote a chapter about children being kidnapped for sacrificial purposes, would you not deny it as a wicked libel?" The congress men kept quiet . . . [And then finally the baffled listener is discovered.] "Go away! Who are you?" one of the Congress volunteers shouted as he returned to his post at the door. Munoo started, blushed a confession of guilt, and capered on his way. (246–247)

The author figure, Katherine Mayo, is a crucial index here. In fact, the structural irony upon which the narrative is based might be summed up as follows: the publication of sensationalist accounts of brutalized Indian children (in the metropole) detracts attention from the reality of child labor (in the periphery).[35] The two events are simultaneous and inextricably connected. A coolie's story is not noteworthy enough to make it into the local and national news—nor is it scandalous enough to warrant mention in Mayo's catalogue of child victims, *Mother India*. But in fact, it is just as the international and national furor over missing (Indian, Hindu, Muslim) children reaches its height that Munoo is abducted by the colonial memsahib, Mrs. Mainwaring, to serve as her houseboy in Simla. Significantly, the word "kidnap" is not used to describe this encounter.

The center of a book, E.M. Forster argues, often has nothing to do with its plot or spatial arrangement. More often than not, "the center" contains authorial commentary on the validity of disparate truth claims. Forster suggests "truth in life versus truth in art" as an example.[36] At the center of *Coolie* is Anand's commentary on the validity of writing historical fiction versus writing history. To apprehend the scene in this register we need to know that Anand shares a certain affinity with the figure of the doorkeeper/Congress wallah. (Anand was, for a while, a member of the Indian Congress Party.[37]) We also need to be familiar with the fact that the literary representation of the central character owes to a "childhood friendship"[38] and that, in fact, the novel is predicated upon a deliberate decision not to transcribe a testimony.[39] In this sense we cannot overlook the significance of the scene of "communication" between the Congress wallah and the small, silent, nameless witness. It is a scene that is replayed in Anand's fictionalized autobiography (there with the figure of a mother as mediator facilitating communication).

What do we make of this active marginalization of the "true story" (testimony) in the interest of staging, indirectly (through literature), the drama by which justice is obstructed and testimony is suppressed? Do we see it as the novelist's case for historical fiction (focalized) from below? Or do we see it as the writer's disclosure of complicity with the very processes that he is critiquing (that is, some testimonies are never collected)?[40] The protocols of the passage (the sequence of rhetorical questions) will not allow us to choose between the two agendas (of history and of fiction). A rhetorical question, as we know, is where "the same grammatical pattern engenders two meanings."[41] In this scene, composed of questions where no answers are required and no witness solicited, Anand involves himself in the scheme of the aporia that he returns to over and over again in *Coolie*: representation for one constituency is predicated upon subalternity for another.

We must keep in mind that *Coolie* was written and published while the author was living in England, having received his doctoral degree in philosophy from the University of London. Is this, then, a condition of possibility of proletarian writing representing the colonial periphery? The author figure (in the above scene) is hardly represented as a welcome character. I am not suggesting that the positions of the American imperialist (sojourning in India) and that of the socialist, colonial intellectual (studying in England) can be deemed equivalent. I am saying that this scene indexes a moment of complicity between the author and the object of his critique. Notice that the textuality of imperial philanthropy disguised as feminist reform is cited as "wicked libel": "If Miss Mayo came to India and wrote a chapter about children being kidnapped for sacrificial purposes, would you not deny it as a wicked libel?" But on the other hand, nationalist discourse is not the answer: "The congressmen kept quiet." This scene is focalized from the perspective of those for whom negotiated political independence means nothing. At its close, we are given the figure of the Congress volunteer who wittingly or unwittingly waves the nondescript coolie out of the picture: "Go away! Who are you?" What can be learned from this attempt to enter into the protocols of the text? In "Can the Subaltern Speak?" Spivak, via a critique of Michel Foucault, notices the slippage between the representing intellectual's desire to render visible the (suppressing) mechanism and his desire to render vocal the individual. Anand consistently guards against this impulse in his (literary) representation of the subaltern. This scene makes intelligible (through the protocols of the text: rhetorical questions, presupposed silences, and so on) the mechanisms by which the child-worker/part-subject of labor is made to unspeak himself.[42]

In *Coolie*, this wordless center is emblematic of other instances where the writer formalizes a pattern of silences. There are, for example, as discussed also in my introduction, moments of "interruption from a source relating 'otherwise' to the main system of meaning unfolding." Munoo reads the export trader's sign, but he is "too young to know the laws of political economy." Here, the defining comment on the global text has to be made by the narrator as a marked aside to the reader, who must know the significance of the corn laws in 1930s India. Another place of interruption (a break in speech) that defines how we read this book is the *meaningless* rumor that disrupts the trade unionist's charter. This writing of course encrypts the exorbitant story that will never make it onto center stage—that of the central character's "kidnapping." Here, in this scene of the failed strike, it is set wild—a narrative without author. Rumor marks the place of subaltern discourse: "the broken accents of a voice defined, 'kidnapped, kidnapped . . . o my son has been kidnapped.'" Significantly, the disembodied voice is gendered: "Only the moaning of a coolie could be heard, a queer, broken moaning like the howling of a she-hyena" (234).

Once again, if "the work of form is revealed in reading," something is to be learned, also, from the moments where the text transgresses its own rhetorical rules.[43] In a novel focalized almost entirely from the perspective of a factory coolie, Anand then gives us this telling episode that stands out as particularly gratuitous (lacking good reason) in terms of the narrative code. The following scene breaks with the general conduct (of presupposed silences staged as rhetorical questions) to give us an answer where none is called for. It represents a space to which the central character has no access: the bosses reasoning (boardroom discussions about transnational corporations, consolidated interests, tariffs, imperial preference, world trade, and other obscure topics). Focalized from the point of view of the ubiquitous "Parsi" messenger boy who sees and hears all, this scene gives away the reasons behind the production of a notice informing the coolies of short work, effective immediately.

A dispatch arrives from "Sir George White" (factory headquarters) in England, prompting the manager to hastily dictate a notice to his scrivener. In the official document to be sent out, the impending season of short time is explained in terms of global economic depression:

> "In view of the present trade depression and currency crisis," Mr. Little dictated, in a slow, deliberate manner, screwing up his eyes and puffing out his cheeks, till the words began to twist and roll like windy rhetoric,[44] "the Board of Directors regrets to announce that in order to keep the plant running and to curtail expenses, the Mills will go on short time immediately. There will

be no work for the fourth week in every month till further notice. No wages will be paid for that week, but the management, having the welfare of the workers at heart, have sanctioned a substantial allowance...." (223)

But afterwards, as Sir Reginald White, the proprietor of the Bombay Mills, arrives on the scene, he intimates that socialist agitation in the home factories in England is connected to the policy of cost-cutting crisis management here. The gaps in the blandly worded company document are filled as he explains, "the Board of Directors had serious news about a threatening crisis at home. And in view of the Company's interests, not only in this mill, but in the Calcutta Jute Mills and the Madras Mines, and to guard against any loss to the shareholders we have had to take this unfortunate decision.... Britain must go through with the Singapore agreement and make the Indian ocean safe for our ships. But the trouble is that these Indians are getting more and more restive, and the socialists at home, you know..." (225). Elsewhere in the story, the impossible aporia of socialist agitation at home being the condition for short work here is perhaps too easily resolved in Anand's caricature of Jimmy Thomas, once a Lancashire mill operative, now the evil foreman who brutalizes factory coolies in sync with newspaper reports on communist agitation:

> Occasionally he kicked a coolie. But that was when he had read in the morning paper the news of a nationalist demonstration, a terrorist outrage or an attempt at seditious communist propaganda which he, as a member of the British race in India, considered to be more of a personal affront than the pursuit of an ideal of freedom on the part of the exploited. He had long since forgotten the days during which he himself had eked out a miserable existence in Lancashire. (217)

The "supplementary" scene of boardroom discussions is also crucially significant in that it introduces into the story the shadowy figures of the Indian capitalists/businessmen who stand to benefit indirectly from Sir Reginald's appeals to the viceroy for a "high tariff on foreign goods."[45] "Did you hear that the Stephenson Mills have been bought by the Jamsetji Jijibhoy group? That makes the Indian Interests in the cotton industry 75 percent to our 25. It is a bad look-out," opines Sir Reginald. Of course the issue of trade wars between British and Indian capitalists is set in a system of knowledge and calculation that is worlds apart from the life and times of a coolie. Once again, the narrator underscores the protagonist's subaltern bafflement: "Munoo, who knew nothing about directors and shareholders and threatening crises, believed that it was Ratan's dismissal that had been the cause of this uproar" (226).

At the heart of Anand's novel is a dilemma for reporter, politician, Marxist, writer, and reader. The question becomes: should we suppress the damaging details to preserve the integrity of the story? At stake is the issue of whether we should edit the testimony of a coolie in order to produce a more manageable account of events (e.g., the failed strike, the management-manufactured communal riots, international working-class solidarity). Indeed, some of us would like to suppress the evidence of the sad misfirings of the socialist message in colonial India altogether, a message delivered, as Chakrabarty so eloquently puts it, "only in a travestied form by the mad and violent agency of imperialism." *Coolie* marks the problem that is discreetly effaced in the craft and analysis of the proletarian novel—the unspeakable margins of peripheral labor.

THE LOGIC OF THE SUPPLEMENT

> This monograph is an attempt to share with the reader the truth about the working classes in India.
> —D. Chaman Lall, *Coolie: The Story of Labor and Capital in India*

With the writing of *Coolie*, Anand follows through with the promise made to T. S. Eliot: he gives us a counternarrative to Kipling's feted boy's adventure story from the perspective of unorganized child labor. But as touched upon in the opening lines of this chapter, Anand's novel is a 1930s rewriting in another sense in that his novel also draws upon a 1932 tract produced by Diwan Chaman Lall titled *Coolie: The Story of Labor and Capital in India*.[46] The foreword to Lall's book explains that the text to follow is "a monograph attempt[ing] to share with the reader the truth about the working classes in India."

The tract itself (composed of two slim volumes filled with typographic errors) reads as a painstaking work of sociology in the pamphleteering tradition whose central preoccupation is "telling the truth." Against the weight of factory inspectors' reports and letters from the Royal Labor Commission, we are repeatedly given counter-examples of "testimony." Throughout Lall's text, insistent statements such as these occur: "The peasants presented me with a pitiful appeal. I give it in its own quaint language" (2), and "I record here four such cases in each of which the peasat [sic] speaks for himself [sic]" (3). The final paragraph of the first chapter, however, is both commentary and prophesy. The writer concludes with a promise:

> But the times are rapidly changing. Peasant revolts are becoming the order of the day. Industrial strife is becoming more and more bitter. The peasant is refusing to pay his rent. The industrial worker is refusing to be made a door's mat for every foot to wipe on. The year 1931 opens with reports of peasant action against money lenders in the Central Provinces, where in several cases the peasants took the law into their own hands and burned down the houses and shops of the money-lenders, and in the United Provinces, where they have taken to a steadfast refusal to pay rent, going even so far as, in some cases, to murder the landlord. A Frankinstein [sic] has been raised in India and there is no knowing how far its shadow will spread throughout the length and breadth of this country. (26)

Lall's hortatory tone, here—"a Frankinstein has been raised in India and there is no knowing how far its shadow will spread throughout the length and breadth of this country"—surely recalls Marx's clarion call opening line of the *Manifesto*. Writing in historical hindsight, Rothermund produces a more tempered summation, considering that in general, "peasant unrest was widespread in the countries of the periphery in the 1930s. But in most cases it remained localised and did not attract international attention." In fact, in the aftermath of the 1930s, a range of anticolonial historians produce meticulously researched case studies documenting (albeit from different theoretical angles) instances of working-class resistance in 1930s India among jute-mill workers in Bengal, coal miners in Bihar, and steelworkers in

Jamshedpur. Somewhere between the pamphleteer's urgency and the historians' measured inventory of dispersed yet interrelated phenomena is the novelist's intervention. In Anand's book, as we see, there are no dramatic episodes of successful industrial action or agrarian revolt, although there is one muted reference to the wheat price index and "political economy."

Before arriving at the textile factory, Munoo finds work at the Grain Market. He works at loading and unloading sacks of cereal to be exported by local merchants. Fascinated by the sounds and names of distant places, "Munoo read[s] the blue Hindustani inscription on the sacks of grain. But [the narrator tells us] he was too young to know the laws of political economy, especially as they govern the export of wheat from India to England." Unlike the scene of closed-door trade discussions, this fragment is focalized from the perspective of the central character—a child-worker. The statement itself, however, is made in the register of an ironic aside to the (Marxist) reader of working-class fiction—a prompt, perhaps, to discover the significance of the corn laws in an international frame.

Mieke Bal reads the narrative logic of an ellipse as follows: "All we can do, sometimes, is logically deduce on the basis of certain information that something has been omitted. That which has been omitted—the contents of the ellipsis—need not be unimportant; on the contrary, the event about which nothing is said may have been so painful that it is precisely for that reason it is being elided. Or the event is so difficult to put into words that it is preferable to maintain complete silence about it."[47] In Anand's *Coolie* the whole story might be summed up in this moment of not knowing the facts (of political economy): the colonial peasantry produce agricultural products for export rather than food for themselves. Anand, in this speaking silence, references and rewrites the textuality of the pamphleteer's angry rhetoric and voluble testimonies. In Lall's pamphlet, the story of the Kangra Hills (Munoo's place of origin) is narrated in terms of famine and abiding hunger:

> In the month of August 1921 a gentleman in charge of the famine relief fund in the Kangra valley wrote as follows of the peasantry of that part: "They take a seer or two of wheat or maize, mix it with about the same quantity of mango-stones and husk of rice and get the three powdered together and eat. Cholera which is

the natural concomitant of famine has reappeared. The power of resistance has gone, and the people have been obliged to live on leaves of various vegetables mixed with some sort of grain.   (8)

In the literary representation of *Coolie*, the history of export agriculture and the politics of human-made famines (in Amartya Sen's terms, the "political economy of hunger") are not referenced. However, in terms of the rhetorical conduct of the text, this place—this scripted silence (where Munoo "reads" the sacks of grain)—calls for supplementation. It quietly but insistently addresses the reader to "give [this] writing its future."[48]

Chapter 2

POSTCOLONIAL SRI LANKA AND "BLACK STRUGGLES FOR SOCIALISM"

Socialist Ethics in Ambalavaner Sivanandan's When Memory Dies

These others, Hardy and Foster and them, he reflected, familiarized us with their cities and villages and the people in them through their tales, but the tales themselves had nothing to say to us. And when they wrote about our countries and our people, though the tales were familiar, the characters were strangers. . . . We had no history, or we had several, mostly not of our doing, or we had forgotten that part of it which was, or it was a part too late to remember: it could only unmake the present.
—Ambalavaner Sivanandan, *When Memory Dies*

It is significant that the idealization of the peasant, in the modern English middle-class tradition, was not extended, when it might have mattered, to the peasants, the plantation workers, the coolies of these occupied societies.
—Raymond Williams, *The Country and the City*

Above all, communalism, like ethnicity, is a pluralist word in a class world. They both describe, but do not tell—are historicist rather than historical.
—Ambalavaner Sivanandan, *Communities of Resistance*

The opposition between the history of labor immigration to the Euro-US metropolitan "centers" of the world and the history of the working class in the manufacturing sector of the postcolonial "Third World" forms the impasse that generally delineates the boundaries of the separate fields of immigration studies and postcolonial studies. However, this provisional distinction (produced in the context of framing institutional objects of investigation) risks reifying an instrumental, structural difference into an absolute, ontological one—forever dwelling upon economisms of comparative advantage and competition, rather than beginning to consider, however shakily, the possibility of a transnational "socialist ethics" in the shadow of trade unionist socialism.

Such an ethics is envisioned as an alternative to deadlocked dualisms of thinking that juxtapose the rational economic self-interest of the national worker against that of the foreign worker. The adjective added category of the *immigrant* worker supplants the naming of the worker—now more so than ever, in the era of remittance economies and outsourcing. Thinking of these (admittedly opposed) categories together is looked upon as ideologically suspect by extremes of left and right alike.[1] But these lines cross, or are forced together, in historical situations, in creative labor organizing, and within the narrative predicaments of working-class literature. For Ambalavaner Sivanandan, where "black is a political color," working in the interest of underclass migrants and (black) working-classes in Britain requires simultaneously addressing stateless immigrant and national—the categories themselves are certainly politically charged—workers in postcolonial Sri Lanka. In *When Memory Dies*, as we will see, the lines of the subject and antisubject of the fabula are made to cross in the narrator's self-annihilating wish for reparative justice.

Sivanandan's concept of "black socialism"—forged, on the one hand, in opposition to Eurocentric Marxism, and on the other, against the divisive culturalism of a *certain* type of (essentialist, narrowly identitarian) ethnic studies—opens up a different set of possibilities for knowledge politics. Toward elaborating the terms of these possibilities, in this chapter I focus on the doubling of the postcolonial/immigrant subject represented in the literary texts and political essays of Sri Lankan Tamil/black activist-writer Ambalavaner Sivanandan (b. 1923). While Sivanandan's own journey is from newly independent "Ceylon" to the imperial metropole of Britain—not North America—nevertheless, the subject position that he theorizes has relevance for U.S. Marxist cultural studies. This is not only because the genealogy that Sivanandan plots for black socialism derives from the political arsenal of U.S., Caribbean, and African pan-Africanist internationalists like W.E.B. Du Bois, C.L.R. James, and Amilcar Cabral; it is also because Sivanandan's writings open us up to new ways of apprehending what has become an unthinkable abstraction in the era of economic globalization: the changing terms of the new international division of labor—in Sivanandan's lexicon, the dialectic of "race and class."

Following up on questions raised in the previous chapter, here my objectives are twofold. There I called attention to how the anticolonial proletarian novel is overlooked within working-class literary historiography. The first part of this chapter describes how Sivanandan's work illuminates the place of this ideological blind spot in Western Marxism. However, moving beyond a consideration of this omission, in this chapter I also focus on the means by which Sivanandan moves away from the language and dicta of trade unionist socialism and left-party politics toward a more abstract and expansive philosophy of socialist ethics. The turn toward socialist ethics marks a break with conventional Eurocentric, masculinist analytics of class as well as with nationalist counternarratives. It opens up ways of articulating class and other collectivities—of asking "How many are we?"—in ways that anticipate contemporary working-class women writers' and feminist thinkers' attempts to conceptualize class as an anti-essentialist category. (Chapter 3 of this book provides a sustained examination of such working-class women's and Marxist feminist critiques, focusing on writers and texts from either side of the international division of labor.)

The strategy behind this sort of organization of class—not framed by the particular historical example of the Industrial Revolution in England but based rather on the idea that the concept of class cannot be understood by generalizing from a particular historical moment— once again relies on a careful reading of some of Marx's later writings. But if the idea of class should not be tied to a particular historical moment, only to be retroactively enshrined as the defining moment of social revolution, the questions persist: "What makes a class?" What constitutes socialist ethics? In Sivanandan's case, the content of socialist ethics derives from the idea of literature and a concept of "the literary." His move from left journalism to socialist ethics also coincides with his turn to literature and the decision to write historical fiction. For Sivanandan (who is best-known, perhaps, for his political essays and analyses), the publication of *When Memory Dies* opens up a different avenue for theorizing class struggle and a philosophy of history. The second objective of this chapter is to try to understand this turn to literature: What ideological—or, possibly, ethical—work does it accomplish?

I read Sivanandan's literary texts and political analysis as supplementing each other in ways that many critics have neglected to examine. There seems to be a clear, categorical divide separating different schools of readership when it comes to Sivanandan. On the one hand, postcolonial scholars focus only on *When Memory Dies*, reading the novel as an epic narrative of class struggles leading up to the Sri Lankan civil war. On the other hand, scholars of black British cultural studies focus exclusively on Sivanandan's critiques of the British government—his analyses of institutionalized racism, labor management, and immigration policy in contemporary Britain. Sivanandan, however, does not subscribe to this cauterized, compartmentalized vision of history. In his fiction as in his political analyses, we notice a doubling of subjects and historical scenes. What do we make of this narrative move? In his novel about the war in Sri Lanka, the life stories of disenfranchised immigrant workers constantly intrude to interrupt and sideline the primary narrative of interethnic violence. In his book *Communities of Resistance: Writings on Black Struggles for Socialism* Sri Lankan history is included as a "case study."[2] This back-and-forth movement between Sri Lanka and black socialism also becomes, for Sivanandan, a back-and-forth movement between history and literature. Ultimately, as we will see, this alternating movement itself becomes allegorized as a figure for reading.

"When was the post-colonial?" asks Stuart Hall. "What should be included and excluded from its frame?"[3] (242). Sivanandan, one of Hall's contemporaries and a "co-worker in the kingdom of culture," embeds the story of postcolonial Sri Lanka in the context of "black struggles for socialism," displacing the (commonly agreed-upon) order of the frame and what lies outside. Sivanandan, prior to Robert Young and his influential theoretical study, conceptualizes postcolonial historical difference in the context of a broader history of internationalism.[4] If Dipesh Chakrabarty's exhortation to the reader is to "provincialize Europe," Sivanandan suggests we go further.[5] We must also provincialize Sri Lanka.

PROVINCIALIZING SRI LANKA

"Was it a smooth transition, your development from teacher in the plantation areas of Sri Lanka to left-wing thinker here in Britain?" This question is posed to Ambalavaner Sivanandan during a 1990s interview (*Communities*, 8). The interviewer is a sympathetic colleague, but it seems significant that the phrasing of the question precludes any discussion of leftist political culture in Sri Lanka (then Ceylon). It also presumes a continental divide between the practice of teaching working-class students in Sri Lanka and the practice of theorizing within Marxist circles in Britain. Moreover, the interviewer comprehends the postcolonial socialist's journey as an evolutionary progress.

Sivanandan, however, recounts his arrival not as an introduction to left political culture but rather as a "double baptism of fire." In the aftermath of the passage of the racist "Sinhala Only" language act of 1956 and the 1958 riots, he left Sri Lanka and entered upon the scene of race war in Britain. In his own words: "That was, I suppose, a double baptism of fire—Sinhalese-Tamil riots there, white-black riots here" (9). This is a much-quoted rendition of events. This synopsis of the author's passage to England is in fact reprinted in the prefatory pages of *When Memory Dies*. While the language and rhetorical strategy of the brief biographical sketch are a necessary corrective to a neo-Orientalist optics that (still entrenched in its civilizing mission) only sees Third World violence, Sivanandan's easy parallelism of separate historical events does not do justice to the breadth and depth of his own later work, which grapples with the complexity of differing ideologies of class, race, and "ethnicity" in the metropolitan center versus the postcolonial, *anticolonial* periphery.

In early pieces of prose writing and left journalism, Sivanandan emphasizes a cause-and-effect, *structural* connection between the exploited working class "here" (in Britain) and the one "there" (in Sri Lanka). As he puts it, writing under the heading "Casualties of Imperialism":

> The economic depredations of multinational capital, the political repression of the regimes that host it ... all combine to effect the brutal dislocation and displacement of people all over the Third World and force them to flee their countries. Whether as economic refugees or as political asylum-seekers is no matter—for, however their arrival at the center may be categorized, their ejection from their countries is, as I have shown, both economic and political at once. To distinguish between them is not just willfully to misunderstand the machinations of imperialism today, but to

pretend that the struggle against imperialism is not also here, at the center, or has nothing to do with workers' struggles here.
(*Communities*, 189)

Beyond linear, causal narratives, *When Memory Dies*, however, might be read as mapping the political différance between ideas of race, class, and Marxism "here" and "there." Specifically, it is a reworking of anecdotal, historical, and sociological evidence into political fiction—into literature's provenance, the so-called ethical universal. The writing of *When Memory Dies* marks the political journalist's turn to a medium other than realist reportage. Beyond personal history and the fact that—as it reads on the title page of his novel—"Sivanandan came to Britain from Ceylon in the wake of the riots of 1958 and walked into the riots of Notting Hill," how can these different, multiple instances of racialization be understood as representative of a collective experience? What is at stake in this movement from the particular to the general (from metropolitan history to Third World political fiction—to Marxism and literature) signifies nothing less than a reorienting of the critical terrains of Marxist historiography and theory, starting from the grounds of an ethics of class struggles in the periphery.

In the concluding chapters of *The Country and the City*, Raymond Williams begins to touch upon the need to examine the politics of modernism in light of the racialization of the international division of labor, but ultimately stops short of closely examining the racism that is a structural, not aberrational, part of the left, liberal paradigm. Centering the example of postcolonial Sri Lanka, the export-oriented tea plantation industry, and other legacies of the colonial division of labor, Sivanandan ultimately engages the provenance not only of bourgeois (Sinhala) nationalist historiography, but also of "left-wing thinking" or "left cultural imperialism," as he formulates it.

WRITING RACE, CLASS, AND (LITERATURE)[6]

One year after the anti-Tamil pogroms of July 1983 in the city of Colombo, Sivanandan first published the essay "Sri Lanka: A Case Study" in the London-based journal that he had founded, *Race and Class*. In 1990 he republished the article as the final chapter in *Communities of Resistance*, an anthology of heterogeneous political writings—reviews, transcripts of interviews, pieces of left journalism, and historical studies. Here we find—strangely, perhaps—that the particular historical case study of postcolonial Sri Lanka constitutes the last word in "black struggles for socialism." In 1997 Sivanandan revisited the text of this monograph once again, this time transforming its phrasing into bits and pieces of dialogue and plotline for an epic novel/part fictionalized memoir set against the backdrop of the ongoing Sri Lankan interethnic war, *When Memory Dies*.

What enables the politics of that reframing? What limits it? What is gained (or lost) for Marxist historiography in this move from the radical particularity of the case study to the supposedly universal properties of "Marxism and Literature"? "Sri Lanka: A Case Study" is an angry piece of writing. It concludes like a manifesto with a call to arms; the final paragraph reads:

> Against that mounting dictatorship stands only the armed resistance of the Tamil freedom-fighter—and whatever the goal in view, their immediate and inevitable task is to continue their unrelenting war against the fascist state.... There is no socialism after liberation; socialism is the process through which liberation is won. (*Communities*, 248)

Sivanandan's novel *When Memory Dies*, however, is written in a different register—not in the tone of a manifesto, but in one of elegiac protest.[7] Counter to the staging of history in the case study, in the closing scene of book 3 the hero is gunned down by an LTTE (Liberation Tigers of Tamil Eelam) "freedom fighter." And Sivanandan rewrites the "no socialism, after liberation" speech, reshuffling the terms as part of an unresolved debate between an LTTE operative and a grassroots activist (the novel's protagonist) struggling to find common ground in socialism—but failing (405–406). The final speech in the book, not incidentally, will be given over to Meena, the girl-child/organic intellectual from the tea estate regions of Sri Lanka.

I resist the contention that the turn to literature signifies a capitulation, an abandoning of an earlier radical—even violent—stance in favor of an uncritical liberal humanism. Rather, the turn to literature enables a different elaboration of radical politics and ethics. In Sivanandan's case, this different elaboration is motivated by a dispute with the idea of "history as fait accompli" that sociological explanations must rely on to ground their truth claims—that is, by a critique of historicism.[8] Elsewhere, in a rousing prose passage on the poverty of the historicist imagination, Sivanandan has noted that "above all, communalism, like ethnicity, is a pluralist word in a class world. They both describe, but do not tell—are historicist rather than historical" (*Communities*, 235). And yet this literary rewriting cannot be understood to be simply equivalent to an exercise in revisionist history.

As mentioned, "Sri Lanka: A Case Study" is an angry piece of writing. In the novel, however, the writer restages the final drama differently. Sivanandan rewords the terms of his manifesto, this time simultaneously knocking the gun out of the LTTE adherent's hands. By the end of the book, we find that Vijayan, the final protagonist of the novel, although he does not live to realize his goal, has foresworn allegiance to militant nationalism and revolutionary violence, dedicating himself instead to teach in a rural school district. Inspired by reading Amilcar Cabral, he resignifies the slogan "Return to the Source," to serve the cultural politics of the struggle at hand. Undoubtedly there are other, more programmatic ways of understanding this ideological shift in the text, especially in the wake of philosophical and tactical changes in organizations like the LTTE (and indeed the Sinhala chauvinist JVP) from socialism to nationalism to violence.[9] But it's also worthwhile to consider Sivanandan's general statements touching upon Marxism and the philosophy of literature.

In Sivanandan's case, the turn to literature, simultaneous with the movement away from the language of manifestos, is a move toward an understanding of the dialectic as quotidian—to be apprehended not in the context of revolutionary moments, but in the struggles of the everyday. As the writer explains it, "that tool of analysis that Marxism gave me in dialectical materialism was 'the moment of a miracle' which in Dylan Thomas's phrase is 'unending lightning' and I was later, much later, to discover with the poets and novelists that the dialectic was not just a tool of analysis but a felt sensibility" (*Communities*, 5). Not incidentally, lines from Dylan Thomas's "Forgotten Mornings" compose the epigraph to book 1 of *When Memory Dies*; the idea resurfaces in a short story by Sivanandan titled "The Man Who Loved the Dialectic."[10] Literary rewriting, then, is not simply equivalent to an exercise in revisionist history, but is an exercise in dialectical thought.[11] The turn to literature also must be seen as Sivanandan's effort to grapple with a Marxist philosophy—from class politics to socialist ethics. But finally and most importantly, the literary turn enables a deterritorializing double focus—a principled, intentional blurring of the lines not permitted in the tenets of history writing, reportage, or, indeed, revolutionary propaganda.

Literature preserves the shifting relationality, the différance of race and class that Sivanandan attempts to illuminate when he writes elsewhere of the ever-changing terms of the international division of labor. Describing his own position, as the organic intellectual of the anticolonial struggle, he writes, negating the concepts of "exile"—and of "domicile":

> For me to feel truly "an exile" would to be exiled from the struggles of the black and Third World peoples I know so well and from whom I come. And the struggle is where I am, the struggle is here and now. But of course, I carry a double consciousness with me: that of my place in this society, my place in the struggle of black, working-class people here and now, and that of my place in the struggles of Third World Peoples in Third World countries both here and there. And I am not exiled from that. . . . And therefore I do not understand the question of exile. I do not understand the question of domicile. (*Communities*, 16)[12]

For Sivanandan, ultimately it is a philosophy of literature and the provenance of the literary that enables the ethical double movement—a worldview that not only "provincializes Europe" (to refer to Dipesh Chakrabarty's intervention) but also, just as importantly, provincializes Sri Lanka—frames the nation in the context of a larger history of socialist internationalism, class politics, and comparative ethnic struggles, worldwide.

TELLING HISTORY

Some might argue that the turn to literature (that I am identifying in Sivanandan) is synonymous with what Marxist critics of poststructuralist theory have decried as the "linguistic turn." According to certain orthodoxies of Marxist literary criticism, formal experimentation (outside realism) would constitute at best a form of sleight of hand and at worst a type of ideological betrayal. Critics like John Berger, for example, seem adamantly against poststructuralist readings of *When Memory Dies*. In his back-cover blurb—admittedly an overdetermined genre of critical appraisal—he writes, "There are no flip evasions, or post-modern copouts. Here [in *When Memory Dies*] you are in life, just as one says 'in love.'" By contrast, Timothy Brennan finds the course of the novel "unsatisfactorily" dictated by the saga form. He would excuse the novel's limitations by redirecting the focus to Sivanandan's writings in other genres. Yet conventional theories of literary historiography (more often than not, merely conveniences of periodization) do not help us to account for the particular ways in which Sivanandan breaks with chronology to establish a relationship between narrative form and the conceptual and ideological content of historical discourse. Rather than a chronicler's saga, *When Memory Dies* might be read as charting the zigzagging prospects and unverifiable outcomes of actively marginalized stories with working-class history and formal labor organizing.

Given its intergenerational scope and richness of historical detail, *When Memory Dies* resists summary. The sheer expanse of time covered presents us with a difficult, if not impossible, task. We are forewarned by the narrator at the outset to expect "no one story, with a beginning and an end, no story that picks up from where the past left off—only bits and shards of stories" (5). And yet, interfering with this qualification, the imperative of the book is to recover what we have now passively forgotten or actively repressed—moments of solidarity, compromise, and forgiveness, remembrances of life and work before the creeping ethnicization of politics and the systematic militarization of daily life in post-Independence Sri Lanka. The novel is at war with itself in terms of its ideological and taxonomic legacy. Some parts read like an archetypal social realist working-class novel; others, however, dream after another way of "telling history." For Sivanandan, literary rewriting—the expansion and annotation of the polemical essay and historical case study—despite certain critics misgivings, permits the exercise of dialectical revisionism (as opposed to relativist second-guessing) of certain entrenched Marxist orthodoxies.

"Historicist histories ... describe but do not tell." To tell, then ("to make a narrative of," might we say?), is to do more than to describe, tally facts, or keep faithful score according to the time line of significant events in nationalist history. In *When Memory Dies*, the historical backdrop changes from early anticolonial labor struggles to the rise (and decline) of the trade union movement, to the compromises of post-Independence left-party politics, to "IMF Capitalism," to the institutionalization of Sinhala Buddhist nationalism, to LTTE violence. The basic plot (rearranged for chronology's sake) traces the biography of a three-part collective subject—father (Sahadevan), son (Rajan), and the son's adopted son (Vijaya/Vijayan)—over a period extending from the 1920s to the contemporary moment in Sri Lanka. Following upon the murder of his wife and his subsequent breakdown, Rajan, the narrator-protagonist, all but drops out of the story with the end of book 2. Vijayan, the hero-protagonist, is depicted as haunted by memories of his murdered mother—more of a presence in his life than his absent father.

Annotating, and at moments disrupting, the primary story line of male bonding/unbonding, however, is a different, dispersed, dislocated kinship narrative of father, sister, and daughter (Sanji, Selamma, and Meena) who are stateless plantation workers facing the threat of "repatriation" to India. Here, within the situation of indentured labor, we see that the Oedipal/familial bond has been broken and reconstituted at the outset. In a novel without a center, the exorbitant vignette of (the child) Sanji's expulsion from school serves as recursive, provisional focal point for the narrator. The character development of Meena, Sanji's daughter (and Vijayan's lover) reads as a counterpoint to this abortive narrative trajectory. The author represents her as an autodidact and organic intellectual of the working class. She gets to pronounce the final word on ethnic fratricide—simultaneously a verdict on nationalism and a eulogy for socialism: "You have killed the only decent thing left in this land.... We'll never be whole again" (410).

Reordered through the lens of Sivanandan's fiction, the exorbitation of the organic intellectual of the stateless plantation working class is made central to the telling of Sri Lankan history.[13] The author contrives a connection between the main actors of the nationalist contest and these others, deemed peripheral to all action. In assessing how and where he breaks with chronology to establish a relationship between form and ideology, we cannot overlook the meaning of the novel's *labored* and unwieldy beginning and interrupted ending. The story opens with a philosophical meditation on a sense of self located in the acknowledgment of a disenfranchised other. Linearity and the "saga form" are in fact dispensed with at the very outset of the novel. In practices of reading as in movements of migration, which do we privilege, origins or destinations? Sivanandan's narrator-protagonist, Rajan, cannot answer this question for himself in any positivistic sense. He starts us off from a muddled place where lines of territorial claims and losses, those dividing victims and conquerors, and even self and other, are more ethically compromised than the accommodations of slogan-shouting peace builders and war mongers alike.

READING INTERNATIONALISM: THE DIALECTIC OF RACE AND CLASS

Sivanandan's cross-generational epic, most often construed as a novel focusing on the Sri Lankan civil war, opens with this unwieldy moment of the narrator-protagonist attempting to articulate an archive of working-class history across dispersed locations—the immigrant writer (in England) and the immigrant worker (in Ceylon). The moment is framed by the author's own history; Rajan, like the author, leaves Ceylon in the wake of anti-Tamil violence of 1958. At the very outset of the novel, we are confronted with a deliberate provocation: Is it possible to read internationalism as transference, and transference as ethical—as the displaced affective basis for the activist intellectual's politics?

The problem of describing internationalism as a "structure of feeling"—in Sivanandan's own words, "the dialectic as a felt sensibility"—becomes the narrative burden of *When Memory Dies*. In context, the story of an estate worker's son who is expelled from the English-medium school is forthcoming in book 2 (following the birth of the narrator). In a book that is primarily ordered into three sequential parts, the marked achrony of the first few pages reveals something about the past and memory before it gets separated out from the narrating self as something objectified, nameable, and discrete—the social. The novel opens out of sequence with an out-of-sync narrator contemplating a strange death wish:

> My memory begins, as always, with the rain—crouched as a small boy against the great wall of the old colonial building that once housed the post office. It frightened me, the great monsoon downpour, and saddened me too, threw me back on my little boy self and its lonelinesses, the growing things in myself I could not tell others about, the first feel of the sadness of a world that kept Sanji from school because he had no shoes. And I welcomed the lightning then, not frightened any more, for it would strike me dead and Sanji would have my shoes, and I would be sad no more . . . in that moment that had gone and come again, it was awe and grief and wonderment crowding in on each other mixed up with Sanji's shoes.

Rajan, the narrator of this passage, is speaking out of turn. According to the book's narrative chronology, his birth has not occurred. Yet this strange (and estranged) figure is also very familiar and proximate in relationship to Sivanandan, the author. Furthermore, the author constructs Rajan as an unreliable narrator (traumatized after losing his wife to a murderous Sinhala mob) who begins telling the story from outside the frame, from a place removed from Sri Lanka—distant England. But conceptually and logically prior to (any) protagonist's story is the space displaced for the cosmopolitan, colonial intellectual: The nonsubject, Sanji, whose absent presence haunts the story from the very outset, happens to be the child of one of the "stateless million," Indian-origin Tamil laborers, originally recruited by the British in the nineteenth century and the first half of the twentieth to work on colonial tea plantations. He belongs to a subaltern class that remains disenfranchised in the aftermath of national independence. The narrator recalls the day his childhood friend was sent home from school. Sanji is denied access to education in an era of free education for all (in postcolonial Sri Lanka) because his parents can't afford to supply him with shoes to go along with the required pristine uniform.

The doubling of the subject and antisubject (of the political and economic migrant) is predicated on a self-reflexive/deauthorizing movement. These two figures converge/disband as a dialectical image. Across time, distance, and class difference, the mise en scène is a moment of fraught overidentification—but one which emblematizes an acknowledgment of the autocritical privilege of narration: wishing someone else into his shoes. The "dialectic as felt sensibility" in the opening iterative movement is a complex recasting of the desire and interests of "double consciousness." The class divisions between the speaking subject (the postcolonial Tamil diasporic intellectual) and the subaltern antisubject (stateless economic migrant) cannot be magically undone by slogans and manifestos: "I don't believe in exile. I don't believe in domicile" resonates differently for the stateless immigrant (in Ceylon). Sivanandan's narrator and alter ego risks communicating what Sivanandan, theorist of black British cultural studies cannot—that internationalism is a feeling of connection based on disconnection.

The narrator goes on to observe, "Other seasons I would come to know—spring and autumn and winter—and other countries where shoes abounded. But the things that crowded in on me that day in the rain, and in many rains after, and made me an exile for the better part of my life, were also the things that connected me to my country and made me want to tell its story" (1). The troping of history writing as survivor's guilt is a strange way of representing the ethical stance of the engaged historian, to be sure. Furthermore, here the speaking subject's own access to collectivity in "other countries" is predicated upon the recognition of the denial of access to the subaltern other in Sri Lanka—glaringly faulty logic, certainly. Sivanandan's critique of historicism proceeds by way of an imagined substitution and an active displacement—an exchange of places between "here" and "there," between colonial subject and organic intellectual, between diaspora and nation. Is this rhetorical maneuver simply to be understood as Sivanandan instrumentalizing the history of up-country Tamils in Sri Lanka?

We have no explicit textual evidence to suggest that the character, Rajan, is identical to Sivanandan. We don't know that he goes on to become politically active in working-class struggles in these "other countries." He fades out of the narrative at the end of book 2, "resurfacing" only for the opening meditation at the beginning of the novel. In *Allegories of Reading*, Paul de Man suggests, however, that "political and autobiographical texts have in common that they share a referential reading-moment explicitly built in within the spectrum of their significations" (278). In a text that is as political as it is autobiographical—

part fictionalized history, part political memoir—this is one such referential reading-moment captured in confessional mode. The colonial intellectual hearkens back to an earlier moment of originary dispersal, forcing a connection between "diasporas old and new."[14]

Rajan's remorseful commentary as it occurs in the novel, then, is very different from the strident postcolonial immigrant credo, demanding legitimation and visibility in the imperial metropolis. It is voiced in a different register than the familiar line "we are here because you were there," or, as Sivanandan maintains in his political essays: "I do not understand the question of exile. I do not understand the question of domicile" (*Communities*, 16). Rather, it is modified—completely reformulated in the service of the subaltern other: "I am here, because he is not" seems to be the formulation of the colonial intellectual in a strange sleight of hand involving cause and (a)ffect. Problematically perhaps, the concept of the literary in terms of Sivanandan's definition (as the graph of différance) can also make visible the difficult fact that representation for one constituency is predicated upon the effacement of another. But knowing this, how do you proceed? Historicist histories dictated by pregiven sociological categories such as race and ethnicity ("pluralist words in a class world") "describe but do not tell." Again, to "tell" then (to make a narrative of) is to do more than to describe or merely tally facts. Thus counter to dominant narratives of Sri Lankan nationalist history, *When Memory Dies* begins by recalling the displaced origins of labor history—not those of archaeological settlement history or those of separatist nationalism.

In a novel that has no center—we are forewarned to expect "no one story, with a beginning and an end, no story that picks up from where the past left off—only bits and shards of stories"—the foreclosed narrative trajectory of the organic intellectual, like the memory of shoes that never were, calls attention to itself through absence. Beyond merely gestural politics or claims of solidarity from a distance, Sivanandan's explicit decision to prioritize stories of estate workers resonates with the efforts of labor historians who would frame Sri Lanka in the context of histories of labor internationalism and the politics of migration. Displacing competing nationalist claims to national territory, *When Memory Dies* recalls us to the fact that Sri Lanka must be understood to be the beneficiary of Indian immigrant labor. Sithaperam Nadesan makes the case explicit, reminding us that "millions of Indians were compelled to migrate to the various colonies of the British Empire. And today we find peoples of Indian origin constituting a considerable part of the populations of many countries, such as Sri Lanka, British Guyana, Trinidad, South Africa, Mauritius, Malaysia, and Fiji."[15] At the beginning of the novel, questions of nation and diaspora are presented as all tangled up with the narrating subject's own feelings of displacement and cathexis. "And therefore I do not understand the question of exile. I do not understand the question of domicile." Again, undoubtedly, the phrase indexes a different reality for the internationalist as opposed to the stateless million plantation workers, and yet while for Giorgio Agamben the refugee marks the paradigmatic figure of the age who brings to crisis the fiction of the sovereignty of the nation-state, Sivanandan would seem to want to underscore that it is the figure of the stateless refugee worker who does so.[16]

"DEHISTORICIZING HISTORY": LABOR HISTORY AS SUPPLEMENT[17]

> "And even what little is left of them you want to send back to India. They never knew India. They were born here. Even the British let us die here and be buried among the tea-bushes for manure, but your people . . ."
> —*When Memory Dies*

The alternating rhythm between prospective and retrospective (new objects and old) is not framed in terms of different spaces (diaspora and mainland/England and Sri Lanka) throughout the novel as it is in the opening scene. (The opening frame narrative is the only segment—descriptions of locale withheld—that is set in England.) And yet, the back-and-forth movement, which is also the motion of reading, propels the critical ethical agency of this book. Elsewhere in the novel, the concept of the dialectic as felt sensibility is illuminated against and through dialectical revisionism as the activity of reading and rereading. (I return to this point at length in the final section). The narrator as "reader" (in the robust sense of the word) is a leitmotif of the novel. Both as trope and plot point, questions of what reading is, who reads, who fails to, who is rendered illegible, *and* who is rendered illiterate become freighted with meaning. Meena, Sanji's daughter, an autodidact and proletarian philosopher in her own right, struggles to acquire the educational opportunities denied to her father. As we see, Sivanandan's own allegory of reading strains, however imperfectly, toward a performative poetic justice for the stateless refugee workers of Sri Lanka's plantation economy.

The year that Ceylon received national independence from Britain, 1948, saw over a million tea plantation workers rendered "stateless" by fiat of the new "post-Independence" state. The catachrestically named Ceylon Citizenship Act (No. 18) disenfranchised an entire social formation of working-class Sri Lankans, officially designated as "recent Indian-origin Tamils," based on where they were born. (The appellation "recent" is itself a misnomer, given that many of those disenfranchised were the descendents of South Indian workers who had been arriving in waves since as early as the 1820s, summoned, cajoled, and in other instances coerced by labor recruiters working in the pay of British tea planters.) The sequence of events unfolded as follows: the famine in Madras (one in a series of agrarian crises in India under British rule) lead to the proletarianization of rural labor and subsequent forced migrations to Ceylon. Endless cycles of debt, hunger, and coercion (or compromise) then compelled the journey along Mannar and the North road to the dismal line rooms of the tea estates.

Among historians of the plantation economy in Sri Lanka, former trade unionist and labor activist Nadesan presents the case most emphatically for understanding Sri Lanka in diasporic relation to India. Not surprisingly, such a perspective is actively marginalized in Sinhala and Tamil nationalist historiographies.[18] Nadesan's account of the history of "Up-country Tamils," however, begins by invoking changing cartographies of labor, and piecing together unforeseen or ignored linkages also with systems of slavery and forced labor.[19]

In 1964 the Sirima-Shastri Pact established elaborate terms for "repatriation" and devised a mathematical formula for apportioning citizenship between donor and recipient states. According to the terms of the agreement, of an estimated 975,000 stateless people, 525,000 ("with their natural increase") were to be "repatriated" to India over a period of several years. Ceylon agreed to grant citizenship to a mere 300,000, along with "their natural increase." The fate of the remaining 150,000-plus was slated to be determined later. While the Indian government balked at the prospect of an influx of repatriates, the Ceylonese government congratulated itself on solving the crisis to the nationalists' satisfaction—for the time being at least. The projected time line for the satisfactory balancing of the equation was set for fifteen years, but the stateless question remains unresolved. Registration and repatriation, both voluntary and coerced, continue in post-Independence Sri Lanka, past sundry election year maneuverings. As of 2003 the UNHCR (United Nations High Commission for Refugees) was continuing its programs of registration and repatriation for Sri Lankans unable to hold property in their own name—noncitizens who have lived their entire lives without a passport, identity card, birth certificate, or bank account. The wording of the 1961 convention, under whose auspices such work is carried out, captures the futility of the endeavor: its mandate is for "the reduction of statelessness."

The history of Up-country Tamils thus testifies to the fact that the inauguration of the "subject of freedom" or of postcolonial "independence" coincides with that of a subject of bonded labor and statelessness. This cruel fact of postcolonial Sri Lankan history is more than the background or setting of Sivanandan's novel; it constitutes the différance at the origin of independence.

Ultimately Sivanandan's *When Memory Dies* must also be read as contributing to the ongoing projects of critiquing historicism and "dehistoricizing history" in Sri Lanka. In the context of recent Sri Lankanist postcolonial theory, "the critique of historicism"—or the critique of the idea that (past) history absolutely determines and dictates present history's political and ethical options for organization and collectivity—is identified almost automatically with David Scott's *Refashioning Futures*. In postcolonial literary studies, it is by now a meaningless piety to point to the fact—although it is still routinely done in the context of revisionist projects—that there are gaps and omissions in the available postcolonial record. Postcolonial fiction is thus marshaled via a poststructuralist reading practice to show how we produce history's concept in the aftermath of colonialism—after epistemic violence.

It must be conceded that, on the one hand, *When Memory Dies* dramatizes a version of this useful but by now familiar political strategy. Book 3 finds the protagonist, Vijay/Vijayan, discovering the economic and philosophical lacunae of the canon and liberal humanism. As he sifts through the books that his father (now a political exile in England) sends him, he meditates on the ideological blind spots: "These others, Hardy and Foster and them, he reflect[s], familiarized us with their cities and villages and the people in them through their tales, but the tales themselves had nothing to say to us. And when they wrote about our countries and our people, though the tales were familiar, the characters were strangers. . . . We had no history, or we had several, mostly not of our doing, or we had forgotten that part of it which was, or it was a part too late to remember: it could only unmake the present" (289). On the other hand, however, beyond this moment in the book, the rhetorical protocols of *When Memory Dies* illuminate a more counterintuitive critique of historicism that also contributes to a specific school of thought within Sri Lankan Marxism.

Less well known than Dipesh Chakrabarty's intervention into "provincializing Europe," perhaps, are the projects of critiquing historicism and "dehistoricizing" history within Sri Lanka. In 1979, with a series of conferences, the Colombo-based Social Scientists Association opened up a general debate into how historians produce history's concept. Papers from this gathering were later collected and published under the title *Ethnicity and Social Change*. This publication then led to the production of other collections, such as *Facets of Ethnicity*—critically important works of activist scholarship combining a wide range of different interdisciplinary theoretical interventions. How do we begin to write a "history of the present" without becoming caught up in the claims and counterclaims that structure the base terms of the nationalist contest? Radhika Coomaraswamy takes on this question in an early piece, titled "Myths Without Conscience: Tamil and Sinhalese Nationalist Writings of the 1980s," in which she observes that too often "issues of justice and oppression get lost in a discourse of fact and counter-fact, [and] ironically, in this struggle for the 'correct' interpretation other more social values are forgotten" (54). Kumari Jayawardena writes about the rise and fall of the labor movement in Sri Lanka, excavating the brief history of an undivided Tamil-Sinhala left and working-class politics in the anticolonial 1920s—which undoubtedly serves as the background setting for much of the first segment of Sivanandan's 1997 novel. Newton Gunasinghe, on the other hand, analyzing the political economy of the ethnic conflict, theorized that in Sinhala and Tamil ethnic formations "class contradictions" are overdetermined, in the Althusserian sense, by ethnic conflict. David Scott's "Dehistoricizing History" invokes this collective project, even as he intervenes to show how some of its best-intentioned practitioners mistook its conditions and constraints.

Sivanandan's book not only builds upon this scholarship but also extends its reach. If *Ethnicity and Social Change* assessed the banal templates for mapping Sri Lankan historiography in terms of mytho-historical chronicles and archaeological settlement history—rescued and resuscitated to validate current territorial claims—*When Memory Dies* dramatizes the irrelevance of origins fetishism altogether, placing as the supplement to the origin (of the book) working-class history and cartographies of labor. It is not incidental, I would argue, that the story begins with a subaltern figure, exorbitant to nationalist histories. That is, the recollection of Sanji, without shoes, barred from attending estate schools—child of one of the "stateless million" tea plantation workers originally recruited by the British—must go "before the beginning" of the story proper. (Historicist) history is irrelevant—especially competing versions of national history, either Tamil or Sinhala—in the context of such a narrative sequencing.

Ultimately Sivanandan's novel needs to be read along with Nadesan's historiography, which connects the history of the Up-country Tamils with the global history of indentured labor and forced migrations. Nadesan's account of the estate workers' struggles is a beautifully heretical statement that is mindful of the lost parts in the telling of the story, especially in a Sri Lanka riven by an interethnic war, where working-class history is daily being erased and reconstructed by political institutions such as the Sinhala Commission. We see how in 2001, for example, this militant nationalist organization issued a curious statement recommending to the government that as a means of righting British colonial wrongs it take measures to retroactively deny citizenship to the descendents of Indian-origin Tamils. A truly ironic use of the epistemology of postcolonialism—here in the service of Sinhala nationalism.

The discontinuous piece of the story that serves as a supplement to the origin has to be understood also in the context of the novel considered as literary rewriting of the earlier case study. Critics like Qadri Ismail, for example, have proposed that Sivanandan's novel is "not historical, but historicist."[20] But then again, most critics (Ismail included) focus on the beginning of the book (chronologically its end), commenting on the pessimism of its outcome. By this point, the protagonist is dead. The death of socialism has been pronounced. But to focus on beginnings—or properly speaking, beginnings as ends—I would argue, is to ignore the text's own rhetorical and political protocols, given that the entire book is about the undecidablity of origins in one sense or another. Origins are in question, for example, if we consider the character-logic of the martyr-hero Vijay/Vijayan: Is he Sinhala or Tamil? By birth, or by socialization? The doubling of his name itself is an undoing of nationalist origin myths, as we know.[21] Or, if we consider narratology itself, the undecidability is aptly emblematized in the signal phrase "socialism is the path to liberation, not just its end" (406). Thus to privilege beginnings, or indeed beginnings as ends, is to resolutely ignore the crucial, urgent motif of "undecidablity" of origins dramatized in the text.

THE TURN TO LITERATURE

> He reached out for his notebook to put his thoughts down; he kept one now, as his mother had; it helped him to talk to himself, to all those other selves of his. "He who sees himself in others and others in himself is no longer alone." Was that the *Gita* or the *Upanishads*? He prided himself on his reading. Perhaps he should be a writer. . . . But for whom would he write? He did not want to write for intellectuals, they made playthings of knowledge. For ordinary people? . . . He understood contradiction out there in society, but he did not grasp it in himself, in people. He had not till now seen conflict as necessary to one's personal growth, as an essential part of life, its motor, as natural as breathing. *He had not seen that the dialectic was also a felt sensibility and, unless he grasped that, he would not be able to change anything.* (291; emphasis mine)

In one of the culminating episodes leading up to the tragic "ending" of *When Memory Dies*, the following conversation takes place between a separatist militant, fighting for a separate state, and Vijayan, a teacher, working-class activist, and, as seen here, believer in socialism. As many with other instances in the novel, it registers as pointedly didactic intrusion—made more interesting if we consider that it is the revision of Sivanandan's earlier essay, "Sri Lanka: A Case Study":

> "What are you fighting for? Yes, yes, for Eelam, I know. But what sort of Eelam?"
>
> "A socialist Eelam, of course."
>
> "But where's the socialism now? . . . It never happens like that, you know, Yogi . . ."
>
> "But then we'll never take power" . . .
>
> "There's that chance, of course, but this way you are bound to end up replacing one tyranny with another. Where's your socialism then? . . . Socialism is the path to liberation, not just its end."

In the final, though not conclusive scene, of the novel, Vijayan is shot down as he attempts to rescue a mistakenly identified "informant" from the fate of a signature LTTE lamppost killing. But in the dialogue above, as elsewhere throughout the novel, we notice a deliberate turning away from revolutionary injunctions toward other meanings and moorings for socialist transformation. The autodidact's discovery of literature—or to put it more precisely, his discovery of a mode of reading—is what leads him to question prescriptive dogmas. In *When Memory Dies*, as we see, what is lost and mourned is not sovereignty or territory as much as it is a shared way of life built on the value of learning as well as a mode of questioning motivated by habits of "reading" in the robust sense of the word.[22]

The turn to reading and specifically the turn to literature becomes the defining trope of the book. Scenes of reading recur throughout. And at the heart of the novel, we are made privy to the precise moment where, eschewing revolutionary violence, Vijayan discovers (as Sivanandan does) the Marxism *of* literature. In terms of plot, this turn occurs when Vijayan finally and firmly abjures the propagandist revolutionary rhetoric of the Marxist university student groups to instead derive a politics from reading Marx, Cabral, and Avayyar. A nonhierarchized, expansive notion of literature which ultimately accommodates a "noncanonical reading of the canon" becomes the provenance of the working-class intellectual's library:

> He understood contradiction out there in society, but he did not grasp it in himself, in people. He had not till now seen conflict as necessary to one's personal growth, as an essential part of life, its motor, as natural as breathing. He had not seen that the dialectic

was also a felt sensibility and, unless he grasped that, he would not be able to change anything. (291)

In other instances as well the work of reading signifies an active mode of engaging the world—a politics of interpretation. The opening scene of book 3 finds Vijayan poring over books and letters sent from England. He puzzles over double meanings and rhetorical figures in Marx:

> Engrossed in the thoughts provoked by his repeated reading of the Communist Manifesto, he stared blankly at the parched land that stretched before his eyes. . . . "A spectre was haunting Europe." "Why a 'spectre,'" he thought inconsequentially. Was he clear about the meaning? Perhaps his English was not as good as he thought. He had looked up the word in the *Concise English Dictionary* that his father sent him from England: "spirit," it meant, "ghost." (237)

Reading, misreading, even actively mistranslating the book extends meaning making beyond the covers into reading the world as the protagonist attempts to distinguish between two different senses of haunting. The living "memory" of his dead mother, not the "spectre" of his absent, yet living, father moves him to action and reflection: "her memory, not her spectre, haunted him now, like an experience whose meaning he had to find, not later but now." Spectres of Marx. Shades of Derrida. Reading, in this sense, signifies a willful, disobedient, transgressive semiosis. "In the same way, the beginner who has learned a new language always retranslates it into his mother tongue: he can only be said to have appropriated the spirit of the new language and to be able to express himself in it freely when he can manipulate it without reference to the old, and when he forgets his original language while using the new one"[23] Later on, Vijayan learns to read Amilcar Cabral in the same way—making the "content transcend the phrase." Cabral's admonition, "Return to the Source," is actively decontextualized and recontextualized to serve the purposes of a more immediate struggle.

The motif of reading-as-translation is ultimately emblematized in a pivotal metacommentary moment where, cutting across Tamil-Sinhala ethnic and linguistic divisions, literary reading figures the concept of internationalism. Even as the pogroms of Black July (July 1983) break out elsewhere in Colombo, Vijayan turns to "reading" Tamil poetry from memory:

> *Karrendha iddathelai naduthey karrom*—the lines of a Tamil verse came to him . . . "the hand dwells where it suckles . . ." but why the hand and not the mouth? Was Avvayar deriding men as lustful creatures . . . and was she concealing it in a play on words because she was poet to the king's court . . . ? How did the couplet go?
>
> *Pirandha iddathelai naduthey pay-the mannom*
> *Karrendha iddathelai naduthey karrom.*
>
> . . . *naduthey* . . . "dwells on" . . . "reaches out" . . . the mind reaches out to the place where it came from . . . did she mean that was all that men thought about or was she speaking of the exile to which she'd been condemned . . . One word with so many meanings, what a beautiful language Tamil was . . . Sinhala too, Sinhala too, the same voluptuousness . . . hopeless to try to understand it in translation. (383)[24]

Distances between national identities and ethnicities are crossed and inhabited in the epistemology of comparative literary reading. In the activity of reading—moving back and forth between the stated meaning and its possible other—Vijayan arrives at an ethical blurring of the lines. It is a curious, though not completely isolated, moment in the text, where language acts, overwriting the language acts of the state.[25] Literary language defamiliarizes and deforms, illuminating uncanny affinities. It permits proximity where distance is contrived. In this miraculous moment of synesthesia where "the mind reaches out" and "the hand suckles," in the paradigmatic doubleness of meaning and authorized confusion of literature, the protagonist sees/reads Sinhala and Tamil together—despite the state-imposed boundaries that deny the parity of status of languages.

Thus in *When Memory Dies* "the turn to literature" is overdetermined in complicated ways. It is part motif, part epistemological shift, part ethical leverage, and part transference—if we consider that here, too, the novel contains recycled, modified content from previous political essays and interviews. And at the center of the novel is the above-mentioned passage where the hero-protagonist forswears the romance of revolutions for the task-oriented, unglamorous, always-incomplete work of the everyday—teaching and organizing. And yet the novel's turn away from revolutionary violence is a risky choice in light of the author's readership. Critics remain divided about the political meaning and utility of this revisionist impulse.

At first glance, some find this activist journalist's attempt at fiction writing altogether unpersuasive: "Every single political event of any significance of twentieth-century Sri Lanka seems to get a mention in these pages," comments Qadri Ismail. "There are other—metonymic, allegorical—condensed ways that the novel has adopted of depicting history. But this text can't take that route. It must write narrative history in fictional guise."[26] Ismail's quick study dismisses the meaning of achrony, iteratism, and the myriad other infidelities and planned inaccuracies of the novel. Other, mostly sympathetic, critics explain the perceived ideological shift in terms of impediments of literary form.[27] Still other critics comment on the "strained pacifism" of the final scene. And yet I would argue that the novel's uncompleted closing scene stages the dialectic as "un-ending lightning." The story breaks off on, however tenuous, the slim grounds of hope, as the gun is knocked out of the commando's hand and the thinking dissident stands poised to take over.

Panning out beyond the focus on reviews and commentary on Sivanandan, the epistemological shift toward literature and "the literary" (away from revolution) also resonates uneasily with broader debates in Marxist historiography. Theorists of Western Marxism have hypothesized that theoretization of Marxism and the turn to epistemological questions have risen in tandem with the decline of Marxist scholarship theorizing revolutionary social movements. The question might even be raised as to whether the epistemological and literary turn in currents of Marxism is analogous with the "embourgeoisement" that others (Aijaz Ahmad, for example) have identified as the neutralizing impulse of postcolonial studies.

Indeed, the semantics of reading and the concept of literature, as well as the desire for literature, accomplish a lot of ideological work for the writer. However, to dismiss this literary turn as a species of crisis management or retrospective "strained pacifism," or even as either an aesthetic or a political failure, would be to overlook the imaginative ways in which this turn is elaborated. In terms of the formal composition of *When Memory Dies*, the arrangement of epigraphs signals a decided shift: the final segment marks a break in the sequencing and selection of canonical literature for epigraph text. While words from Dylan Thomas precede book 1 and authorize the narrative to follow, and a line from Gerard Manley Hopkins heads off book 2, book 3 invokes itself—a dialogic exchange between Uncle Para and Vijay—in a performative moment of self-constitution as literature.

In terms of political semiosis, the turn to literature is juxtaposed with stories of working-class intellectuals and proletarian philosophers who are denied access to education. As we see, who reads and whose writing is received as literary are questions that pertain not only to the subject's story, but also to that of the repressed subaltern subject of *When Memory Dies*. The narratological meaning of reading, then, hinges just as much upon those works of working-class literature that will not be written. It relates just as much to codings of dyslexia. Counter to the authorized reading list selected for the education and cultivation of the postcolonial subject—"Hardy and Foster and them"—there are other anonymous texts that capture the meaning of the country and the city in critically intimate ways but will not find their way to readers' bookshelves. "The third-world novel will not offer the satisfactions of Proust or Joyce," Jameson argues. But Vijay is moved by an immigrant plantation worker's poetry:

> One of them was a poet, you know. . . . I met him once, and recently a mutual friend sent me a poem of his, I have forgotten his name. . . . He gave me eyes to see my country with, his country, he was born here, but by government definition he was not a citizen, just a number in the agreed quota of "coolie Tamils" that India would take back. (255)

CODA: HISTORY AND ALLEGORIES OF READING

We keep returning to this point. Book 3 of *When Memory Dies* is marked by the turn to literature and scenes of reading. In the first scene we encounter the protagonist Vijayan poring over books and letters sent home by his father. It is difficult to speak of allegories of reading, however, without first acknowledging that any scene of reading is overdetermined historically, politically, and ethically when we recall a seminal event in the history of postcolonial Sri Lanka: the state-supervised burning of the Jaffna public library. Writing insightfully about the event in the context of canons of Tamil cultural nationalism, Vasuki Nesiah calls attention to the fact that it was perceived not only as

> a material attack on the building, the books, and the manuscripts stored in it [but] even more significantly, a symbolic attack against the value the Tamil community placed on learning. In this narrative [she argues] the core of "loss" experienced by Jaffna was that this was an attack against a culture of intellectual striving and a long tradition of academic achievement.[28]

Questioning cultural nationalism as an end in itself, she underscores the point that "the symbolism at stake in the burning of the public library may not have been the ruin of a mythologized ancient culture of learning, but the ruin of *a public space for a culture of questioning and resistance*. Libraries are here markers not of academic heroism, but a space for ideas and questions, of public debates and contested histories" (2; emphasis mine).

When Memory Dies indexes the historic burning of the Jaffna public library as a moment where the thread of history becomes dechronologized. But that is only one end of the story. The other is imparted to us by Stuart Hall in his preface to *A Different Hunger*, Sivanandan's collection of writings on black resistance (gathered under that haunting title phrase) wherein he recounts the seminal role of the IRR (Institute of Race Relations) librarian Sivanandan during the growing compartmentalization of black struggles in 1960s Britain. He explains that

> behind these essays [in *A Different Hunger*] lies the history of the [IRR] Institute itself: the focal point for "race relations" research in the early days; then like CARD (the Campaign Against Racial Discrimination), polarized and fractured by the growing politicization of black struggles in the 1960s; the critical moment when

the "race relations industry" was first identified, and its project analyzed—these are crucial moments, at each of which Sivanandan played a critical role. Few know the story of how he simply hijacked the Institute from under their very noses; took the material resources (books, journals, pamphlets, filing cards and connections) which he has helped, painfully, to accumulate, packed them up, and walked out with them, as it were, under his arm; transferring them to a less salubrious and less respectable part of town, bearing the official title (to the establishment's intense annoyance) with him. . . . Few librarians have achieved so striking—and brazen—an appropriation/expropriation of the tools and materials of their trade. (xi)

It is between these two moments, different but asymmetrically related—one archive lost, another rescued—that the terrains of socialist ethics versus race and class politics are mapped out in the middle ground of literature and in practices of reading in the robust sense.

Chapter 3

GENDER, GENRE, AND GLOBALIZATION

Proletarian revolutions, however, ... constantly engage in self-criticism, and in repeated interruptions of their own course.

—Karl Marx

Yet the word "proletarian"—one who serves the state with nothing but his [sic] offspring (OED)—continues to carry an effaced mark of sexuality.

—Gayatri Chakravorty Spivak

And where is there time to remember, to sift, to weigh, to estimate, to total? I will start and there will be an interruption and I will have to gather it all together again.

—Tillie Olsen

This chapter asks what happens when we shift our emphasis from working-class literature understood as categorized by systemic accounts of labor history, to working-class literature defined by ethico-political questions. Proletarian writers such as Tillie Olsen—from 1930s North America—as well as writers with strong socialist sympathies—such as Mahasweta Devi from postcolonial West Bengal—figure a critique of historicism in their writing, reminding us that measures of chronology, important dates, periods, and "events" do not let us into quiet moments that are "too late" or "too early"—into secret places where chance meetings and haphazard alignments take place. They do not lead us into quiet moments that cannot be read like a message. Such texts illuminate the possibilities of "ethical singularity" rather than the logic of ethical universality and master narratives.[1]

The emphasis on the concept of literature and an ethics of historical materialism are inescapably intertwined. Literature is categorically antihistoricist. Its concept refuses particularism in favor of the "singular and unverifiable." Its history is aleatory, not progressive—international, not insular. Precisely because literature is historical, not historicist in this way, as Raymond Williams puts it, "many of the active values of 'literature' have then to be seen, not as tied to the concept, which came to limit as well as to summarize them, but as elements of a continuing and changing practice which already substantially, and now at the level of theoretical redefinition, is moving beyond its old forms" (*Marxism*, 54). Too often, a consideration of the literariness of working-class literature is either overlooked, hastily assimilated into familiar Frankfurt school debates on aesthetics and politics, or indeed dismissed outright as elitist. I am suggesting, however, that a rhetorical analysis of figural logic and the literariness of such texts must be made to supplement the logic of periodized case studies.

History is not synonymous with the past, nor is it reducible to historiography. And, once again, "Marxism is not a historicism."[2] The latter, particularly concise formulation belongs to Louis Althusser, who calls for a critical epistemological reading of the object of history in Marx. In *Reading Capital* he argues his case by initially analyzing the politics of the turn to historicism and humanism by Antonio Gramsci and others as a "vital reaction" against the mechanism and economism of the Second International. Acknowledging these debates between major theoreticians of a particular period and the justified—if ultimately mistaken—basis for their critique, however, he then goes on to painstakingly elaborate the significant ways in which Marx leads us to a different mode of conceptualizing history and progress when he rethinks the concept of Hegelian totality, opening up breaks and disjunctures in the concept of developmentalist logic. Whereas "the Hegelian totality presupposes an original, primary essence that lies behind the complex appearance that it has produced by externalization in history," the Marxist "totality" is a decentered structure. And thus, as Althusser puts it, "the reduction of and identification of the peculiar history of science to the history of organic ideology and politico-economic history ultimately reduces science to history as its 'essence'" (133). Althusser wished to make Marx contemporary even as he sought to prevent Marx (and Marxism) from merely becoming slogans for validating left-party politics of the day. And yet the discussion of ethics remains a lacuna in his corpus. The interminable contest between subject and structure, "agency"—any form of agency—versus the immanent logic of capital, is driven to a stalemate, even in his later writings.[3] The feminist critique of historicism (proposed in this chapter) owes to thinkers like Althusser and Balibar but also builds on the simple facts that Marx's texts on class remain unfinished and that it is a mistake to posit reified theories of capital and class relations or stagist modes of production narratives based on any specific historical instance. Such a critique proposes a comparative (but not cultural relativist) approach to the changing object of working-class writing and suggests the ethico-political agency of a dispersed collective subject of feminism.

The isolated study of the discrete historical event—whether we consider the metropolitan financial centers of Europe and the United States (the 1929 stock market crash) or rural Naxalbari (the 1967 Naxalite rebellion)—irreducibly limits the scope of working-class literature to a particular, resplendent period in organized labor—a moment of crisis or planned rural insurgency. But what happens after the revolution, after national independence, after the communists are in power? This chapter trains the focus on women writers from different moments in the literature of labor, whose writings—novels, short fiction, poetry, and periodicals—explicitly engage questions of historicism. Through a literary-critical analysis of women's texts from noncontiguous spaces within the international division of labor, I attempt to rethink the category of proletarian literature with attention to specific questions of gender, genre, and the politics of history. My texts range from a "classic" work of proletarian fiction from the 1930s United States to socialist fiction in contemporary communist West Bengal, to serialized pieces of poetry, prose, and reportage in radical periodicals of a collective of worker-writers in contemporary, neocolonial Sri Lanka. Specific writers considered are Tillie Olsen (1912 or 1913–2007), Mahasweta Devi (b. 1926), and the Dabindu Collective (est. 1984).

GENDER, GENRE, AND GLOBALIZATION

Proletarian writing as a movement has been identified with the period of the 1930s, the decade of international socialism. And yet it was hardly a formal institution.—as Michael Denning puts it, "proletarian literature was a formation in Raymond Williams's sense"[4]—but rather a strategic alliance of workers, writers, readers, and political activists who came together in formal and informal settings: Marxist study groups, May Day rallies, national and international writers' conferences, etc. This concept of proletarian writing as a changing "formation" as opposed to a static institution—anti-essentialist and nonidentitarian in its very origins and "structure"—poses a problem for the academic subdivision of labor in universities. (Admittedly, the adjectives modifying Williams's words, "formation" and "structure" are my own, but I perceive an opening for thinking anti-essentialism here.)

How do we begin to conceive of this interminably provisional and shifting terrain as an object of study? Williams writes that "since such formations relate, inevitably, to real social structures, and yet have highly variable and often oblique relations with formally discernible social institutions, any social and cultural analysis of them requires procedures radically different from those developed for institutions" (*Marxism*, 119). The study of the changing *formation* of proletarian writing, not limited to the period of the 1930s or indeed to nineteenth-century industrial capitalism, exceeds the grasp of specialized programs of study conventionally demarked (solely) by genre, period, and nation. Anticipating the way in which the "disciplining" of such a formation might happen, Williams warns against a pedagogy where

> many of those in real contact with such formations and their work retreat to an indifferent emphasis on the complexity of cultural activity. Others altogether deny (even theoretically) the relation of such formations and such work to the social process and especially the material social process. Others again, when the historical reality of the formations is grasped, render this back to ideal constructions—national traditions, literary and artistic traditions, histories of ideas, psychological types, spiritual archetypes—... (119)

We might say that in terms of the cultural politics of working-class studies, E. P. Thompson's figure of "the freeborn Englishman" remains an "ideal construction," not only emblematic of the British working class, but also significant generally for the field of working-class historiography.⁵ From within traditions of Indian Marxism, Dipesh Chakrabarty's important intervention, *Rethinking Working-Class History*, presents the other side of the story of the Industrial Revolution and the organized working classes in England—that of the colonial working class (in this case, in Bengal).⁶ However, in the current economic conjuncture of globalization what we understand as the "new international division of labor" is predicated on the cheap labor of (mainly) women workers in neocolonial countries with national economic policies of export-oriented industrialization. And yet, *proletarian writing*, according to the old system of signs and notations, remains synonymous with icons and codes of masculinity and the metropole.

Arguably, in the contemporary historical moment, the "new proletariat"⁷ is best represented by the figure of the woman worker in the periphery. Separate from organized labor in industrialized countries of the North, the occluded agent of production in this "postindustrial" age is the super-exploited worker in postcolonial, "developing" countries with extraverted, rather than autocentric, economies.⁸ In the terms of government-issued business brochures targeted at foreign direct investment, she is sold as "cheap," "docile," and as "famous for her manual dexterity." In terms of U.S. feminism, she cannot be easily written into labor history because she represents, disturbingly, the containment of the wage-bargaining power of struggling women workers closer to home.⁹ (Tillie Olsen's "I Want You Women Up North to Know" is an interesting exception. But more on this in an upcoming section.) In terms of nationalist historians and trade unionists, she is *not* identified with the revolutionary conjuncture. In fact, proletarian literature seems unable to produce a script for her. She seems ill-fitted to the narrative conventions, especially when we consider that the dominant archetypes and idealized constructs—the available language (despite the interventions of feminist genre critics) is limited. Spivak, in her *Critique of Postcolonial Reason*, frames the problem in this way: "we see [in] the establishment of the International Workingmen's Association . . . a foreclosure of the woman who will be the agent of Marxism today in the inevitable docketing of European as 'international' and organized internationality as men's."¹⁰

This chapter is an attempt to open up questions of genre as well as debates on aesthetics and politics in the service of this figure excluded from the literary-critical calculus. It builds on the intuition of U.S.

feminist critics who have astutely drawn our attention to the fact that "'30s feminism"—its conventions, notations, ideologies and ethics—has been overlooked in the history of ideas forging ahead toward the logical conclusion of postmodernist, antifoundationalist variations, even by some trends within single-issue postcolonial feminisms. What gets lost in the ideological break between the old left and the new is (1) the Marxist-feminist critique of the autonomous subject; (2) how to think a comparative, not competitive, model for internationalized feminism; (3) how to think feminism and class struggles outside reified narratives of organized resistance.

Too often, in literature and criticism alike, the working class is seen and represented as masculine, metropolitan, and revolutionary. Women's texts of nonrevolutionary socialism, however, present us with new figures and concepts for thinking unorganized resistance, everyday experience, and the shape of the ethical within globalization. Bracketing these anomalous, unfinished, dialogic, anticipatory texts, theoreticians of proletarian literature confront the problem that its celebrated narratives are tied to the logic of revolutions and the mindset that is supposed to accompany them. Since the literary internationalism of the "radical" 1930s, the development of proletarian literature beyond short-term political agitation, codings of crisis, and revolutionary romanticism remains an issue for the political and literary history of working-class writing. According to a corpus of representative texts and standard, minimal Marxist definitions, the "proletariat" of proletarian literature is by definition revolutionary, and by implication, male; this is the specific subset of the working class entrusted with the historic mission of abolishing the class system. Nonrepresentative texts by proletarian women writers from different historical periods propose a more counterintuitive model, one not connected to the conditions and constraints of the revolutionary conjuncture but to other measurements and templates for thinking socialist ethics.

The genre of proletarian literature remains to be analyzed in connection with the changing terms of gender and sexuality. In her important contribution to feminist historiography of women's working-class texts, *Labor and Desire,* Paula Rabinowitz exposes the ideological biases of prevailing 1930s generic taxonomies where codes of proletarian realism, naturalism, and the idea of the (rational) subject come to be automatically associated with masculinity and, by extension, proletarian writing, whereas techniques of modernism and/or realist (domestic) fiction and any and all depictions of interiority are associated with women's writing. More than a simple recounting of the forgotten numbers of women proletarian writers, Rabinowitz's broader epistemological critique acknowledges the pitfalls of an essentialist logic (subscribed to by certain feminist critics themselves) that reifies a dichotomous rendering of difference refracted through the oppositions between realism and modernism; factory and home; male and female. Ultimately, however, Rabinowitz, along with other contemporary feminist historians of the genre, falls prey to the terms of her own critique. While unmasking the politics securing the privilege of the 1930s male literary-critical establishment and their rules of genre, she replaces this standard of judgment with the criteria of liberal feminism. That is, the project of feminist historiography becomes the recovery of the lost subject, sometimes part of "the search for our literary foremothers."

Infused with this mission, which becomes inextricably personal, the feminist critic is quick to recognize in the writings of women worker-writers and organic intellectuals of the period versions of the bildungsroman, arguably the norm of high feminist criticism allied to the later mainstream Euro-American idea of consciousness raising. Olsen's *Yonnondio: From the Thirties*, understood to be a hallmark text of U.S. literary radicalism, for example, has been construed (misconstrued, I will argue) as an example of a novel of self-formation.[11] Along these lines, what has been overlooked in a certain tradition of materialist-feminist historiographic practice is the *rejection* of the idea of the individual subject at the very core of texts by proletarian writers.

In the opening section of my chapter, I will read, in relationship to the works of North American proletarian writer Tillie Olsen, a selection of poems, political commentary, and short fiction produced by the worker-writers of the Dabindu Collective, from the Katunayake free-trade-zone region in Sri Lanka. The period under consideration is 1984 to 2001, which covers the passage of Dabindu's transformation from a workers' collective organized loosely around the free-trade-zone periodical and other forms of alternative organizing into an internationally funded NGO. Neither Olsen nor the writers of the Dabindu Collective chose the form of a bildungsroman as they undertook to represent the nonsubject of history. Each writer in her own way undercuts the "the development" of an essentialist feminine consciousness. Rather, what is at stake for these *proletarian* writers (from different sides of the international divide) is the critique of the subject, as well as a critique of historicist thinking. In the place of the style of the individualist utterance, elliptical marks, interruptions, and interferences take the measure of moments, not monuments. A concept of a nonindividual subjectivity brings these writers together under the rules of a different sociology of form. Anti-essentialism and the decentered subject are considered to be the provenance of deconstruction or high postmodernism, but the calculus changes when we consider feminist working-class texts as our object. Ultimately, both Dabindu and Olsen undo the concept of working-class writing as a canonical genre or even as a unitary authorial construct and instead keep it alive as an "oppositional transformative."[12]

RETHINKING WORKING-CLASS LITERATURE

Consider this curious passage in Olsen's *Yonnondio: From the Thirties*[13]—a moment of speech interference that communicates the writer's resistance to the transformation of the working-class novel into a fetishized, canonical object. At a critical juncture an angry voice interrupts the story: "And could you not make a cameo of this and pin it onto your aesthetic hearts? So sharp it is, so clear, so classic" (20). In terms of Olsen's plot, the speech interrupts at a point where a terrible mining accident has occurred in a small mining town in Wyoming. The ominous death whistle has blown, and the members of the mining families are standing about, gathered in tense suspense to discover who has been lost to the explosion and who will be lifted up from the rubble. At this point the focalization of the scene shifts away from Mazie, the girl-child subject of the story, to a disembodied voice that cuts in to save the episode from the literary critic's desire to crystallize the moment into a "classic." During this moment of text interference, the separation between what is constituted "the social"—the historical event, always in the past—and "the personal"—in Raymond Williams's words, "this, here, now, alive, active, 'subjective' always in the present"—is momentarily collapsed.[14]

The narrator's discourse breaks abruptly, with the third-person past tense—the value-neutral, objective prose of history—becoming instead an immediate, direct, angry address to the reader-critic:

> Surely it is classical enough for you—the Greek marble of the women, the simple, flowing lines of sorrow, carved so rigid and eternal. Surely it is original enough—these grotesques, this thing with the foot missing, this gargoyle with half the face gone and the arm. . . . You will have the cameo? Call it Rascoe, Wyoming, any of the thousand mine towns in America, the night of a mine blowup . . . [*and then, answering her rhetorical question regarding the aesthetics and politics of representing working-class struggles, the speaker concludes*] A cameo of this, then. Blood clot of the dying sunset and the hush. No sobs, no word spoken. Sorrow is tongueless. (20–21)

In *Marxism and the Philosophy of Language,* Volosinov defines "speech interference" as the "merging of two *differently* oriented speech acts; [in which we sense] the *integrity* and *resistance* of the reported message behind the author's transmission."[15] In this autoreferential passage, punctuated by deictic indices, as elsewhere in Olsen's *Yonnondio,* an impossible ethical paradox is made visible: might something be irretrievably lost when Olsen's book, "this" writing, acquires the status of a canonical, "classical" object? The rhetorics of this passage, the prose-poetry of its language, allows the writer to say something unsayable in the voice-consciousness of her characters, struggling for representation and visibility. Indeed, such a declaration would be unthinkable for an impoverished labor activist and writer struggling for recognition and validation during the hard times of Depression-era America. Yet the language performs this impossible task.

Is it possible to represent without monumentalizing a necessarily provisional structure? How do you capture "all that is present and moving"? (Williams, *Marxism,* 128). Olsen outlines the terms of a representational strategy for working-class writing other than reportorial realism, on the one hand, or romantic idealism, on the other. She turns to a philosophy of literature, rather than a system of official history, to figure the terms of an ethos of working-class writing that is *not* defined in relationship to a moment of crisis or a single, emblematic instance, but is connected, instead, to other durations. "This" literature is not a monument to casualties of labor history, but rather it is categorically unfinished, anti-essential: not a Greek statue, but "this thing with the foot missing." A conceptual shift from historical prose to literary language is most transparently underscored in the anonymous protest letter that signs off the segment: "Dear Company [the unsigned letter reads]. Your men are imprisoned in a tomb of hunger, of death wages. Your men are strangling for breath—the walls of your company town have clamped out the air of freedom" (*Yonnondio*, 20). A movement is charted from the philosophy of History to that of Literature as the "buried" workers become allegories of history and the "facts" of the past are transformed into a "larger" figural logic.

Postcolonial Sri Lanka, transnational corporations, and the writings of the export-oriented garment industry worker-writers might seem extraneous to the moment that Olsen writes about in the 1930s United States, but the poetry, short fiction, and serialized novels of the monthly free-trade-zone newspaper—always unfinished, always awaiting the next supplement—seem to figure the dilemma addressed in *Yonnondio* (and also later in Olsen's short stories, "I Stand Here Ironing" and "Tell Me a Riddle"[16]). Of what is history made as it happens? How do we write about the necessarily disappearing objects of working-class literature without sentimentalizing them—without freezing them into emblematic objects? This chapter introduces the periodicals of the Sri Lankan free-trade-zone workers as a supplement—that is, as both supplying a gap and adding an excess—to the rhetorics of the working-class novel of the Europe and the United States. But as I begin this section on contemporary Sri Lankan working-class writing, I want to keep in mind the difficult lesson of Olsen's *Yonnondio*. Even as the patheticized figure of the "nimble fingered" garment industry worker threatens to become a "classic"—acquires a certain iconic status within contemporary discourses on globalization and the feminization of labor—I want to be mindful of the lost parts in the telling of the story. In a Sri Lanka riven by an interethnic war, working-class history is daily being erased and reconstructed by political institutions such as the Sinhala Commission.[17] To this end, I do not construe the (Sinhala) *Dabindu* periodicals as *the* representative example of modern industrial fiction, but rather as one example, among the many ignored texts of labor at the limits of metropolitan discourse studies, within the changing terms of the international division of labor.

In *Yonnondio*, the text itself is a split subject. In her epigraph Olsen marks that her unfinished book, published in 1974, is pieced together from rough drafts begun in 1932, "in arduous partnership," as she puts it, "with that long ago writer." With regard to *Dabindu* I ask: How is the subject put together in these stories and poems from post-Independence Sri Lanka? How is woman as subject *for* history imagined? In Olsen's staging of the diachronic autobiographical subject we are given the writer straining to reconnect with a past self, the working-class subject from the forgotten 1930s. By contrast, in *Dabindu* we are presented with a heterogeneous collective subject, a group of women free-trade-zone workers writing in and against the history of the present—within globalization and counterglobalist struggles. And yet, while the text of the free-trade-zone periodical is produced by a "collective," it does not offer us a model for a "synchronic" subject in the readily available sense; that is to say, it does not represent some seamless cultural unity of contemporary women's working-class struggles. Rather, the subject of *Dabindu* figures a "unity-in-dispersal"—heterogeneity and contradictions gathered under a collective signature.[18] Writings are contributed by named and sometimes unnamed garment factory workers and mediated by the interventions of volunteer editors. The very concept of (private) authorship becomes unstable in the context of its publication history and material production, evoking perhaps the situation that Terry Eagleton describes when he proposes that "community and cooperative publishing enterprises are associated projects, concerned not simply with a literature wedded to alternative social values, *but with one which challenges and changes the existing social relations between writers, publishers, readers and other literary workers*" (216; my emphasis).[19] He goes on to describe a concept of (British) working-class writing that portends the interrogation of unitary authorship and, indeed, "ruling *definitions* of literature."

Eagleton (as always) is preoccupied with the example of the worker-writers' movement in Britain, but the point resonates with the example of the free-trade-zone worker-writers collective also. If we consider the form of the free-trade-zone newspapers, we see that the text itself is a creative mishmash of genres—bits and pieces of political analysis and cultural critique interspersed with romantic melodrama, nationalist poetry, letters, didactic leftist literature, reportage on local strikes, and international labor news. In considering content, it is important to note that while the periodical is composed of writing contributed by garment factory workers, pieces are sometimes edited and selected by feminist activists and cultural workers. While these two constituencies (of feminism and the working class) are not always mutually exclusive, as Kumudini Samuel points out, the periodical's editors belong to different formations within organized feminism in Sri Lanka, reflecting *Dabindu*'s shifting political tenor over the span of different editions.[20] Kumudhini Rosa, one of the conveners of the collective and the founding editor of the periodical, explains *Dabindu*'s historical conjuncture in these terms: "In Sri Lanka, the new wave of the women's movement arose in the late 1970s, at the same time as the FTZ (Free Trade Zone)" (75).[21] Along these lines—and also in its current incarnation as an internationally (and locally) funded NGO—it goes without saying that the Dabindu Collective categorically cannot lay claim to some ideologically uncontaminated space outside relations of capital and class within globalization.[22]

Thus a seamless or idealistic concept of "the collective" gives way to a more complex, contemporary historical transaction between class politics and feminism. Just as we mark that Olsen's 1930s *Yonnondio* comes to us in some way mediated by the author's own hand—guided by the projects and interests of 1970s U.S. feminism, we note that *Dabindu*, too, is mediated by changing waves of feminism within globalization. But then again, arguably, neither Olsen nor *Dabindu* (the collective signature) claims to offer us direct, unmediated access to some authentic working-class "voice from the factories." Instead, they both illuminate a vital, if overlooked, exchange between Marxism and feminism in different historical conjunctures. *Dabindu*, perhaps, presents us with a particular type of collective subject—resolutely nonindividual in its figuration. Following signs of anti-bildung and speech interferences, I will attempt to trace the itinerary of such a collective subject in my close readings of these short stories, poems, and serialized novels. But first, in the absence of a formalized institution resembling the working-class novel, and given that *Dabindu* and global feminism are not immediately part of the history of other Sri Lankan traditions of working-class writing—for example, Tamil protest literature and oral narratives composed by laborers of the tea plantation regions—it becomes necessary to begin by saying something about the protocols of the text—as well as something of the history of the present.

"ALL THAT IS PRESENT AND MOVING": SRI LANKAN FREE-TRADE-ZONE PERIODICALS

Most of the signs in contemporary historical war-torn Sri Lanka mean "crisis." As I sort through research materials from previous summers, archival papers, handwritten notes from interviews, I come across a photograph that recalls me to a place where the writing on the walls reads: "Mavbima Koti Kate! Sinhalayini Avadivav!"[23] The urgency of this message is belied, however, by the subtext of a watchmaker sitting directly under the poster. Oblivious to the blarings of racist, nationalist propaganda overhead, he appears to be putting into order the remains of old, broken timepieces—curls of wristbands and cracked faces. Shaded by the awning of his stall, against the backdrop of that raucous lettering, it looks as if he is selling crisis.

This conspicuously odd figure, exorbitant to the time frame and setting of nationalist histories, represents something about the calculated untimeliness of this project. My research into forms of working-class literature does not conform to the expedient demands of the day. Lawyers, policy makers, and human rights activists turn their attention to constitutional reform and relief work. Instead, my objective is to collect examples of literature by garment industry workers: letters sent home by foreign domestic laborers, and literature of and by the tea plantation workers. Instead of the founding documents of the nation-state, I turn my attention to the working-class writings of the garment industry factory workers whose stories, essays, and poems are defined by narrative durations other than "crisis."

The free-trade-zone paper *Dabindu* (*Sweat*)[24] traces its origins to a date of little-known historic significance in September 1984, when a group of women workers, newly employed in the free-trade-zone regions, joined together with cultural workers and grassroots labor activists to devise an alternative means of communicating in a climate where trade unions were effectively prohibited and speech was censored. Sri Lanka's first free-trade-zone region was created in 1978 under the advisement of the World Bank and International Monetary

Fund as part of the conditions for global aid. These plans were implemented by the rightist UNP (United National Party) government, whose national economic policies charted a shift from welfarism to development. Dismantling the infrastructure of labor laws put into place as the result of the hard-won gains of the 1930s anticolonial working-class movement, the new free-trade regime of the United National Party promised investment protection, tax holidays, and the availability of cheap labor to foreign capital.

Seven years after the first factories were built and operational, the Dabindu Collective first met to discuss the strange, separate space that they inhabited. Here, by fiat of the GCEC (Greater Colombo Economic Commission), their workplaces were declared exempt from the Trade Unions Ordinance and the Maternity Benefits Ordinance, as well as the Factories Ordinance, among other laws of the country.

In the beginning there were no resources for a printing press. The founding members of the group pieced together a first edition from photocopies of anonymous letters, protest poems, testimonials, and worker biographies. They distributed these copies free of charge among the cramped quarters of the boardinghouses where many of the garment factory workers lived. After the first installment, it was discovered that the paper would find its way down the assembly line to factory notice boards. In other instances, it would be smuggled into the premises slipped in between the sheets of the dailies that they used as wrapping paper for their meager lunches. From the time of the first meeting in September 1984, regular publication was discontinued just once, for a three-month period in 1989, coinciding with the second JVP uprising following the disappearances and murders of some of the worker-activists connected with the collective.[25] During that time *Dabindu* was proscribed as an antigovernment publication. Since the old days of forbidden pages smuggled into the factory, the periodical has received some measure of visibility with the Dabindu Collective's transformation into a local NGO.

The newspaper was originally conceptualized as a medium for interrogating false rumors, for publishing workers' correspondences, factory reports, and news of struggles with management, and for bringing together national and international labor news. It was also, however, conceived as means of publishing the preliminary "beginning/amateur" literary efforts of worker-writers. The preface to the

1988 International Women's Day commemorative booklet titled *Stri nirmana* (Women's writing)[26] addresses a general feminist readership: "Therefore, because [the writings] found here are only amateur creative efforts ["*Adhunika*" *nirmana*—also in some traditions of literary history, the word for "modern"], we hope in the event of shortcomings and failures for your unbiased response."[27] In their creative writings, the garment workers formed a political picture of an organization of society counter to the new mythologies constructed by the state, which simply extolled the virtues of their obedience and manual dexterity.

For example, in poems such as "Apatada nidahasak natha" (For us, there is no freedom)[28] they write themselves as set apart from the declarations of independence sounded by political parties in postcolonial Sri Lanka. The unsigned poem, appearing on the cover of the February 1998 edition, published to coincide with postcolonial celebrations of fifty years of freedom, is a critique of the nationalist rhetoric of independence as well as an exposition of the terms of economic imperialism. The first two stanzas read:

Although fifty years ago today
This land received its freedom
O for the sisters of the zone
There is still no freedom from enslavement

Today, as then, under foreign rule
They are
Like prisoners
O, when do they become free?

The writing is a mix of colloquial and literary Sinhala. Each stanza registers a different meter. On some occasions we find words shortened with a literary license according to some metrical scheme that is impossible to isolate, indicating signs of collaboration—text interferences.

Recent studies of the *Dabindu* papers have focused mainly on segments of their prose writings as sociological evidence of working-class consciousness among the women of the Sri Lankan garment industry. There are, for example, such wonderful texts as grotesque cartoons personifying the World Bank, comparative studies of the exploited garment industry workers in Bangladesh, and opinionated discussion pieces on the international implications of U.S. child labor legislation.[29] However, in an otherwise close reading of the vocabulary of "class" in the free-trade-zone factories of Katunayake, anthropologists Sandya Hewamanne and James Brow briefly dismiss the fiction pages, generalizing, "In their fiction writings, however, the heroines unfailingly overcome the pressures of outside forces to uphold moral values. . . . It could be that some of the writings are addressed to a general readership in an attempt to convey the message that there are 'moral heroines' within the FTZ."[30]

But in addition to their tales of moral heroines, the *Dabindu* periodicals encompass a vast heterogeneity of narrative forms, ranging from worker biographies and realist reportage to short stories about recanting JVP insurgents, romantic melodramas with the interethnic civil war as their backdrop, didactic stories critical of Sinhala ethnonationalism, poems dedicated to soldiers on the frontlines, poems addressing the Tamil tea plantation workers, free-verse (*Nisandas*) poetry addressing that abstract entity named the MNC (Multinational Corporation/Bahujathika Samagama), socialist fiction celebrating great Russian and Latin American Marxist leaders, love stories and other elliptical utterances, and perhaps most poignantly, stories and poems mourning lost opportunities for higher education in the university system.[31]

These bits and pieces may not be particularly useful in the context of projects of data retrieval for United Nations statistical reports on gender and free trade. Still, while much has been written about the internationalization of production and the feminization of labor by anthropologists and economists focusing on these poems and stories—the less useful parts, summarily dismissed by social investigators—I return to my central question: How is woman as subject for history constituted in these different writings? What if any recurring conventions and notations make up the figuration of her identity? In "For us, there is no freedom," we discern the traces of a nonindividual subject in the irregular lines and erratic rhythms of the unsigned poem. On the other hand, "Vagrant wishes/Padada pathum" (Vagabond wishes [Perera]), appearing in the June 1994 edition, imagines the abstract entity of the multinational corporation as a speaking subject whose sovereign speech act brings into being the terrible order of things. The poem reads in colloquial Sinhala:

Garment[32] for girls
Army for boys
Heavenly comforts for us . . .
Say the Multinationals
Together with those-who-lay-waste-to-the-country . . .[33]

"Wishes" illustrates a brief anatomy of the national sexual division of labor in terms of the militarization of the state. Its form is quite simply a short list of actors in a staging of post-Independence Sri Lankan history. The list includes working-class women of the export-oriented garment industry, men of the Sri Lankan armed forces fighting a savage war to maintain a unitary state, multinational corporations (*bahu jathika samagam*) and a set of unnamed agents: "those who ruin/lay waste to the country."

The English translation fails to capture the stark brevity of that final line as well as the planned slippage between the words for those who "rule" (*deshapalana/palaka*), and those who "ruin" (*deshapaluvan*). In the context of contemporary historiography, the poem is crucially significant in that it shifts the focus of dominant narratives of the Tamil-Sinhala interethnic conflict, placing the blame not on Tamil separatist nationalism, but on the governing elite who collude with global capital to perpetuate the war industry. Perera's poem uncovers a hidden complicity between "free trade," the slogan of the MNC, and "freedom," the patriotic rhetoric of the postcolonial Sinhala-Buddhist government. (Less "literary" techniques mediate the language of the antiwar statement of the Committee for Democracy and Justice in Sri Lanka published in the 1995 September/October edition.[34])

"Vagrant wishes," written in the short, staccato language of the pamphleteering tradition, represents the macropolitics of nationalism-as-an-alibi-for-global-capitalism in terms of a compact, accessible, gendered logic. Deepika Thrima Vitana's 1994 "Chintanaya nidahas nam" (Thinking freedom),[35] on the other hand, dramatizes the micropolitics of internalized gendering in a modernist short story that stages the interior monologue of a former "Marxist" insurgent. The time frame is the present, after the 1989 abortive JVP insurgency in the southern part of Sri Lanka. The protagonist, Sahra, is the only one in a group of operatives who manages to escape her captor, and only after an army officer brands her face with his cigarette, leaving her permanently disfigured. The description of this scarring, however, is withheld in the order of narrative sequencing. Starting with the opening scene, in which we see Sahra walking out on her lover, the story moves backward and forward as bits and pieces of the heroine's life story are given as a series of retroversions through reported speech, but without quotation marks. The title, here translated as "Thinking freedom,"[36] also underscores a movement in the text where the former JVP recruit gives up the phraseology of mechanical Marxism—the *harabara vachana, tharaka vada* (heavy duty words, and logical arguments) of "the organization" to discover her "self" through a process of uncollected thoughts and disconnected sentences—a collection of textual interferences, rather than the speech of the autonomous, intending subject.

Sahra remembers episodes of university life, of leaving the university to work full time for "the organization," a failed love affair, the scarring of her face. Rooted to the spot by the river where the primary action of the story takes place, she also inhabits the present. She overhears village women discussing the marks on her face: "One of those '*Che Guevara*' types, when these words beat against Sahra's ears she feels incredible pain. That she had committed herself on behalf of their children no one seemed to acknowledge." In the final turn of the story, Sahra contemplates her reflection in the water and resolves to no longer ask for validation from disaffected party ideologues or grieving family members. "If she died in that jungle—that would have been something. Now how do you keep an unmarriageable woman in the house": Their comment is a statement, rather than a question. In the closing scene, the protagonist counters with her own philosophy of Marxism, feminism, and history as she reconstructs her image in the water: "She began to feel the strong need for independence of thought. There is no possibility of returning to University to continue studies. Well, whatever happens, tomorrow, by first light [I] must go to the fair and find some greens, potatoes, yams. Life is beautiful but there must also be independence of thought. She saw on her face a strange beauty from under the water."

Ultimately, Vitana's short story connects the narrative of the gendered revolutionary working-class subject to a different duration than either "crisis" or "development" (the proletarian female bildungsroman). Rather, "Chintanaya" (along with S. Udyalata Menike's

"Mai Dinaya" [May Day]) is an autocritical text of nonrevolutionary socialism. The protagonist's final thoughts register as a hymn to ordinariness—a rededication to inglorious, mundane affairs. Ultimately "Chintanaya" strains to connect the rhythms of the daily task to the historic event of the revolutionary conjuncture. Vitana's protagonist, like the indomitable figure of the mother in Olsen's "I Stand Here Ironing," measures "history" and socialist ethics not in terms of the logic of revolutions, but in the unceasing back-and-forth movements of daily life that construct and erase the present.[37]

Over and against the wide-ranging and anomalous texts discussed here, I find it particularly telling that the best-known *Dabindu* poem, originally published in the 1987 July–August edition of the periodical and since reproduced in local- and foreign-development NGO and human rights publications, is K. G. Jayasundera Menike's realist testimonial, which describes with play-by-play precision the factory scene at Star Garments.[38] Here we find stanzas organized by segments of clock time, as Menike's poem faithfully replicates the mind-numbing mechanical rhythm of the working day at a garment factory. I would suggest that caught within this exacting tempo, bound to the factory floor, we cannot begin to imagine different times and other measures for thinking collectivities beyond trade unionist socialism and class politics as usual.

Still, despite the unresolved critical debate on Marxist aesthetics, the relationship between working-class writing and literary realism continues to be taken as dogma. Tony Davies writes, "That relationship, in one strong tradition, is simply taken for granted. According to this view, working-class writing is realistic in the most unpremeditated and unselfconscious fashion: autobiographical, documentary, or commemorative, rooted in the experience of family, community, locality, it 'tells it as it is,' (or, more often was) in plain words, valued for their sincerity and simple truth."[39] Still, beyond realism and the genre of testimonial writing, then, how are the truth claims of working-class literature constructed—and according to what terms? These working-class women have been dubbed by some as "the good girls of Sri Lankan modernity."[40] But they actively write against such crisis-management myths of the state. We might ask how, in fact, they themselves define the interruption that is the "modern" (*adhunika*)— that is the new. Theirs, as we see, are collaborative writings, not self-writing in any smooth, seamless way. They are not necessarily rooted in family or locality. Strategic a-chrony, not clock time or nation-building projects, constitute their measure. In the *Dabindu* periodicals, I believe that perhaps the most politically imaginative (but at the same time tenuously situated) writings are a group of Sinhala poems, stories, and letters addressing and identifying with the stateless Tamil women workers of the up-country tea plantations/estates.

Some pieces haphazardly blur the lines between collective identity and class interest. For example, in one segment of a long-running, anonymous epistolary novel, one protagonist (a free-trade-zone factory worker) compares her marginalization to the disenfranchisement of Indian-origin "recent" Tamils:

> Just like those plantation workers . . . They, too, were brought over from India . . . got their work done by them . . . After that they were discarded like dirt . . . Did anyone think about what happens to these people? . . . No . . . How many years has this been going on? Still these people don't have citizenship . . . That's how we are. (*Hasuna* [Letter] 7)

The historical analogy is forced. Despite numerous palliative reform measures, ever since 1948 (the year of Ceylon's independence from Britain), countless numbers of Indian-origin Tamils by birth and descent have been denied national citizenship. Here the narrator reaches for a comparison, invoking a national scandal to give meaning to her own sense of social betrayal.

Other texts approach the plantation workers' struggles more cautiously, acknowledging limitations and marking communication failings. "From zone to plantation" ("Kalapayen vathukarayata"), for example, resists the ethically compromised stance of recognition through assimilation.[41] The exergue preceding the heading identifies this writing as the second part of a serialized letter, but there is no specific addressee. "Put together," not "written by," as the credits disclose, it disclaims unitary authorship and, as such, metonymically mirrors the bricolage aesthetic of the *Dabindu* page. Part reportage, part analysis, part journal entry, embedded speeches (translated, we are told, into Tamil by Sinhala-speaking Tamil activists) take on the challenge of opening a collective dialogue in the face of race war (*jathi vadaya*). As one labor activist puts it, calling for solidarity in alienation, "I too am a garment factory worker. I don't own what I produce. Plantation workers are the same. Production has no caste, race, or religion. And yet we remain divided in that way" (9). From the margins, though, a personal observation (submitted by "the compiler") provides a quiet counterpoint to slogans. Upon entering the line rooms she notes:

> They welcomed us with love. But how do we inquire about their day-to-day lives? We don't understand Tamil. But this doesn't pose a problem for us because Arumugam speaks Sinhalese. The other brothers and sisters that accompanied us could also speak both Sinhala and Tamil. I felt a sense of shame because the only language I know is Sinhalese. (8)

Counter to the communalizing ploys of the Sinhala commission, texts such as these, as well as others like "The tea plantation worker-woman" ("Vathu kamkaru striya") and "Tear drops from the hills" ("Kandurelle kandulu binduva") (both written in the voice-consciousness of the plantation worker) imagine cartographies of labor that attempt to displace competing nationalist imaginaries.

"I WANT YOU WOMEN UP NORTH TO KNOW"

The rhetorical protocols of Tillie Olsen's texts—interruptions interspersed with "heteroglossic crossfire"—certainly resemble the writing (or, properly speaking, the "graph") of the *Dabindu* page. And it is tempting to claim the necessarily collaborative aspect of the unfinished text, writing under the sign of text interferences—whether it be the "serialized poetics" of the free-trade-zone periodical awaiting the next installment, or writing cut short because of the inexorable regulation of the working day and the demands of others (*Yonnondio*)—as categorically feminist. However, to focus only on formal similarities as transparent signs of ideological content is to replay, albeit in a different way, the historicism of those who ordain postmodernism the cultural logic of capital.[42] By simple reversal, the form of feminist interruption becomes "the prose" of counterglobalization.

Not withstanding the fact that the literature of labor and especially the literature of women's labor have been overlooked in literary historiographies charting the passage from realism to postmodernism, we risk collapsing a formalism into an ontology if we claim some seamless unity between the aesthetics and politics of *Dabindu* and Tillie Olsen. There is no organic connection between these texts. Indeed, separated by time and geography, these two very different examples of working-class literature are positioned such that they seem to illustrate perfectly what Michael Hardt and Antonio Negri might describe as the failure of proletarian internationalism today—the incommunicability and *untranslatability* of different working-class struggles via a common system of meaning making. As they put it: "There is no common language of struggles that could 'translate' the particular language of each into a cosmopolitan language. Struggles in other parts of the world and even our own struggles seem to be written in an incomprehensible foreign language" (*Empire*, 57). Furthermore, even as they bracket feminism and the global South as constitutive objects in their study of globalization, Hardt and Negri advance the case that when proletarian internationalism was alive and active it was so because "international solidarity had to be recognized not as an act of charity or altruism for the good of others, a noble sacrifice for another national working class, but rather as proper to and inseparable from each national proletariat's own desire and struggle for liberation" (49–50).[43]

But this rationale does not account for today's emergent "new trade union initiatives," bringing together different "national" labor unions across the North–South divide (India and the United States, for example) to produce a unified platform against the divisive ploys of outsourcing.[44] Neither, in fact, does it account for the ethico-political strategy of Olsen's 1934 "I Want You Women Up North to Know," written in the interest of the garment factory worker of the "global South," in this case, Chicana women in the U.S. garment industry. Olsen writes not in the service of the U.S. working class, but on behalf of a heterogeneous, collective subject of feminism. What do we make of texts such as these, which negotiate the countercurrents of "intranational class differences?" Via a reading of Olsen's poem, this section of my chapter considers global feminism as a language—properly speaking, a translation or mediation, never pure, not always clear, sometimes ideologically compromised—that facilitates communication (amid misfirings) across the North–South divide.

If, as Hardt and Negri contend, internationalism needs to be recognized not as altruism, but as self-interest, Olsen's "I Want You Women Up North to Know" occupies an uneasy position in the canon of literary internationalism. Based on Felipe Ibarro's letter to *New Masses* (1934), Olsen's poem, at a very rudimentary level, reads as antisweatshop boycott politics. Ibarro documents labor violations based on evidence gathered from interviews with Chicana workers in San Antonio. In an interesting variation upon the genre of workers' correspondence poetry, Olsen the working-class poet rewrites the activist journalist's impassioned rhetoric, translating it into lines of poetry. But the first stanza follows Ibarro's opening salvo almost word for word:

I want you women up north to know
how those dainty children's dresses you buy
    at macy's, wanamakers, gimbels, marshall fields,
are dyed in blood, are stitched in wasting flesh,
down in San Antonio, "where sunshine spends the winter."

The central metaphor, predictably perhaps, translates women's bodies into commodities. But the narrative logic of the poem also relies on another metaphoric scheme—alternative regionalisms—depicting an economic and ideological divide between "the North" and "the South." Several decades before the documents of the Brandt Commission mapped the world in the simplest, starkest terms, divided between rich nations (the North) and poor (the South), Olsen adopts their rhetorical strategy, investing the historical North–South divide in the United States with new meaning—one that is all too familiar to us, now, in the aftermath of hurricane Katrina.

Written during a period of hard-won gains for the U.S. labor movement, at the height of proletarian internationalism, Olsen's poem anticipates the age of comparative advantage, multifiber agreements, and NAFTA. As Charlotte Nekola and others have noticed, " 'I Want You Women up North to Know,' about Mexican needle workers, is unusual [in the context of standard surveys of 1930s literature] in that it not only details the conditions of work itself, but also outlines the relationship of third world workers to a capitalist economy" (132). Here Olsen takes it upon herself to write in the class interest— although, significantly, *not* in the voice-consciousness—of Mexican American workers. She calls our attention to ever-shifting contours of cartographies of labor reminiscent, perhaps, of Antonio Gramsci's concept metaphor of "the South," or of Raymond Williams' construct of "the country and the city." According to Olsen's narrative of global capital, the country, here, is down south, where workers are exploited; the city, in this context (up north), identifies the metropolitan centers of consumption. New York, Chicago, and Boston are explicitly named in Ibarro's letter. (Note that Olsen herself is living in San Francisco at this time.) Olsen assigns "the North" a subject position and connects it with the figure of the American Woman-as-Consumer. The last two lines are an exact replica of Ibarro's oath: "I tell you this can't last forever / I swear it won't."

There are other significant moments, however, where Olsen's writing departs from exacting fidelity to the original, taking on an ideological and ethical discursive life of its own. In Ibarro's letter as in Olsen's poem, the North–South divide is inscribed as Northern (women consumers) versus Southern (women workers); the poem, however, beyond naming these women according to their documented names (as Catalina Rodriguez, Maria Vasquez, Catalina Torres, and Ambrosa Espinoza), does not hypostasize national difference. Ibarro makes a point to call attention to the fact that these superexploited women are "*American-born* Mexican" (emphasis mine). But in what might seem a questionable omission from within the ideological and disciplinary maneuvers of (liberal) multiculturalism and identity politics, Olsen does not comment on cultural, ethnic, or indeed national difference in her narrative.[45] Some might make the case that, twice removed from the lived context of their stories and struggles, Olsen is merely ventriloquizing these women. But I would argue that her position might better be understood in terms of a system of socialist ethics put in the service of the worker as opposed to an ethics of the immigrant worker—or the *legal* (American-born) immigrant worker. Elsewhere, as we know, she writes critically of the current overemphasis on race, ethnicity, and identity politics. Overall, in this, her first publication, oversimplification of terms becomes her ethico-political strategy. The women "Up North" constitute a faceless monolith, but the Southern women are named, given subjectivity—sometimes collectively ("maria catalina ambrosa"), sometimes individually. All the Northern women are consumers; the Southern women are workers; but the working-class poet is brave? Ultimately, we do well, as we read Olsen's 1930s poem, to keep in mind the richness and complexity of Chicana protest poetry as a necessary supplement to discourses on borders and borderlands—collective selves and others.[46]

Olsen's own critique of individualism and identity politics cuts across period and genre divisions. While her novel and poem are appraised and studied separately, a comparative study illuminates linkages as well as divergences between history and an ideology of form. Thus it is interesting to compare the reception and discursive life of *Yonnondio* with that of "I Want You Women Up North to Know," her first publication. Olsen (then Lerner) was twenty-one (or twenty-two) when her poem first appeared in *Partisan Review*. Its theme of divisions and differences not withstanding, "I Want You Women Up North to Know" finds a home in feminist working-class studies. *Yonnondio* is generally celebrated as the hallmark text of U.S. literary radicalism. It is widely anthologized in authoritative retrospective collections of the period. What does it mean to celebrate the cultural legacy of the U.S. left in this moment? While hardly expansive, Olsen's corpus of texts provides constant counterpoints to an agenda of triumphalist recovery projects and celebrations of self-interest. And as such, it is immediately relevant to the critical task facing feminism in globalization today. In her poem, as in *Yonnondio*, once again, there is a hesitation around the commodification of resistance—a question as to how "this" (her own) writing might be received and formalized. Once again there is a warning note addressed to "the bourgeois poet." If in *Yonnondio* the message to the corporation cannot/will not be sent, here it will be, but must needs be rerouted via the Northern woman as consumer. Marking its shortcomings, "I Want You Women Up North to Know" is unique in that it anticipates with uncanny prescience feminist negotiations within globalization.

"REPEATED INTERRUPTIONS": HISTORY AND ETHICS IN MAHASWETA DEVI

Chotti Munda's life is one story after another.

—Mahasweta Devi

"Proletarian revolutions," Marx writes, "constantly engage in self-criticism, and in repeated interruptions of their own course" (*Surveys*, 150). Here the adjective "proletarian" is charged with a specific disembodied, abstract meaning. It becomes synonymous with the process of autocritique. Marx invokes this meaning again in his postface to the second edition of *Capital*, volume 1, where he links dialectical thought to "revolutionary" critique: "in so far as such a critique represents a class, it can only represent the class whose historical task is the overthrow of the capitalist mode of production and the final abolition of all classes—the proletariat" (98). Then again, later in the same text, we encounter the stuff of this "critique": "It does not let itself be impressed by anything, being in its very essence critical and revolutionary" (103). In such moments of exergues and revision, the meaning of "revolution" is transformed, even as "proletarian" comes to signify not merely the real working-class (or even that specific subset of the working class entrusted with the historic mission of abolishing class society) but also the agency—*"in so far as* such a critique represents a class"—of historical materialism. Such revolutions are autocritical and antidevelopmentalist, *and thus* are long-lived. They are conceptualized as "repeated interruptions," constantly sidelining the path of capital.

Serialized form (as in the *Dabindu* periodicals) generates repeated interruptions, and the rhetorical protocols of Tillie Olsen's texts, as we have seen, resemble those of *Dabindu*'s writings. Building on Marx's elaboration of "the proletarian," this final section of the chapter considers "interruption" as a structural, not aberrational, aspect of a specifically feminist proletarian aesthetic and ethic. It is not open-ended messianicity, but the open-endedness of proletarian (in this sense) "revolutions" that is captured by Indian writer and tribal rights activist Mahasweta Devi's works. Her writing and activism emerges within and against over thirty years of left front rule in the communist state of West Bengal in India. In the preceding section, I read Olsen's field-defining literature from the 1930s alongside the *Dabindu* writings representing the new proletariat within globalization. There the incongruous pairing of the single-author novel with the collectively authored and edited free-trade-zone periodical was intended to call attention to the figure of a collective subject and the critique of individualism shared by different *changing* traditions of women's and feminist texts of labor. This concluding section considers how Devi's aesthetics and ethics of interruption extend the reach of such a Marxist-feminist critique of historicism.

A consideration of moments of revision and supplementation (like Marx's postface to the second edition of *Capital*) animates retrospective battles over the political and theoretical provenance of the "real" Karl Marx. Was he a humanist—a structuralist? Is his intellectual legacy properly validated and countersigned in the work of Antonio Gramsci or that of Louis Althusser? (I return to this question below.) It doesn't even occur to us, however, to consider how a Devi (or a Spivak, we might add) might extend the afterlife of Western Marxism. Born in 1926 in East Bengal (contemporary Bangladesh), Devi came of age intellectually and politically during anticolonial struggles against the British, but was also witness to the CPI (Communist Party India)-initiated peasant movements in Tebhaga, Kakdwip, and (later, in 1967) Naxalbari. Marx, caught within the historicism of his own milieu—industrial-imperial Britain—was unable to think outside certain ideological blind spots of his time. And yet, as attentive poststructuralist readers of *Capital* have shown, Marx's method—his self-reflexive attention to the gaps and hesitations in his own thought—at the very least suggests an itinerary for mapping an autocritical Marx(ism) beyond the conditions and constraints that produced the historical individual. Both formally and conceptually, however, Devi's writings are categorically unfinished texts connected to the longue durée. Validated by a longer "proletarian moment" than the "Red Decade" of Europe and the United States, her writing nevertheless is radically antitriumphalist.

The journalistic prose of her memorial tribute to CPI leader Asoke Bose sets a context for her investment in a type of nonrevolutionary socialism and her own "ethics of interruption." Writing the text of a memorial tribute in collaboration with her brother, she observes,

> For us Asoke Bose is not a mere leader of a short-lived movement that failed years ago. It has been proved time and again in the history of peasant struggles in this country that failure can be more glorious than victory. Who remembers the names of the victors of these struggles? Or of those who defeated Birsa Munda and Sidhu Kanhu? It's the defeated who continue to live in our minds. The name of Kakdwip has become a part of this history and has provided inspiration to movements of later periods and will continue to do so. Regimes change, but the struggle continues.[47]

In her literary texts she dramatizes this critical agency of failure and uncompleted mourning. Her stories play with differential time—alignments and misalignments, repetition as transformative recurrence.

As we know, Marx's final texts on class remain unfinished. Whose script of history, then, should determine the context of general theories of capitalism—of an ethics of socialism? Can we speak of a global ethics of time—of historical materialism? Which history? Whose time? Even as we think in terms of Marxism and (comparative) literature, what should be the frame of reference for making comparative moral judgments about modes of production and the logic of culture? "Time, complex time, how can a *computer* possibly *process* this time and give birth to a *data-sheet*" (156)? The question is raised in Mahasweta Devi's "Pterodactyl, Puran Sahay, and Pirtha," which depicts the appearance of a pterodactyl in contemporary postcolonial India.

Devi's realist novella addresses debates in Marxism, shifting the burden of questions from grounds of history to questions of ethics. Again, "Marxism is not a historicism": Placed in context, Althusser's famous but polemical statement refers to a quarrel with Antonio Gramsci—properly speaking, it refers to a quarrel with lesser practitioners' interpretations of Gramsci—who tended to reduce theory to historically specific programs of action and agendas of reform. As mentioned before, Althusser sought to prevent Marx (and Marxism) from merely becoming slogans for validating left-party politics of the day. As such, although Althusser accepts Gramsci's "leftist" humanist reaction as a strategic response to the economisms and mechanism of Second International doxa, he cannot allow Marxism to be understood *merely* as a programmatic call to arms. But "historicism" in Althusser's lexicon also refers to *a specific* ideology of history that conforms to a narrative logic of successive stages, continuity, and determinism. Marxism cannot be handcuffed to history—either specific failures in state socialism, or momentary successes like the making of the English working class. It is a general theory of changing capital and class relations over time. And yet, if Marxism is not a historicism, from what does it derive its content? What should be its morphology? Althusser, for the most part, leaves us hanging with his partial insight. It is the burden of this book to show that unwittingly, perhaps, somewhere between his critique against reformism and revolution, a consideration of Althusser's—mistaken, some would argue—anti-Gramsci polemics leads the Marxist reader to a middle ground: the need for a theory (and practice) of socialist ethics. As Perry Anderson puts it, "The notorious absence of anything approaching such an ethics within the accumulated corpus of historical materialism—its regular displacement by either politics or aesthetics—lends to this project a peculiar point and force."[48]

Mahasweta Devi, writing in the aftermath of revolution (1968; Naxalbari), and yet, hearkening to the threat of organized leftist brutality (2007; Nandigram), would seem to echo Althusser's cautionary statement. Her "Pterodactyl" and "The Fairy Tale of Mohanpur" are both "myth and analysis" of a particular Indian left tradition too hastily assimilated into legends of revolution, on the one hand, and into knowledge bureaucratized by left-party politics *and* managerial NGO culture, on the other. But while—as I've mentioned before—Althusser opens up the provenance of Marxism for us through his reading of Marx beyond the historical particularism of Marx's own milieu, nowhere in Althusser's own corpus do we find an ethical alternative to "historicism." There is in fact a gesture of equivocation that concedes some ground to possibilities opened up by the "Third World"—but only provisionally:

> Even today, this "humanism" and "historicism" find genuinely revolutionary echoes in the political struggles waged by the people of the Third World to conquer and defend their political independence and set out on the socialist road. But these ideological and political advantages themselves, as Lenin admirably

discerned, are offset by certain effects of the *logic* that they set in motion, which eventually and inevitably produce idealist and empiricist temptations in economic and political conceptions and practice—if they do not, given a favorable conjuncture, induce, by a paradoxical but still necessary inversion, conceptions which are tainted with reformism and opportunism, or quite simply revisionist. (*Reading Capital*, 141)

Devi's literary texts on West Bengal, supplemented by Spivak's elaborations of Marxism and feminism, articulate a connection between a politics of comparativism, the critique of historicism, and the turn to ethics. If historicism is the parsing of history as seamless, continuous, and tending toward "the global," the critique of historicism makes visible the narrative and logical mechanism by which we produce such an apprehension of history. The counterintuitive lesson of "Pterodactyl" might be that we must look beyond the epiphenomenal headlines of the period, as well as short stories of revolution, to the longer-term logics and uncertain outcomes of history. Here history is understood as "the ordinary," the nonevent—it is daily repetition understood as transformative recurrence.

A brief plot summary sets the context for my reading: A pterodactyl—or properly speaking, a creature closely resembling the exact specs of the science textbooks—has been sighted in the famine-ravaged area of Pirtha, India, "where . . . eighty thousand tribals among the one million, one hundred and seven thousand, three hundred and eighty-one people of the district live" (98). If the well-meaning reporter and dedicated left-front government representative were to document the media event, no doubt attention would be focused on a habitually neglected area and aid money would come pouring in. But in consultation with tribal "representatives," the decision is made not to capitalize on this phenomenon. Eventually, the creature dies, having communicated a cryptic message to Bhikia, a mute tribal boy. "Pirtha," it is claimed, "is the place where reporters go mad." Empirical investigations into current events are confounded. Puran, the journalist, cannot understand the message, but intuits the lesson to be learned: "We have lost somewhere, to Bhikia's people, to Pirtha. By comparison with the ancient civilizations modern progress is much more barbaric at heart. . . . We have slowly destroyed a continent in the name of civilization.... To build it you must love beyond reason for a long time" (195). Devi's pterodactyl does not lend itself to the marketing ploys of the postcolonial culture industry. "This time is out of joint." It is not *safely* "post"colonial. Shankar, the "native informant," explains to the reporter and his friend, "We are late by many, many moons. Now no one can show us any help" (117). Neither the postcolonial state nor the new imperial philanthropy of NGOs can provide redress or remuneration to the tribal aboriginals, even if they wished to: "The government does not even know that there are human beings in Pirtha" (117). The Pirtha tribals remain delayed and deferred. They remain to be "scheduled" and "denotified" into independence along with other "scheduled castes," awaiting the minimal measures of affirmative action devised by the postcolonial state.

Devi's writing directs attention beyond the conjunctural limits of "the revolution" to the daily, unglamorous, unrewarding, unfinished business of the everyday. Her novella and activist journalism (some of which is compiled in *Dust on the Road*) conceptualize an epistemological break from monumental time marked by explosive (global/newsworthy) events to time registered as transformative repetition—in fact, untimeliness. In terms of structure, her writing breaks with the representation of linear time and progressive narrative-sequences. Even at the level of the sentence, there is no subject or (obvious) syntax, just parataxis held together loosely by alliteration. "Pterodactyl, Puran Sahay, and Pirtha," the heading, becomes emblematic of a signature rhetorical strategy deployed throughout the text. Time is represented as *décalage* (dislocation). Breaks and interruptions cannot be easily sorted out by devices of periodization or literary history. A moment of speech interference, reminiscent of the moment discussed in *Yonnondio*, enjoins the reader to reflect on the ethico-political agenda of "this" writing. This is not "science fiction" (nor is it "national allegory"). The narrative of the pterodactyl sighting—on the eve of the enforced liberalization of the Indian economy—in 1987 neoliberal India is something else.

At the heart of "Pterodactyl" is this angry, *chastising* outburst commenting on the cultural politics of class struggle, literature, and the way we parse literary history.

> But oh the first and last living messenger from the prehistoric world! This too is the implacable and cruel truth that time will

advance, that the wheels of time will destroy much as they advance. You cannot turn the eighteenth to the seventeenth, however hard you try. Only the creators of science fiction can do that. The boys and girls who are of the *"cute"* and *"oh baby"* and *"oh boy"* brand and who are constant escapists in the mind get an adulterated joy when they read those stories. But in India, or in the world, what is *"tidy," just* fine, smooth? Such things exist for the few. For the many, time means a struggle red in tooth and claw and the struggle does not mean the same thing all the time. Time, complex time, how can a *computer* possibly *process* this time and give birth to *a data sheet*? (156)

Deictic indices are both implicit and explicit in this passage. Here and now, "this" is the literature of struggle, a cruel truth—not utopian "science fiction." This does not belong under the heading of "Postmodernism; or, The Cultural Logic of Late Capitalism." (In fact, Devi's fiction opens up different ways of reading and engaging Jameson's classic texts in Marxist theory.) According to the narrator at least, conventions and notations of architectural historicism or theories of time–space compression cannot account for the unceasing dialectical revisionism of "the everyday." Time travel is the provenance of "escapist" science fiction. And there is an unmistakable American accent ("cute," "oh boy," "oh baby") to the brand of fantasy disavowed. But contrary to a genre of postcolonial revisionist history, neither is "Pterodactyl" a romantic, romanticizing journey back in time to some prebourgeois, precolonial idyllic past. In Devi's novella (as in contemporary Indian history) the caste-Hindu postcolonial subject is colonizer and usurper of aboriginal lands. As such the ethical objectives and aims of Devi's texts transgress the provincialism of some South Asian (area studies–based) subaltern studies approaches that (despite their best impulses) tidily equate historicism with Eurocentrism. "But in India, or in the world, what is 'tidy,' *just* fine, smooth?" Devi's is a rough, uneven, global comparativism, where the breaks and articulations are designed to show. Her pterodactyl is a figure for an ethics of historical materialism. Over and against reformism *and* revolution, beyond just the decentering of the subject of the moment, Devi's writing proposes an autocritical aesthetics and ethics.

There is, for example, this precarious moment in Devi's novella—one which resembles, on the surface at least, a kind of unapologetic cultural relativism. We don't know what to make of Shankar's decision to refuse aid from those committed to painstaking infrastructure building. We also don't quite know how to read the decision to withhold the transcript of the truthful report and to submit, instead, an edited "false" one, omitting details of the pterodactyl. A rationale is spelled out (but not spoken) in Puran's thoughts:

> Bhikia, I don't want anyone to know of our dreadful discovery, because if we let them know there will be an invasion of the *media* of the inquisitive world. You will be shown on television, and the soul's warning message, the terrifying news of the tribal being of Pirtha, will all lose their perspective, by many analyses the rodent and the rhododendron will be proven the same. And who can tell, all the countries of the world will conduct investigations out of Pirtha everywhere, into the last forest, last cave. (162)

"By many analyses the rodent and the rhododendron will be proven the same." The silent admonition makes perfect sense on one level: global capital-logic opens up spaces and economies, making them continuous and available for exploitation under one (world) trade regime, forcing recognition of the other through assimilation. But on another level, Puran's warning runs counter to the text's own protocols and politics—coming riskily close to reifying historical differences as static monuments. To refuse the telos of globalization (as Hegelian "transculturation" or world history) is one thing. But feminism and comparative literature also contrive connections across distances and differences. At first glance, Puran's ethical stance does not square with either the politics of form or the broader ideological and political vision elaborated by Devi. (Elsewhere in this novella, we see that against prevailing leftist moralism, she depicts journalists and local activists bypassing NGO strategists and working instead with ethical *state* officials.) Overall, through parataxis/alliteration Devi suggests imaginative, counterintuitive, heterodox connections and collectivities. Here, the insistence on logical, coordinated sequencing seems opposed to such creative alignments and misalignments. Upon closer scrutiny, however, we see that Puran's warning speaks to Mahasweta's commentary on the Marxian question of *value*—more specifically, the question of how value is produced and expressed in exchange relations. As such, Puran's demurral takes us into the heart of the productive problem of historicism in Marx—his elaboration of the emergence of the *differential* "value-form."

Puran's insistence on the incommensurability of "the rodent and the rhododendron" recalls us to basic foundational tenets of *Capital*, volume 1. To posit a relation of value you need at least two *different* commodities. In Marx's lexicon, "value" constitutes "that simple and contentless thing" that mediates between differences. There is, however, an implicit political corollary to Marx's discussions on the commodity form and the value relation that arises as a consequence. Marx (the Hegelian Marx, some would qualify—Marx had other moments) believed that the logic of the commodity form encrypted a universal emancipatory narrative in the unfolding of its internal logic: he believed that "[t]he secret of the expression of value, namely the equality and equivalence of all kinds of labor, . . . could not be deciphered until the concept of human equality had already acquired a permanence of a fixed popular opinion" (152). (Thus England becomes his example for elucidating capital relations.) Capital logic needs as its predication a society that has collectively internalized ideals of liberalism and equal standing as its foundation. The value-form—a basis for comparing and thus making equal two entirely different commodities—can arise only though a process of abstraction. But to "abstract"—to defetishize the concrete—in this way is also to necessarily dehumanize and dehistoricize by arbitrarily creating equivalence. To do so is to elide historical differences and cultural particularities in order to produce a common measure for comparison. Arguably, the process of abstraction in itself is intrinsically neither "good" nor "bad." This dialectical tension between the universal and the particular is as much the ethical leverage of socialism as it is the driving force of capital maximization. Spivak, reading Marx through Derrida, will call this relationship "pharmakonic"—poison taken as medicine.

Through this cryptic statement made in Puran's voice-consciousness, Devi's novella engages just this thorny question of value—especially pertinent to how we produce the value-coding of the object of history. The rodent and the rhododendron are unequal. Adamantly maintaining their incommensurability must accomplish some specific ideological (or ethical) work. What if we were to begin by dismissing the premise of equality and liberalism to begin with? What if we were to begin, instead, with the insertion into responsibility, rather than liberalism and individual rights? The pterodactyl as a figure for tribal culture represents responsibility as freedom and individuality as separation. "There is no escape, we were torn apart so long ago, in fragments in atoms, we are scattered everywhere" (161), someone mourns. It is not clear who. To be autonomous individuals marks the painful dispersal of the disparate parts of a collective subject. Devi asks us to conceive of this starting point as a brilliant lost opportunity—not for capitalism, but for socialist ethics. In *Rethinking Working-Class History: Bengal, 1890–1940*, Dipesh Chakrabarty, too, begins to unpack this proposition when he observes that "the bourgeois idea of 'equality,' incorporating as it does concepts of 'individual rights,' 'contract,' and 'possessive individualism,' has extremely serious and grave limitations that are necessarily inimical to the construction of any socialist, communitarian ethic and order" (xii). He questions what might be learned from other resistant collectivities *devalued* by capitalism. But ultimately he, too, remains caught up in a historicist trap of his own, as he demarcates the space of resistant collectivities and communitarian ethics as "precapitalist." Devi's pterodactyl, on the other hand, is not precapitalist. It figures as a sign of other times outside *in* capitalism. Logically outside the temporality of factory discipline and the measurements of (a labor theory of) value, it represents the unthinkable abstraction of "difference without hierarchy"—and also the ideal of feminism and comparative literature.

The meditation on the rodent and the rhododendron cuts deeper and closer than the earlier self-reflexive passage commenting on the cultural politics of genre and a literature of struggle. Puran's statement, in fact, gets to the heart of the matter: how we make comparative judgments about historical value. E. P. Thompson—though conflating history with the past and mixing morals with values—touches upon the difficulty of grasping the a priori value-coding of history when he observes that "progress is a concept either meaningless or worse, when imputed as an attribute *to* the past, which can only acquire a meaning from a particular position in the present, a position of value in search of its own genealogy."[49] "[B]y many analyses the rodent and the rhododendron will be proven the same" is a statement that flouts empirical measurements and places pressure on how we produce that slipperiest, most abstract, and nonteleological of Marxist concepts—value. As such, it must be understood as a mirror text of the fabula. The illegibility and untranslatability of the pterodactyl might be misread by some as a signature postcolonial device—a valorization of an "ethics of alterity." But, in effect, the pterodactyl cannot be valorized. It is outside the scheme of value. It represents a starting point for histories of socialism—difference without hierarchy.

Thus "Pterodactyl" rests stubbornly on a blatantly illiberal premise: the resistance to neoliberal globalization and development. Devi's reconstitution of the object of labor history through the perspective of tribal adivasis confronts and disputes the famous affirmation of *Empire*, where Hardt and Negri claim that "Empire is better in the same way that Marx insists that capitalism is better than the forms of society and modes of production that came before it" (43). The pterodactyl cannot speak but "[w]hat does it want to tell? We are extinct by the inevitable natural geological evolution. You too are endangered. [*The addressee, here, is the human/journalist.*] You too will become extinct in nuclear explosions, or in war, or in the aggressive advance of the strong as it obliterates the weak, which finally turns you naked, barbaric, primitive, think if you are going forward or back" (157).

"Pterodactyl" read through the critical interpretive lens of Marxist-feminist critic (and Devi's translator) Spivak opens up other possibilities. As she puts it, "Today Marx's ghost needs stronger offerings than Human Rights with economics worked in, or the open-ended messianicity of the future anterior, or even 'responsibility' (choice or being called) in the Western tradition. The need is to turn toward ethical practices—care of others as care of the self—that were '*defective* for capitalism.'"[50] The formulation charts an interesting development in the chronology of Spivak's own writings. If in "Can the Subaltern Speak?" she opposed the ethical decentering of the sovereign subject via a meaning of class suggested by Marx's "Eighteenth Brumaire" to certain standard signature moves of poststructuralism, there she stopped short of following through with this theoretical opening in terms of an ethical alternative. Here, building on Foucault's third volume on the history of sexuality, she turns to the question of socialist ethics—specifically a collective subject articulating Derridian responsibility-based ethics with Foucault's posthumanist humanism.

Spivak's own symptomatic reading of Marx builds upon the counterintuitive implications of Althusser's exegesis, not taken up by most Marxist (or subaltern studies) scholars. Marx could not envision other modes of collectivity (beyond the party form and trade unionist socialism) outside bourgeois liberal traditions of equality and rights. Devi refracted through Spivak (feminism as translation) suggests that we must harness those "residual" sometimes hierarchical, gender-compromised ("defective") modes—failed modes for capitalist progress—in the service of an ethics of historical materialism and a vision for other collectivities. Here, as elsewhere, Devi and Spivak venture into dangerous terrain when they imply that we may have to (in some instances, at least) instrumentalize feudality in the service of fighting feudalism *and* capitalism. Resource-rich, rights-based societies may have something to learn from (sometimes gender-compromised) responsibility-based cultures. The content of an ethics of historical materialism is not ideologically pure. Upon first take, the silent message of the pterodactyl intuited by (not communicated to) Puran seems rather anticlimactic, almost banal and melodramatic, in fact: "To build it you must love beyond reason for a long time" (195). "Only love, a tremendous, excruciating explosive love can still dedicate us to this work when the century's sun is in the Western sky, otherwise aggressive civilization will have to pay a price" (196). Elsewhere, in conversation with her translator and collaborator, the author, Devi, repeats this mandate: "Our double task is to resist 'development' actively and to learn to love" (*Imaginary Maps*, xxii).

"Love beyond reason" does not quite compute in Althusser's calculus of structural causality. But Devi's concept of "love," as it is developed in her novella and other writings, provides Spivak with the basis for elaborating a concept of socialist ethics. Akin to, but some paces removed from, an extension of Levinasian ethics, Spivak parses such love as the encounter of "ethical singularity": this is the "secret encounter" of imperfect communication that transpires in the interstices of history-making events, in something like normality, between equals—not subject and object of benevolence. In other words, such an ethical exchange can occur only in the tempo of the everyday between interlocutors—not historian and native informant, nor journalist and source. It cannot take place in crisis mode in the register of moral exhibitionism; the message of the pterodactyl cannot be read like a manifesto or be made "actionable" like a state agenda. Such an encounter cannot be confused with the event that galvanizes short-term coalitional politics and forges provisional links between activists and subalterns in the moment of crisis.

Such nonteleological dialogic relationships of ethical singularity constitute daily repair work undoing internalized gendering. "The slow effort of ethical responding" is measured by other speeds than those of the revolutionary conjuncture or mode of production narratives. It lasts beyond media events, well after the ink dries on official reports and newspaper pages become obsolete. Such labored practice, "which is neither 'mass contact' nor engagement with the common sense of the people," must supplement collective action, Spivak proposes: "Most political movements fail in the long run because of the absence of this engagement" (xxv). And yet, the goal of this effortful striving can never be (completely) realized. There is no moral "payoff." Something is always lost/held back, despite the best intentions of both respondents involved. (It is in this sense that the encounter is "secret"—because of the lost bits, parts inaccessible to the subjects themselves). Thus the condition of this relationship is loss. Its outcome is uncertainty. But this acknowledgment cannot forestall the commitment to action. Elsewhere in her *Critique of Postcolonial Reason*, Spivak builds on Derridian responsibility-based ethics to propose that "the promise of justice must attend not only to the seduction of power, but also to the anguish that knowledge must suppress difference as well as différance, that a fully just world is impossible, forever deferred and different from our projections, the undecidable in the face of which we must risk the decision that we can hear the other" (199). Here we see that in Spivak's formulation, "ethical" perhaps replaces "historical" in the system of ideas operating "historical materialism."

Perry Anderson hypothesizes that the reason the founders of historical materialism were so wary of "ethical discussions of socialism . . . is their tendency to become substitutes for explanatory accounts of history." However, to be "ethical" in the context of ethical singularity is not necessarily commensurate with doing good or being good according to a prescribed set of morals or established precepts. Rather, it might be understood as acting in the hope of justice in the absence of guarantees, ideological sanction (histories of left-party politics), or institutional validation. Singularity, in this sense, is repetition with a difference. It is not identical with individualism or exceptionalism, as in commonly available received notions. Where the individual is indivisible, singularity is divisible and relational. Thus "the everyday" is singular because it epitomizes repetition with difference—transformative recurrence. Ethical singularity is focused on the task, not the event.[51] But most importantly, ethical singularity, predicated on the impossibility of "winning," is not proposed in lieu of collective struggle. Rather, as Spivak puts it, ethical singularity is what needs to happen in the everyday, in the aftermath of the revolution: "For a collective struggle *supplemented* by the *impossibility* of full ethical engagement—not in the rationalist sense of 'doing the right thing,' but in the more familiar sense of 'love' in the one on one way for each human being—the future is always around the corner, there is no victory, but only victories that are also warnings" (xxv). In Devi's "Pterodactyl," "Love" (responsibility-based ethics, ethico-political negotiations of the everyday), it is hoped, will sustain the revolutionary event beyond its duration. It must disrupt the telos of "aggressive civilization" and competing stages in the developmentalist logic of modes of production narratives.

The pterodactyl itself becomes a figure for the critique of teleological history. We don't know if it is from the past, the present, or the future. (Based on available scientific evidence, it is unclear as to precisely which era this "current" Pirtha variant of the winged creature hails from: "[Pterodactylus, pteranodon, pterodactyl!]" Puran wonders.) Nonessentialist in its morphology, mapping a planetary internationalism *before* national maps ever existed, it is an impossible retrospective glance at the present. Its message depicts an antihumanist ethics derived from nature—"man's body without organs"—where history *is* geology and temporality cannot be value-coded as history.

> How transparent the dark, how liquid, melting bit by bit. Everything can be seen in such darkness. No, I don't want even to touch you, you are outside my wisdom, reason, and feelings who can place his hand at the axial moment of the end of the third phase of the Mesozoic and the beginnings of the Cenozoic geological ages? (156)

The rhetorical question goes unanswered. Puran, the journalist, cannot grasp its concept.

It is crucially significant that Devi's pterodactyl cannot be empirically verified. Devi's pterodactyl, like the revolution, will not be televised. It is illegible—the antithesis of historio*graphy* as such. But, *therefore*, it figures an abstract ethics of historical materialism. History is not reducible to historiography. "Marxism is not a historicism," Devi would agree. In making their case, Althusser and Balibar reject schools of thought that canonize Marx as an empiricist historian of the British working class, but stop short of extending the implications of their critical exegesis further. A certain formation of postcolonial Marxist studies takes off from this formulation, opening up Marx toward other histories of labor and social movements—but they care little for "ethics," emphasizing, instead, questions of politics. On the other hand, criticism by certain schools of postcolonial scholarship simply equates Marxism with Eurocentrism. Spivak's and Devi's intervention is some paces removed from these trajectories within Marxism and cultural studies. Their collaboration/translation supplements the theoretical vacuum left in the wake of the epistemic break between the (early) "humanist" Marx and the later "political" one, with their proposed turn to socialist ethics.

While the line between aesthetics and politics in never firm, nor straight, Mahasweta's text mediated by Spivak's translation/ethics proposes a supplement to Marxism, beyond Marx. Devi's pterodactyl, as we see, is a break in structure, but it does not inaugurate *a* politics of the subject in any uncomplicated way: (along with Puran Sahay and Pirtha,) the pterodactyl is the part-subject of ethics. The logic of its figuration proposes an autocritical ethics of historical materialism that can never be fully recovered, only partially reconstructed:

> One person eats well by keeping five hundred starving, one person graduates college while six hundred remain illiterate, and one person buys an apartment keeping how many people homeless, such complicated *ratios*. No *ratio* has ever been calculated from the position of people like Bhikia. The position from which *computer*, information ministry, and *media* of the inquisitive world see the situation depends on the will of the current social and state systems. And it is by the will of this system that

the educated person is unwilling to think. This system considers original thought an "exterminable threat." This system forcibly occupies the thinking cells of the brain and makes a body brush his teeth with Forhan's toothpaste. Sometimes makes him or her say that India is proudly on the way to becoming the biggest power in the Third World. Again sometimes it makes one crazy with the idea that the first duty is to change the name of the state. The system wants, and people "dance like wooden dolls." But the first obligation is to calculate the ratio from the position of people like Bhikia. Without that effort Independence has grown to be forty years old. (161–162)

"The system wants, and people 'dance like wooden dolls.'" Subjectivity is assigned to the system, here. The inexorable arithmetics of poverty call for an ethics of historical materialism. And, indeed, here as elsewhere, echoes of Walter Benjamin's theses on the philosophy of history seem to abound. But the comparison cannot be made too glibly. The angel of history is not the same as the pterodactyl.

"Pterodactyl" ends with the journalist leaving Pirtha. The story breaks off abruptly, as Devi stages it; Puran stops a truck, "steps up," and passes out of the frame. What remains to be done is left for the tribal adivasis, who have categorically refused NGO assistance and state aid. Shankar speaks for the collective subject, articulating the present (the event of the pterodactyl) with the present continuous—the quotidian tasks of the everyday: "We will do what we used to do. We've got water, we'll work the field. One thing is true, we must plant the Khajra that keeps us alive. If Baola keeps us alive, we must plant Baola. Otherwise everything will be desert, and we will have to leave" (184). Questions of feminist agency and historiography seem outside the narrative proper, unless we consider that Puran (who must abandon the task of simply documenting) might be understood as an alter ego for Devi herself.

In *Dust on the Road*, a compilation of Mahasweta's journalistic writings, we uncover the author's own thesis on the philosophy of history during a moment where she confronts a shocking statue of a tribal hero, Birsa Munda, depicted in chains. "Why did the artist have to be so faithful to the photograph?" she asks, decrying the aesthetics and politics of a representational strategy bound by a blind fidelity to documentary realism and the official historical record.[52] Throughout the corpus of her writings, Mahasweta Devi elaborates the object of postcolonial historiography in terms of ethical questions rather than historicist preoccupations. Thus her objective is not simply the "recovery" of lost objects of (subaltern) history through the privileging of narratives of tribal (or peasant) resistance movements. Central to her capturing an ethics of history is a philosophy of "fiction," not journalistic accuracy or documentary realism.

In "The Fairy Tale of Mohanpur" (1999), the critique of official historiography and of the Naxalite revolution is figured in the character-person of Andi, and the critical agency of "repeated interruptions" is explicitly gendered—also a structural and structuring aspect of the story. If in "Pterodactyl" interruptions occur as periodic breaks and rifts at the level of the syntactical unit of the sentence, here the very concept of "repeated interruptions" becomes formalized in the figure of irony—"permanent parabasis or a source relating otherwise."[53] In this case, an old blind woman's "fairy tale" history and women's everyday ethical negotiations disrupt and derail the trajectory of masculinist left-party politics and trade unionist socialism in the communist state of West Bengal. "Andi" (the blind one) marks the place of the parabasis, which reveals "a sudden discontinuity between two rhetorical codes": tragedy and wish fulfillment; revolution and the everyday; politics and ethics. Formally, Devi gives us the narrative of a hopeless tragedy undermined, somehow, by the voice-consciousness and blurred vision of an *unbearably* hopeful, completely clueless optimist. (Every dismal happening is reversed in Andi's mind, "jes like a fairy tale one by one!" [104].) Conceptually, Andi's experience of time and of women's collectivity undermines the plot trajectory of the primary fabula: the struggle of the communist trade unionist (Gobindo) to unionize sharecroppers in the rural electorate. Gobindo's history is that of the storied Naxalite movement of the late 1960s. The "fairy tale" is set in an experience of time completely antithetical to revolutionary consciousness. It exists solely in the head of an irrepressible aging woman's overactive imagination.

A word of background first. As mentioned before, Devi's story must be read as a rethinking of a specific historicist tradition of literary radicalism in postcolonial West Bengal—a genre of historical fiction commemorating the Naxalite movement. The name, Naxalite, retrospectively constitutes the designation for a supporter of the militant, "revolutionary" Communist Party of India (Marxist-Leninist) (CPI-ML). But the word (and corresponding ideology, Naxalism) derives from Naxalbari, a village in northern West Bengal that in May 1967 was the scene of a peasant uprising against landlords and police. The event of the Naxalbari rebellion marks a watershed moment in the official annals of not only Indian left-party politics but also Marxist (and Maoist) theory and practice. The peasant-based Naxalite movement quickly catches on as the stuff of an international cultural imaginary—though hardly approaching what the talisman of May 1968 accomplishes for Western Marxism and, thereafter, "political ethics." Marxist writers and critics have, however, already questioned its ideological significance for Indian Marxism and revolutionary thought in general—especially in the wake of Nandigram and Singur. In his *Present History of West Bengal*, Partha Chatterjee comments ironically on a genre of literary radicalism: "If the decade of the seventies did not quite turn out to be the decade of revolution, it does seem to have ended up as the decade of books on revolution."[54]

Devi—at least since 1974, when she published *Mother of 1084*, and then *Agnigarbha* (a novel and a collection of short stories dealing explicitly with the historical background of the Naxalite struggle) in 1978—seems to have moved away from the endeavor of documenting accounts of rural uprisings toward a very different project. In her more recent fiction, counter to her ongoing historical research into agrarian movements, she illuminates the successes and losses that occur in the uneventful day-to-day lives of the rural poor. Spivak mentions one critic who, isolating the final scene in "Douloti the Bountiful," regards this other trend as illustrative of the "jaded pessimism of the postcolonial middle class."[55] But as we know from placing Devi within context, she is adamantly against romanticizing lost causes or fetishizing subalternity. In "The Fairy Tale of Mohanpur," Devi attends to the narrative of the gendered subaltern, set apart from organized agrarian movements—in the aftermath of Naxalbari.

The eccentric center, not subject, of this story "about" the struggles of sharecroppers in contemporary rural West Bengal is an old woman whose wild imagination and terrible hunger know no bounds. No one listens to Andi's stories about Mohanpur before the time of famine. Her failing eyesight and frequent memory lapses make her an unreliable witness. But as the narrative opens we are drawn into the knowledge of a secret history: "Old Andi alone knows the fairy tale of Mohanpur. In which fairy tale there are paddy stacks in every house." Andi "remembers" history the way it never was.

Narratalogically, Devi constructs Andi as the donor, not the subject, of the story, "who must wear the functional appearance of the protagonist in order to perform [a] quite different actantial function."[56] Andi's inaccurate, non*realist* vision provides the basis for the narrative, although she is not the subject of left-party politics. It is while taking "this screw-loose body" to hospital for eye surgery that the protagonist, Gobindo, a dedicated CP village worker, happens upon a trail of wrongdoing sanctioned by the system. "I won't give a damn for the Pat-ty. Your time for seeing straight has also come," Gobindo tells the government-appointed doctors (102). Thus Andi's blindness sets the terms for a recurring metaphor that holds together the different pieces of the story: history is a way of seeing, a mode of focalization. Beyond propagandist histories and party slogans, the rural activist *also* learns another way of seeing, by becoming attentive to feminist practices of ethical responsibility outside the sad failings of the socialist message.

Without romanticizing Andi's way of seeing/remembering the lost object of the past, Devi elaborates the metaphor of history as an optics by making Gobindo's story parallel to the story of Andi's eye operation. Ultimately, the dedicated leftist, too, requires a vision adjustment: regarding the daily struggles of the sharecroppers, he is asked by a patient old villager, "It has been, it is always, it is now, it will be, still you say it can't be. Why don't you understand what you see?" (87). Ultimately, Gobindo learns the limits of trade unionist politics and ignorant goodwill when he is made aware of the harsh retaliatory schemes of the party-sanctioned head of the panchayat. "He no longer asks Andi's sons to leap into the sharecroppers movement" (88), but he learns instead from the dynamism of other collectivities born of the daily intimacies and binding kinship of women's labor. The social worker learns ethical responsibility from observing the relationship between Andi and the (unnamed) eldest daughter-in-law.

While "old Andi alone knows the fairy tale of Mohanpur," her daughter-in-law is the only member of the village community who shares with her an affection for the past. She recalls with fondness her induction into the household as a girl-bride when "[Andi] would mind [her] with candy and sweet balls" (98). The relationship between the old woman and the younger is defined by other durations, set apart also from the "bad times" that everyone else recalls, including the narrator. And while a sharply coded, gendered division of labor organizes rural life in Mohanpur, here gendered hierarchies between women are lovingly reversed. Their bond is defined by the changing dynamics of responsibility-based ethics, rather than the timing of crisis management or oedipal narratives. When Andi's situation worsens, the well-intentioned social worker only sees an added burden: "All this falls on you now," he says to the daughter-in-law (98). But she quietly *chooses* responsibility, in contrast to Andi's son, who, as the narrator tells us, "reveals his filial affection by way of . . . grand declaration[s]"—speeches chastising Andi for her voracious appetite. "I can't lose my mother for fish," he maintains before going to the field (76). The two women are also connected by the daily rhythms of household work, overlooked as invisible labor in the broader context of the sharecroppers struggle. In fact, as Devi depicts it, the daughter-in-law expresses her affection by giving her old, blind mother-in-law a variety of tasks. The following radically unsentimental scene is illustrative of this "fierce love":

You Mustn't cry at all . . .
 Mustn't Cry?
 No. Didn't I tell you to wind me the string by measuring with your hands?
 I can't do it, my love.
 You can. Who says you are of no use? Then who is mixing cow-dung and coaldust balls? (96)

In terms of a sequence of events, it is upon witnessing this exchange that Gobindo is moved to action.

The history of the Naxalbari revolt is in the interstices of "Fairy Tale." We know, for example, that the short-tempered Gobindo is a product of "Naksali days." The rhetorical conduct of the text also works against a simple reading of Andi's unequivocal instrumentality. As Mahasweta stages it, focalization shifts from the character of Andi to that of Gobindo, and then back to Andi in the final scene. The story ends with, according to the rhetorical conduct of the narrative, a paralepsis (information that should be left aside), an internal focalization containing Andi's unconscious thoughts. Whatever the outcome of the operation, and the indices are ominous, as everything fades to black, Devi leaves us with an impossible in-sight into the subaltern unconscious.[57] Ironically, it so happens that Andi's fictions have come to pass: "'everything jes like a fairy tale one by one!'" In a gesture of *ironic* reversal, commented upon in the split voice of a speech interference, narrative agency is given back to the donor and the unreliable narrator is proven right. Might this be read as a comment on the limits of historicism? As Spivak has reminded us elsewhere, "the subaltern is necessarily the absolute limit of the place where history is narrativized into logic" (*Other Worlds*, 207).

Some feminist readings of capital logic remain caught up in a historicist bind. Cynthia Enloe, in her contribution to *Women, Men, and the International Division of Labor*, appears cautious about either glibly eliding or reifying differences, when for example, she writes, "Women textile workers live *in history*." Arguably, however, she does reproduce the elements of a certain developmental narrative when she hypothesizes that

> women being recruited from the countryside to work for the new textile factories in the Third World in many ways are experiencing some of the same hopes, frustrations and risks that their Western sisters did 150 years ago—removal from their families, regimentation of factory organization, wage payments, female companionship, incentives for literacy, textile dust, job layoffs, crowded boarding houses, tension from piecework payment, loneliness.[58]

(We might say that Julia Kristeva's "Women's Time" is perhaps an extreme example of this specific [Euro]centric sequencing of gender and the philosophy of history.) In contrast to the narrative logic of global sisterhood on the one hand, or Eurocentrism on the other, in this chapter I have tried to be attentive to comparative critiques of historicism within feminist texts from different, discontinuous moments in the international division of labor, which persists in spite of the conjunctural changes inaugurated by globalization. Ranging from the rethinking of nationalist historiography in Sri Lankan working-class periodicals, to a critique of the romanticizing of categories of working-class and subaltern in texts by Tillie Olsen and Mahasweta Devi, these examples of women's "proletarian" fiction prompt us to refigure the narrativization of history—not according to teleological narratives but in connection with counterintuitive measures—according to different "presents" and discursive unities. The logic of the "secret encounter," not the "revolutionary conjuncture," organizes these writings. Beyond evolutionary schemas and brief histories of crisis, these texts from India, Sri Lanka, and the United States are ultimately defined by other durations—unfinished, unverifiable outcomes and ethico-political agendas beyond statist realms of rational planning. In the *Dabindu* periodicals, for example, once again, perhaps the most politically imaginative writings are the group of Sinhala poems addressing and identifying with the stateless Tamil women workers of the Up-country tea plantations. Written fruitlessly, perhaps, across the Tamil–Sinhala linguistic divide, a perfect example of *destinerrance*—a message irreducibly errant from the intended receiver—reaching . . . reaching . . . these poems at least gesture to the possibility of a working-class internationalism and other modes of collectivity.[59] Along these lines, perhaps Spivak's concept of the impossible "secret encounter" will also bring us back to Marx in *Capital*, volume 3, where he writes of the timing of the future anterior "realm of freedom," which "only begins beyond [the realm of necessity/sphere of production] *though it can only flourish with this realm of necessity as its basis.*"[60]

Chapter 4

SOCIALIZED LABOR AND THE CRITIQUE OF IDENTITY POLITICS

Bessie Head's A Question of Power

> I think my work at *Boiteko* is more valuable than working in a factory.
> —Mmatsela Ditshego, *Serowe, Village of the Rain Wind*

> Love is two people mutually feeding each other.
> —Bessie Head, *A Question of Power*

BIOGRAPHY IS NOT DESTINY

In 1964 Bessie Head (1937–1986) left the cities and townships of South Africa, never to return. Her destination was the village of Serowe in Bechunaland—soon to be renamed Botswana. There she secured work as a primary-school teacher, and later, along with other volunteer trainees of the Swaneng project, studied sustainable farming techniques.

Head left South Africa in the wake of the fallout of the Treason Trial period, when leftist, pan-Africanist, and other dissident writers and activists like Nelson Mandela, Robert Sobukwe, and Dennis Brutus were confronted with the choice of imprisonment or exile. Despite her repudiation of *organized* left-party politics, she was denied a passport because of her connections to the PAC (Pan-Africanist Congress) but managed to secure a one-way exit visa. In Serowe she was officially designated a stateless person and remained a refugee for fifteen years—even as her writing began to attract international attention. (*A Question of Power* was short-listed for the Booker Prize in 1974.) Until she received Botswanan citizenship, in 1979, her identity papers consisted of a United Nations Refugee Travel document.

In the same year that she left, Head penned a letter to the Ugandan monthly journal *Transition*:

> Dear Sir,
> I am enclosing a subscription slip. To me, at least, *Transition* is a kind of home. It seems to be fighting neither for communism or capitalism. I am rather out of things and slick slogans and I do not feel, as a communist has to, that I could have all the solutions to end starvation and fix the world right—nor as a capitalist, who feels pretty wonderful and secure with a million dollars.
> (*Woman*, 43)[1]

While Head's letters are a genre unto themselves, this one appears hastily written. It displays none of the spare elegance of missives sent to Alice Walker, Toni Morrison, or Michelle Cliff, or anything of the explosive high drama of letters sent to Randolph Vigne—the exiled editor of the *New African*, and Head's personal friend. But I cite it here it because it is instructive, nevertheless.

"To me, at least, *Transition* is a kind of home": set in its transparently obvious immediate context, Head's affirmation of the East African journal as "home" refers, of course, to a sense of artistic and intellectual community—the "practice of diaspora," experienced in the dialogic exchanges of writing in periodicals.[2] While she lived in Johannesburg, Head worked as a reporter for the *Gold City Post* (later the *Post*), which shared office space with *Drum* magazine. Head's own essays, short stories, and poetry appeared in *Transition* as well as in the *New African* and the *New Statesman*. While she didn't "feel as a communist has to, that [she must] have all the solutions to end starvation," the implications of her work with local agricultural cooperatives would later be recognized as extending beyond the vision and ideals claimed here. When we consider Head's comment in the wider, general context of her corpus of writings, it affirms another set of complex, multiply overdetermined meanings about diaspora, internationalism, economic migrancy, and political exile—as well as narrative logic.

"Proletarian revolutions," Marx writes, "constantly engage in self-criticism, and in repeated interruptions of their own course" (*Surveys*, 150). But what is it to inhabit interruption? Paradoxically, Head finds both a historical and a narrative sense of continuity in the figural logic of "repeated interruptions." Liminal figures that inhabit the stops and starts of serialized form, the security and surety of pauses in letters crossed, that somehow, impossibly, cathect *destinerrance* recur in Head's autobiographical as well as in her fictional "mixed genre" writings. "Well there it is. I would like to write the story of the man and his wife who never took the train journey, but I can't," she concludes in a short 1962 article published in the *New African*. This curiously contradictory statement, a direct address to the reader, immediately follows the short story she has just written about a man from District Six, Cape Town's "colored" ghetto,[3] who gets on a train and then off again, finding that he cannot take the trip to Durban. It is a recurring motif in the life and work of Bessie Head—the scene of metropolitan migration placed under erasure. "Peculiar shuttling movements" (as Head herself describes them) and being-in-transition as the underpinnings of both a formalism *and* an ontology are the challenges that Head poses to Marxist literary historiography. Head's ethos, more than those of any other writer studied in this book, mimes the productive possibilities of the proletarian aesthetic. The tentative projected title for her autobiography (never published) was *Living on an Horizon*.

Head's writing privileges neither beginnings, midpoints, nor endings, but rather figures and forms in transit, under erasure—asymptotic lines approaching the limit case. Counter to this impetus, most Head scholars begin by dramatizing the strange circumstances of her birth and the sensationalist details of her "false start" in life.[4] I would argue that this biographical lensing of her work does it an injustice. An analogy might be made with critical exegeses of Althusser's antihumanism that begin with lurid details of murder and madness or with appraisals of Benjamin that attempt to assemble into coherence the dispersed collectivity of his "theses on the philosophy of history" by reading them through the partial prism of the culminating event of a suicide at Port Bou. Such selective biographical detail as is generally summoned up to "set the context," while immediately engaging interest, too easily overdetermines Head's literary, historical, and philosophical contributions to the history of ideas.

Head's contemporary critics, especially those with "pure political credentials," attempted to read her subjectivity and ideological investments in these regressive, retrograde ways. Lewis Nkosi, one of the luminaries of the *Drum* intelligentsia (and her contemporary) explains Head's theoretical and literary "syncretism" as the genetic intellectual legacy of her mixed ancestry rather than the complicated, compromised product of ideological and creative choices. In his itinerary of South African literary historiography, titled *Tasks and Masks*, he maintains that "again and again Bessie Head returns to this vision of a 'power-hungry' and 'exclusive' Africa; but her obsession with this theme, one suspects, is rooted in her insecurity as a mulatto, shared, too, in a less desperate measure, by other colored South Africans" (101).[5] Such "diagnoses" might well recall contemporary sociologists' interpretations of Du Bois's political strategy of "double consciousness."[6] Bracketing, for the moment at least, questions of syncretism—and of that staple of postcolonial studies, "hybridity"—my study, instead, takes for its focal point, a *relatively* undervalued, undertheorized aspect of Head's writing: her contributions to the literature of labor and to a philosophy of socialist ethics. In the organizational scheme of this book, Head becomes a key figure in illuminating the ideological blind spot in dominant trends of Marxism, postcolonial, and globalization studies—the social space of the rural.

The textual figure of Bessie Head and many of the characters who people her fiction represent the reversal of a familiar trope in the literature of labor-in-globalization as well as in working-class literature in general: that of the metropolitan immigrant. In the *Politics of Modernism*, Raymond Williams refers to "a wave of working-class novels" where "the majority . . . included that form— . . . that [D.H.] Lawrence movement of walking towards the city with all your life ahead of you" (186). The subject position of the immigrant refugee-writer moving from the city to the country remains outside this provenance. Bessie Head—born in South Africa, compelled to move to neighboring Botswana, denied government grants to study agriculture, and even denied citizenship (until 1979)—reverses and displaces the archetype. At different times, there were plans afoot (some real, some imagined) for Head to move to Britain, India, Israel, Kenya, Norway, Sweden, the

United States, and Zambia. None of these materialized. In 1973 the Norwegian government offered her citizenship. She first accepted, but then retracted her acceptance three months later, ultimately electing to stay and write in a place where she was denied sponsorship.

Such a subject remains outside the rationale of a calculus that equates the narrative of globalization with the passage of the new immigrant to the global city. While her fellow literary exiles make the storied journey to the metropolitan centers of the globe—New York, London, and Paris—Head moves north, without crossing the North-South divide, to the village of Serowe in Botswana, charting a rural migration. As she puts it in her own words: "Botswana is so close to South Africa that barely a night's journey by train separates them" (*Woman*, 66). In her oral history, *Serowe, Village of the Rain Wind*, she recovers the stories of population movements and tribal migrations, hauntingly named "ruins" in reference to the traces of living left behind. It is the trajectory of these other migrations, these other movements, that figure in many of Head's texts. Her novels and short stories trace the logic of a narrative telos different even from the pattern set by canonical postcolonial writers like Tayeb Salih (whose work Head so admired) with his *Season of Migration to the North* (1969), the story of the European-trained, postcolonial intellectual's return to the country of origin. Rob Nixon has written of Head's life and writings as tracing the shape of a "rural transnationalism."[7] Not the cosmopolitan spaces adopted by her cohort, but the social networks of the village of Serowe provide the inspiration for Head's writings on race, class, and the politics of universalism.

In the context of the tabulation of different trajectories of labor history—industrial, migrant, rural—perhaps the most instructive lesson of Head's writing is that it moves us away from the empiricism of generalizations about the working class and theories of social classes tied to the factory floor to more abstract considerations and relational forms of historical agency opened up against and through questions of "labor power" and "socialized labor." If she had world enough and time to reflect further upon the implications of her piecemeal narrativizing and theorizing, perhaps this organic intellectual might be read not only as a wildly innovative, risk-taking novelist but also as a political philosopher of the ontology and subjectivity of work. Anthony O'Brien writes, "Whether Head would or should have gone further than the radicalism of the NGO, given a wider political experience than her few years as a young adult in South Africa and among the refugees of Francistown, Batswana, and South Africa and her mature years working with Patrick Van Rensburg for community development in Serowe, I cannot say; but labeling her apolitical has always seemed bizarrely wrong."[8] In "Diasporas Old and New" Spivak makes the point that if we give to Noeleen Heyzer's *Working Women of Southeast Asia* the same attention that we would afford to Heidegger or Derrida, we would read her painstaking work of activist research as an ethical document.[9] In the same spirit, I say that if we learned to read Head with the proper attention, we would read her for the ways in which she gets the extended implications of Althusser's polemics that are lost to Althusser himself, in her restaging of the dialectical dyads of humanism and historicism and structure and subject in the service of the collective subject of socialized labor.[10]

Head's best-known book—and the focus of this chapter—*A Question of Power*, is Marxist in irrefutable ways. Its approach is dialectical, tentative, open-ended, and ceaselessly critical of its own founding presuppositions. And yet I would resist the impulse to systematically demonstrate how and where Bessie Head tidily maps onto narratives of the humanist versus antihumanist Marx or onto explanatory frameworks pitting Marx the theorist and Marx the empiricist historian against each other—even though she can be. Rather, in my own allegory of reading, I hope to show how Head extends the interruptive, disruptive ideals of the itinerant Marx to other spaces and places—psychic and otherwise—that he could not imagine.

In this chapter I begin with a rereading of the ghost story in *A Question of Power* as a way of entering into the "peculiar, paradoxical notion" of the social—not universal—in Head. I proceed by way of discussing the importance of "the rural" for Head's visions of social class, radical ecology, and planetarity—not cosmopolitanism. Bessie Head's model of agricultural reform and her writings on *Boiteko* (voluntary cooperative labor) give rise to thinking how cooperation inaugurates the use of socialized labor as, necessarily, deindividualized, dehumanized, *spectralized* labor—"the ghostliness of the body" (Spivak). For Marxist philosophers like Hardt and Negri, abstract labor (renamed *immaterial labor*) finds its felicitous expression in the disembodied abstracting activities that occur with "computational thinking," perhaps best emblematized in the information age.[11] But in Head's *A Question of Power*, information overload is figured as the problem, and the felicitous (or rather, ethical) model for abstraction in globalization is staged against and through figures of rural life and social and affective relations of (agricultural) work. My reading aims to show how *A Question of Power* brings into relief a curious, puzzling Marxist subtext—a theory of anti-essentialism grounded in the labor theory of value, one which also bears upon the historical antiracist class struggles of which Head is a part.

RACE, CLASS, AND "INTANGIBLE FORMS" IN *A QUESTION OF POWER*

The ethical is not a problem of knowledge but a problem of relation.... You crave to let history haunt you as a ghost or ghosts, with the ungraspable incorporation of a ghostly body, and the uncontrollable, sporadic, and unanticipatable periodicity of haunting, in the impossible frame of the absolute chance of the gift of time, if there is any. It is not, then, a past that was necessarily once present that is sought. The main effort is to compute with the software of other pasts rather than reference one's own hallucinatory heritage for the sake of the politics of identitarian competition. —Gayatri Chakravorty Spivak, *Ghostwriting*

"There's something haunting me," she said, slowly. "A past where I loved many people, but the quality of that love was so high, the memories, the images have a way of floating towards me with soft, undemanding faces. The shadowy figures seem merely content to put themselves in my arms and go to sleep, with complete trust: Here I am secure. Here I am safe. I have a peculiar sensation of sleeping with a whole lot of people in my arms."
—Bessie Head, *A Question of Power*

A refugee recently arrived from South Africa, "befuddled by the tablets prescribed for a mental breakdown," starts seeing "ghosts" (*Question*, 13). In Head's *A Question of Power*, where the text itself is a split subject, the following passage dramatizes where and how the subject comes apart:

The chair was empty. She had never seen a ghost in her life. She was not given to "seeing" things. The world had always been two-dimensional, flat and straight with things she could see and feel. This recurred for several nights, and she simply reasoned that whatever it was was not a danger to her life. Let it sit if it wanted to. Oh, no, whatever it was wanted to introduce itself at some stage, because one night she was lying staring at the dark when it seemed as though her head simply filled out into a large horizon. It gave her a strange feeling of things being there right inside her and yet projected at the same time at a distance away from her. She was not sure if she were awake or asleep, and often after that the dividing line between dream perceptions and waking reality was to become confused.

The form of a man totally filled the large horizon in front of her. He was sitting sideways.... [*Eventually the materialization addresses itself to her. It asks:*] "Will you stay here for some time?" (22)

Here "Home" becomes "Unhomely."[12] Later we learn that this "ghost" (named "Sello") has a nonidentical, real-life counterpart who happens to be a well-respected member of the Motabeng village community.

Identity politics becomes a moot point in the sudden, surreal equation of distance and proximity. The protagonist's head thins into a dividing line separating earth and sky—also the self and the world. In a startling dramatization of "double consciousness" she becomes the limits of perception, "the horizon," from which objects, the self, and other subjects are experienced. In a primary narrative in which origins stories are repudiated at both the formal and ideological levels, this surreal moment substitutes for a focal point. It marks the center of the novel—a place, as alluded to before, that has nothing to do with spatial arrangement of the plot but rather refers to the locus containing authorial annotation on the validity of disparate truth claims. Form mimes content in this instance. Head represents the center as a decentering. This pivotal scene undoes the spatial opposition between interiority and exteriority, abstract and material, and imagination and "the social." All bounds of ownership and claims to rights are transgressed at the outset. The situation of host and guest are reversed and displaced in the eerie question: "Will you stay here for some time?" The episode quietly sets up the motif of Marxist contradictions explored in Head's novel—abstract, yet material; global, yet local; universal, yet particular.

The "breakdown," in one register, undoubtedly signifies pain and trauma. But separating literary representation and creative practice from case study or diagnosis, we see that it must also be read as the conditions of possibility for reimagining "the social" through a new dialectical relationship of the self and the world. The extended conceit of *A Question of Power* asks the reader to make a virtue of schizophrenia in the service of ideals of internationalism. Moving us back and forth between Marx and Freud, Freud and Marx, Head's novel constantly switches registers between ghost story, self-help talk therapy, and philosophical meditations on the ontology and subjectivity of work. As we shall see, the emblematic scene of self-estrangement/doubling will be played out across different (though sometimes overlapping) discursive fields of knowledge: Marxism, psychoanalysis, and literature. Ghosts, hauntings, mental breakdown, spatial confusion, *"intangible forms"* that flit in and out of realism and reality, bending time and space—all figures representing the collapse of dividing lines between interiority and exteriority—are tropings of "the social" in the paradoxical sense that Head envisions it. In Head, as in Marx, "the social" becomes staged against and through "the abstract."

"The like-ness of ghosts is invisible," Thomas Keenan reminds us in his rhetorical analysis of Marx's concept metaphors.[13] The cross-reading of Marx and Head (rather than Freud and Head, or Fanon and Head, the obvious comparisons) reveals something telling about the geometry of identity and difference in the unthought commonplaces of the everyday: in commodity exchange, the act of abstraction equalizes categorically different use-values, producing universality out of disparate heterogeneity. In Head's mind-bending scene involving the traffic in "intangible forms" (and, if we place it in context, elsewhere in *A Question of Power*), she casts light on the buried implications of Marx's explanations of the "spectral social." In the encounter with Sello, where boundaries are transgressed and defining properties are exchanged, this translation of differences becomes an index of "the social." Might the de-essentializing of identity that occurs/must occur in the rational dynamics of commodity exchange somehow be set to work in the service of a changing calculus of socialist ethics? Marx was not equipped to take his philosophical intuition all the way toward the envisioning of an antiracist politics. In her figuration of a necessarily dis-propriated subject, as prefiguring "other collectivities" (as we shall see as the book unfolds), Bessie Head takes us there. The defining logical *and ethical* paradox of *A Question of Power* is that "the recovery" of (an a priori social) self is predicated on "the breakdown" of "the race" subject. *A Question of Power* stages this agon as one long, protracted, *painful* speech interference.[14]

What ideological or ethical work is accomplished in the representation of a dehumanized, commodified part-subject in this way? Where, if at all, do the concepts of materiality and race figure in what has been described as Head's "ethics of universality"? At one level, *A Question of Power* tackles more general questions than those of gender and race: morphology and chromatism are challenged at this point in the story (quite early on), where the protagonist is represented as being invaded by *intangible forms*. Placed within context, however, we see that the episode with Sello certainly prefigures the complex, rich meditation on difference and ontology that recurs through Head's writing. Where does the inside end, and the outside begin? Frantz Fanon, compelled by a related set of political, historical, and ideological imperatives, posed a similar set of propositions in asymmetrically related terms. Fanon's signature ethical and analytical apparatus—in *Black Skin, White Masks*, at least—remained psychoanalysis. His expanded theoretical framework, however, presupposed the dialectic of the self and the world—of structure and subject.[15] Pushing the limits of thought in counterintuitive directions, he wanted us to consider the "epidermalization of race" and the interiority of skin.

As the problem is staged in *A Question of Power*, also, "race" cannot be adduced in chromatist labels ("black, white, Cape Town 'colored'"). Rather, it is mapped in topographies of inner landscapes. It is manifested in internalized hierarchies and invisible signs that are illegible on the surface. What really are the legible, legitimate markings of race *and class*? What is at stake in representing these concepts as almost unintelligibly abstract questions of power (including labor power)—invisible, internal, rather than visibly inscribed on the body, or readable like a slogan: a metonymic "fist in the air"? For Elizabeth (the protagonist) the question becomes how to grasp the concept of race in the abstract. What might race mean in the context of ever-shifting constituencies of *relative* minorities—in terms of changing maps of the international division of labor? How do we see beyond the currency of politicized meanings of race even as—to quote Mahmood Mamdani—"victims become killers"?[16] The answers to these questions are urgent ones for Head. In her reply to South Africa's 1975 Censorship Index she writes against simple solutions that legitimize by reversal: "It involves a broader question than mere protest—it is a question of evil as a whole. We are likely to remove one horror and replace it with another, and those of us who have suffered much do not relish the endless wail of human misery. My writing is not on anybody's bandwagon. It is on the sidelines" (*Woman*, 61). The incredible foresight of Head lies in her ability to project and cathect such an untenable situation from the subject position of the victim. At stake is safeguarding the ideals of labor and literary internationalism from nationalism—even its oppositional guises.

Head's *intangible forms* are not ghosts, exactly, or even (counterposed to this explanation) the protagonist's "delusions" or "symptoms." (Tom, a Peace Corps volunteer, registers the intangible presence in the room. He, too, can hear Sello's voice assenting or dissenting, as the case may warrant.) In *A Question of Power* that which is abstract ("to do with or existing in thought rather than practice; not tangible or concrete") is not confined to individual consciousness. Minimal dictionary definitions don't hold. In the Marxist lexicon, however (as in Head's staging), the mysterious activity of abstraction reveals rather than conceals social relations of exchange. Abstraction is the process by which differences are elided or equalized in the service of producing sameness across different use-values. It is the sublation of difference(s) that makes social exchange (in the realm of commodity capitalism) possible. In *Capital*, volume 3, Marx describes the process neutrally as "entail[ing] the disappearance of the different commodity forms of labor. They can no longer be distinguished, but are altogether reduced to the same kind of labor, human labor in the abstract" (128). It produces the same "phantom-like objectivity" across national and industrial divisions. In *Capital*, volume 3, we encounter the productive problem of abstraction once again, this time as ethico-political leverage for socialist initiatives. Abstraction is not simply synonymous with extraction. But what sort of activity is abstraction? Who abstracts? Not the factory owner—or a human subject. Where does it figure in working-class literature? If Slavoj Žižek explains the process of abstraction that takes place in the unconscious as being homologous with the concept of "abstraction" that takes place in commodity exchange, *A Question of Power* reads as literary representation of the counterintuitive concept.[17] The dialogic push and pull of the emblematic scene (involving Sello and the split subject exchanging and assimilating shapes) is annotated by the dynamic of the structural motors of the text. Its "peculiar shuttling" movement keeps switching us back and forth between surreal scenarios of the mind and the prosaic realities of international civil society planning in newly independent Botswana.

In Marx's unfinished "Trinity Formula Chapter," of volume 3 of *Capital*, we come the closest we ever get to suggestions regarding the political utility of abstraction:

> Lastly, as the third in the league ["third," that is, in the "trinity" of capital, land, and labor], a mere specter—labour, which is nothing but an abstraction and taken by itself cannot exist at all, or, if we take what is actually meant here, the entire productive activity of man, through which his metabolic interchange with nature is mediated. But this is not only divested of any social form and specific character; even in its mere natural existence, independent of society, it is lifted right out of society altogether and defined as the externalization and confirmation of life equally for a man who is not yet social and for a man as socialized in some way or other. (954)

According to this calculation, socialized labor becomes the computation of an abstract average. How do you represent an abstraction aesthetically, philosophically, politically? In *Capital*, volume 1, Marx must make recourse to anthropomorphic projections to explain the counterintuitive workings of abstraction in commodity relations. In *Capital*, volume 2, though, he switches to formulas, figures, and notations. Wording changes, and concepts are annotated as the chapter on "the commodity" becomes reformulated as the chapter on "the circuit of commodity *capital*." Here we find Marx breaking things down into their value composition ($C'-M'-C \ldots P \ldots C'$), figuring a rationalized (necessarily dehumanized) way of expressing human labor as the source of surplus value. The notation C' (not C) reveals the source to be the peculiar commodity of labor power—categorically not a subject, merely the superadequating part that creates surplus value for capitalism.

Following this trajectory of recalibrated meanings and shifting modes of address across the Marxian corpus, in *Capital*, volume 3, we begin to register the philosophical charge lent to "abstraction," "the abstract," and spectral "abstract labor" in Marx's later texts. Abstract labor *is* social labor: "Even in its mere natural existence, independent of society, it is lifted right out of society altogether and defined as the externalization and confirmation of life equally for a man who is not yet social and for a man as socialized in some way or other" (954). No longer dealing in revolutionary manifestos, nor simple, straightforward (retroactively Lukacsian) critiques against reification, Marx here invokes the spectrality of labor power—what Spivak paraphrases as "the ghostliness of the body."

Different interpretations of abstract labor, socialized labor, and labor power divide Marxist theorists along divergent lines. For some, "abstract labor," as it is described in *Capital*, volume 1, simply confirms Marx's inability to think (historical) difference. It secures another nail in the coffin of the Eurocentric Marx. And yet, for others, the concept of socialized labor opens up Marx's texts toward thinking the basis of a critique of identity politics at the heart of his intersecting theories on value and the commodity form.[18] Some paces apart from Althusser's chronology and mapping of the epistemic break between the (early) humanist and (late) antihumanist Marx, Spivak proposes another reading: there exist two distinctly different senses of "the social" in Marx's writing across different modes of address and different types of works. While one meaning refers to the conventional humanist sense, the other refers to the abstract rationalization of work as labor power (as outlined in the formulas for circuits in *Capital*, volume 2). The second sense of the social necessarily requires an estranged relationship to the self. The worker can understand the peculiar commodity of labor power only by being "improper to oneself," or "by abstracting from one's existentiality." When the Marx of *Capital*, volume 2, breaks things down into their value components, translating labor power into capital, he asserts it (this spectral thing, this variable capacity for labor) as the agent of valorization. Understood in this counterintuitive sense, labor power (as part-object, as commodity), not theories of the subject (the race-specific worker of this or that national working class) predicate the basis for the historical agency of socialist ethics.

"The product of work is work," writes Marx. "If local industries can help people, then we can help local industries," observes a cooperative worker in *A Question of Power*. Even as the explicit itinerary for socialist ethics gets lost in the epistemic and theoretical vacuum that opens up between the two senses of the social, I propose that Head's novel is one instance of writing that mediates the gap in between. In *A Question of Power*, also, it is the decentered part-object of labor power, *not* a unified coherent subject, that guarantees the identity of this writing—categorically an anti-bildungs. But if in Marx the links between the two interwoven senses of the abstract and the social stretch across a widely dispersed corpus and debated post-Marxist scholarship, in Head's novel we encounter the dialectical image to the negatively coded scene of haunting/"hauntopology"[19] toward the provisional denouement of the book. The entire sign system changes as "breakdown" is recoded as "cure," when Elizabeth returns from the sanatorium to her work with the garden cooperatives. In the passage that follows, the loss of boundaries signifies something radically different from the preceding dystopian *inside* scene. Outside imperatives—global poverty, the food crisis, small-scale experimental agricultural reform initiatives—disorient the ghost story from the outside, looking in. Self-estrangement is recalibrated as the experience of socialist ethics in the open-ended negotiations of "the everyday" world:

> Maybe, the work she and Sello had done together had introduced a softness and tenderness into mankind's history. The flowers, the animals, the everyday events of people's lives had been exalted by them. . . . She had struck at the spring of it, the source of it, that night. They had perfected together the ideal of sharing everything and then perfectly shared everything with all mankind.
>
> To rediscover that love was like suddenly being transported to a super-state of life. It was the point at which all personal love had died in them. It was the point at which there were no private hungers to be kissed, loved, adored. And yet there was a feeling of being kissed by everything; by the air, the soft flow of

life, people's smiles and friendships; and, propelled forward by the acquisition of this vast and universal love, they had moved among men again and again and told them they loved them. That was the essential nature of their love for each other. It had included all mankind, and so many things could be said about it, but the most important was that it equalized all things and all men. (202)[20]

Rendered in the register of prose-poetry, this beautiful, breathless passage contrasts sharply with the previous depiction of haunted space. The spectral/social paradoxically denies and affirms Elizabeth's individuality: "It equalized all men and all things." The schema of Head's "ethics of universality" requires the breakdown of the opposition between humans and "things." It is a precarious balance between sanity and madness, to be sure, and it is uncertain whether Head's protagonist will be able to cathect the place of this phantom objectivity, but within the narrative and ethical logic of the text, this counterintuitive "abnormal" sense of the self and the social is ultimately celebrated:

> Elizabeth could never do anything normally. She had a permanently giddy head. She had reeled towards death. She turned and reeled towards life. She reeled blissfully happy, up the dusty brown road, down the pathway into the valley area of the local-industries project. She paused at the garden gate. Kenosi stood on a trench-bed upturning the soil with a fork. A small boy was watering. A man was preparing a new trench-bed. (203)

"For Bessie Head," notes Jacqueline Rose, ". . . inside the head is the place where you can make the links or points of connection—both deadly and of universal potential—which are invisible to the cultural, historical, and racial differentiations aboveground."[21] Rose's reading of *A Question of Power* remains one of the best critical expositions of the peculiar, paradoxical notions of "universality" (also coded as "contingency") and "humanism" (coded also as "the supernatural") explored by Head. And yet, Rose's careful interrogation of the founding presuppositions of psychoanalysis at work in producing *any* literary-critical analysis of Head's novel still only considers figures that extend the limits of interiority *and* universality, starting from the inside, moving out. It cannot occur to her to compute the same problem from the other direction—from the outside, moving in.

Excluding commentary on scenes depicting cooperative labor and collective decision making, Rose confines herself to an extended study of one aspect of the text's signature undecidability: Is this a ghost story, or trauma narrative? Her reading focuses on the fact that for Head, "universality is part of interiority," discounting the "thousand . . . stories" involving "intangible, unpraised efforts" to establish an autocritical politics of labor internationalism. And yet, as we know, for Elizabeth, "It wasn't any kind of physical stamina that kept her going, but a vague, instinctive pattern of normal human decencies combined with the work she did, the people she met each day and the unfolding project with exciting inventive possibilities" (*Question*, 149). "There were a thousand such stories to tell of life in Motabeng, of tentative efforts of people of totally foreign backgrounds made to work together and understand each other's humanity; that needed analyzing—intangible, unpraised efforts to establish the brotherhood of man" (*Question*, 158). Head's critique of humanism and universality, in fact, relies on the description of this abstract quality (and quantity). It relies on the figural representation of the unrepresentable—not of some phantasmatic synchronicity of the Botswanan agricultural working class, nor of concept metaphors for the "multitude," nor of simple human-interest stories of NGO culture, but of some intangible, yet binding substance—socialized labor. "The exchange abstraction is not thought, but it has the form of thought": Žižek builds upon Alfred Sohn-Rethel's formulation as he poses his own set of questions regarding the frame which delimits the boundary to Marx's concept of the rational social.[22] Bessie Head does not enter into Slavoj Žižek's discussion.

INTERNATIONALISM AND SCHIZOPHRENIA[23]

Bessie Head's *A Question of Power* asks us to make a virtue out of schizophrenia in the service of internationalism. If at one level of the story an inability to claim origins is proposed to be at the base of Head's protagonist's psychosis, at another level, "dispropriation" and self-estrangement are validated, even idealized. How do we read this? "I've got my concentration elsewhere," says Elizabeth (the protagonist) to her interlocutor, Tom. "It's on mankind in general, and black people fit in there, not as special freaks and oddities outside the scheme of things, with labels like Black Power or any other rubbish of that kind" (*Question*, 133). If we consider questions of sociology of form, we notice that Head's text itself is a divided subject. What are the politics of this piecemeal narrative?

The part-subject of Marxism is something other than the split subject of psychoanalysis. Jameson elucidates the political stakes of this categorical, conceptual divide:

> From a Marxist point of view, this experience of the decentering of the subject and theories, essentially psychoanalytic, which have been devised to map it are to be seen as the signs of the dissolution of an essentially bourgeois ideology of the subject and of the psychic unity of identity (what used to be called bourgeois "individualism"); but we may admit the descriptive value of the poststructuralist critique of the "subject" without necessarily endorsing the schizophrenic ideal it has tended to project. For Marxism, indeed, only the emergence of a post-individualistic social world, only the reinvention of the collective and the associative, can concretely achieve the "decentering" of the individual subject called for by such diagnoses; only a new and original form of collective social life can overcome the isolation and monadic autonomy of the older bourgeois subjects. (*Political Unconscious*, 125)

Jameson reads the decentered subject as precursor and precondition to another—that of the Marxist collective subject. There is an implicit logic of progression to this explanation. The collective subject is presumed in the future anterior of Marx's "realm of freedom." It is the shape of things to follow, in the aftermath of the disappearing subject. Bessie Head, however, holds together both concepts (individual and collective, structure and subject) in her book, as a dialectical dyad of madness and "recovery." "Love and work, work and love, that's all there is," writes Freud. *A Question of Power* dramatizes the alternating sequences of this axiom in terms of the mental theater of a South African–born refugee's breakdown on the one hand, and in terms of stories of NGO culture and development schemes in newly independent Botswana, on the other.

My reading in this chapter makes a case for understanding how Head extends the reach of debates in literary historiography even as she moves beyond the provenance of U.S., Frankfurt School, and French Marxist theory. The ethical leverage of self-estrangement can also be the condition of/for collective agency if the worker can see herself as part-subject of labor power in the dialectical doing/undoing of the everyday. But any theory of the ethico-political utility of the divided subject (inasmuch as Head can be regarded a South African writer) must take into consideration the aesthetic and critical production of its immediate proximate, historical milieu. Apart from discussions in high postmodernism, the split/decentered/divided subject as an aesthetic and ethical ideal has its own complicated genealogy in South African literary criticism. In Njabulo Ndebele's classic exegesis *The Rediscovery of the Ordinary*, a case is made against the popular currency of a particular species of Apartheid-era South African protest literature whose Brechtian estranging techniques are read and consumed differently across the ideological, class, and racial divide. Assessing the problem of audience vis-à-vis the political and ethical value of a genre predicated on documenting spectacular events of violence, he writes:

> The aesthetics of reading this literature, for the black reader, is recognition, understanding, historical documentation, and indictment. All these go together. For the white audience, on the other hand, what has been called "protest literature" can, to borrow from Brecht, be considered a spectacular "alienation effect"; a literature that refuses to be enjoyed precisely because it challenges conventional methods of literary representation, and that it painfully shows up the ogre to himself. (46)

Against the sloganeering and posturing of a certain corpus of avowedly political writing that consolidates its status on the basis of "devaluing or ignoring interiority," Ndebele advocates for a genre that makes use of "the vitality of the tension generated by the dialectic between the personal and the public" (55). While there is no explicit evidence to confirm that Head read Ndebele (she attributes her own investment in the politics of the "ordinary" and the "irrelevant" to the writings and life story of Bertolt Brecht), *A Question of Power* reads as a response to his critique. It also resonates as a response to Henri Lefebvre's questions: "Are not the surreal, the extraordinary, the surprising, even the magical, also part of the real? Why wouldn't the concept of everydayness reveal the ordinary in the extraordinary?" Kelwyn Sole revisits Lefebvre (in conjunction with a reading of Ndebele) in his reassessment of how Ndebele's theoretical legacy has been (at best) misconstrued, or even (at worst) hijacked, by certain schools of contemporary theory—uncritical celebrants of "culturalist and humanist discourses of the quotidian."[24] He describes and decries the fetishism of the decentered subject underwritten by a move by South Africanist literary critics in the 1990s to deconstruct liberal humanism and erect in its place "a new humanism." As he puts it, this is "one they hope will bypass both the legacy of apartheid's antihumanism, as well as antihumanist strains in the poststructuralist theory they have up to this point invoked" (186). Sole's is a scathing critique of an ahistorical and apolitical validation of "hybridity" even as multiculturalism is invoked as a state-planning and labor management mechanism.

Referencing these key debates but returning us to the productive possibilities of a *historical* critique of humanism, Mark Sanders asks, "Do some historical instances exemplify more than others the dispropriative, transformative force of assuming responsibility for the other, and responsibility for the others' responsibility?" (8).[25] Head's concept of alienated belonging, hauntingly captured in the final paradoxical figure of the book (I will return to this) anticipates the "ethics of dispropriation" elaborated in his literary-critical analysis of the language of the documents of the TRC (Truth and Reconciliation Commission). Sanders's focus is the "theology of *Ubuntu*" (derived from the Zulu idiom, mistranslated in the TRC document, but parsed by Sanders as "a human being is a human being through human beings; or "the being human of human being is realized through his or her being (human) through human beings" [15]). Sanders makes his argument against received notions and common mistranslations of *ubuntu* as simply "humaneness," "human dignity," "personhood," or "morality" ("people are people through other people" is the translation included in the document). Such an oversimplified explanation for *ubuntu* as a "prescription for the precedence of the collective," he argues, "conceals the dispropriation at the root" (13).

Alluding to the polemics of South African literary history, but working through the rhetorics and politics of the TRC documents, Sanders excavates a powerful figure for self-estranging responsibility-based—as opposed to proprietary rights-based—ethics that ultimately recalls us to Head's prescient Apartheid-era novel. *Ubuntu,* correctly understood, supposes an access to collectivity where "both parties are *exiled from their "proper" selves*" (Sanders, 14). At the close of Head's book we encounter such a figure of radical dispropriation: "As she fell asleep," the narrator tells us, Elizabeth "placed one soft hand over her land. It was a gesture of belonging" (206). Not possession—or possessive individualism—but a disconnected connection to the refugee's place of asylum (Botswana, in this case) validates her claim. We have come full circle. The final counterintuitive image of nonpropietary belonging is anticipated in the opening frame of the book:

> It seemed almost incidental that he was African. . . . It was as though his soul was a jigsaw; one more piece being put into place. . . . He loved each particle of earth around him, the everyday event of sunrise, the people and the animals of the village of Motabeng; perhaps his love included the whole universe. He said to himself that evening: I might have died before I found this freedom of heart. (*Question,* 11)

Identity, propriety, and individualism aren't central to the narrator's scheme of "universality." The novel, which is structured as an antibildungs from the outset, begins with the voice-consciousness of a nonexistent figure (the product of the protagonist's imagination). Race and gender are not rendered unimportant, inasmuch as they are conceptualized as "incidental." It is outside the scope of this chapter to discuss in depth the precise ways in which Head's counterintuitive notions of humanism shape, frame, and disrupt fixed founding narratives of human rights and, specifically, those of the contemporary TRC (although I return to Head's peculiar, paradoxical notions of humanism and universality via Jacqueline Rose). My argument takes as its departure point the question of how the part-subject is put together in terms of the rhetorical code of Head's text. A brief plot summary sets the context for my reading.

In *A Question of Power*, the othering of the self is proposed as the cure to "madness." The text's tripartite structure mimes a divided subject. Part 1 corresponds to Sello, part 2 is headed "Dan," and part 3 is named "Elizabeth." As alluded to before, the opening gambit of the narrative makes the individual protagonist's story "incidental." The very first line of Head's book establishes its eccentric protocols. It begins with the voice-consciousness of the nonexistent Sello. We are pushed off-center and are kept at this remove all the way. As the book begins, we are caught up with someone else's story—not that of the protagonist's—in medias res: "It seemed almost incidental that he was African. So vast had his inner perceptions grown over the years that he preferred an identification with mankind to an identification with a particular environment.... The man's name was Sello. A woman in the village of Motabeng paralleled his inner development" (11). The narrative unit comprising the first few pages serves as a mise en abyme. It stages the part-subject of labor power to be elaborated in different levels of the story—interior (mental breakdown) and exterior (agricultural development projects).

The story unfolds as an a-chronic chronology of periods of mental instability, hauntings, and fantastic visions interrupted by the peace and calm of narratives of gardening and political discussions with friends. Parabasis and parataxis organize the text's rhetorical conduct. Its narrative resists summary, by design. But rearranging the dechronologized thread in the service of sequence, we might summarize the moves of the story as follows: The protagonist, Elizabeth, is compelled to leave South Africa on an exit permit because of her rumored involvement with a proscribed political party. She secures work as a teacher in Botswana, where she is officially designated a stateless person and granted refugee status. She and a son (from a failed marriage) take up residence in a mud hut in Motabeng—a remote inland village, modeled on Serowe. Three months after her arrival strange things start to happen. She becomes host to a series of nightly visitors. The monk-robed Sello is the first to materialize. His foil, Dan Molomo, a sex-crazed megalomaniac, follows. An entire operatic cast of characters takes up residence soon after—including Sello's retinue of alter egos, Dan's entourage of sexual partners, and the competing characters of the Madonna and the Medusa. Some beats after our initial introduction to the first of these characters it becomes clear that Sello belongs to Elizabeth's inner landscape. It gradually becomes evident that the protagonist is suffering from a breakdown.

The text, however, refuses to fix a determining cause for madness. Is her madness the fulfillment of one of Dan's prophesies? His voice predicts that she will inevitably commit suicide. Is it in response to the call of her mother's ghost? (The mother's biography is given in the register of sanctifying sentimentalism. As the narrator tells it, her mother, an English woman, transgressed the Immorality Act in having sex with black man and *as a result* was declared insane and essentially incarcerated in a hospital. The protagonist, like Head herself, is born in a mental asylum. She grows up in the care of a colored woman, and only upon adolescence learns about her birth mother and the scandal of "miscegenation," when the missionary school principal casually imparts this piece of backstory to her.) The ghost of her mother appeals to the protagonist's yearning for connection. Madness offers her access to collectivity: "Do you think I can bear the stigma of insanity alone? Share it with me," pleads the voice (15). The story that follows might be read as a gratuitous answer to this rhetorical question. No information is given about her father, beyond the fact that he is a "stable boy." Yet another possibility is posed: In terms of social semiosis, is madness, logically, the psychology of colonialism? "A lot of refugees have nervous breakdowns," ventures a fellow stateless person. This explanation also hangs in the ether. But the text won't assign priority to these competing aetiologies. Madness, mothers, and origins stories—at the risk of sounding a little redundant—cathect the place of undetermined origins in *A Question of Power*.

The splintering of the ego is represented as torturous pain, but at the same time "making strange," willful self-estrangement, as elaborated against and, through the psychology of work, is put forward as a saving grace. At certain points the provisionally separate worlds coded "inside" and "outside" overlap with negative results. On one occasion, goaded by the voices in her head, Elizabeth attacks a Botswanan postal clerk, on another, she posts a notice accusing Sello of sleeping with his daughter, and on another, she *attacks* Mrs. Jones, a "leftist" apostate turned Christian missionary. Following each incident, Elizabeth ends up in hospital. The drama of Sello and Dan continues, unchecked by sleeping pills and other medications. In contrast to the garish symbolism and abstract expressionism of the interior drama, however, we are given interludes of realism and bits and pieces of dialogue—stories involving the inauguration of the local industries project spearheaded by "the Eugene man"—a Danish developmentalist. Other dialogical exchanges that provide a constant contrapuntal theme to the harsh grating monologues in her head involve narratives of shared meals and the collective decision-making process involved in setting the price for cooperative goods. These brief moments of equilibrium—Jacqueline Rose describes *A Question of Power* as "writing by battery assault"—are achieved in discussions about work activities. Philosophical exchanges and political debates with Tom, the Peace Corps volunteer from America, as they dig trench beds for garden vegetables; sequences describing work undertaken by Kenosi, her Botswanan helpmate from the village; meditations on global food production and sustainable agriculture; expositions on the value composition and price breakdown of commodities for sale in the local industries store: these are narrative segments that disrupt and derail the primary narrative of breakdown and recovery.

Most critics of Head's novel privilege psychoanalysis as an interpretative framework. They focus exclusively on the mind-bending, surreal narratives of interiority and the signs and symbols of the unconscious as the key to understanding Head's peculiar, paradoxical notions of universality and humanism. My reading, instead, works through the sociology of form to arrive at an interpretation of the Marxist subtext of *A Question of Power*. But what does it mean, in the context of my reading, marking the pitfalls of postmodernism, to nevertheless propose the part-subject as "a cure"—or at least as a pharmakon—of sorts? My argument hinges on a rereading of what is by now a classic piece of psychoanalytic literary criticism on Head's *A Question of Power*—Jacqueline Rose's "On the Universality of Madness," which I alluded to briefly earlier in this chapter.

In her brilliant reading of the multiple paradoxical meanings of "universality" in Head's *A Question of Power*—"where universality as a concept starts to break up under scrutiny" (412)—it seems odd that Rose overlooks the ways in which this problematic is inextricably connected with another unrepresentable abstraction—not the empirically verifiable "working class," but Marx's abstract average of socialized labor. While discerning that a claim to universality is the other side of a critique of identitarianism that is at the very heart of

Head's novel, Rose does not engage with a very Marxist subtext that reverses and displaces the concept of identity politics in Head: voluntary cooperative labor. The text is clear that cooperation inaugurates the use of labor power as in Marx—rather than compiling an aggregation of private labor. In fact, "Love is two people mutually feeding each other"—the statement upon which the text turns, that brings into effect the protagonist's cure—might *also* be read in connection with the commitment to internationalism and sustainable agriculture. It is also the credo voiced by the cooperative farming volunteer: "What do billions of people in the world need? Food. That's why I went into agriculture" (Head, *Question*, 135). In another register then, the key to the protagonist's recovery, "the lever [which springs her] out of hell" (198), is socialized labor and responsibility-based ethics narrativized as the saving grace of unlikely friendships (sometimes between historical enemies)—predicated upon a devastatingly simple premise: sharing food. This is the turning point in the story. It is also where the text seems to be repeating itself on two *seemingly* different levels, economic and philosophical.

Rose's discussion of the problematics of universality and liberal humanism in *A Question of Power* marginalizes the story of cooperative labor brigades in Motabeng village. She focuses exclusively on the episodes of madness and the narrative of interiority. And yet it is this other, *outside* narrative that extends the notion of universality and Head's critique of identity politics in relationship with a (socialist) ethics. My reading, indebted to Rose's meticulous, close reading of Head's ethics of universality, suggests that Head's critique of identitarianism is advanced also by the *impersonal* narrative of yet another invisible abstraction—"labor power." While it is true that "for Bessie Head, therefore, inside the head is the place where you can make the links or points of connection—both deadly and of universal potential—which are invisible to the cultural, historical, and racial differentiations aboveground" (Rose, 415), my argument contends that we must also look elsewhere, toward Head's representation of Motabeng village and to the politics of unlikely friendships *in* globalization for ways in which they lend the concept of the "universal" to her narrative. ("There were a thousand such stories to tell of life in Motabeng, of tentative efforts people of totally foreign backgrounds made to work together and understand each other's humanity; that needed analysing—intangible, unpraised efforts to establish the brotherhood of man" [158].) Anthony O'Brien has written that "the gardening cooperatives that grew up around the school [have] marked the spirit of her work . . . more than has been noticed—beyond becoming a healing theme in *A Question of Power*" (217). As mentioned before, Rob Nixon writes of Bessie Head's "rural transnationalism."[26] By suggesting that Head's figuration of the rural and socialized labor is inextricably connected to her critique of identitarianism, I build upon these openings suggested by O'Brien and Nixon, while also calling attention to a powerful Marxist philosophical subtext that undergirds the mundane, uneventful rhythms of cooperative farming: "Nature is Man's body-without-organs."[27] Beyond simply reading the supplementary narratives of the cooperative brigades as the resolution to the protagonist's inner conflict, I am proposing that the narrativization of cooperative farming in rural Botswana provides us with a starting point for thinking Head's "ethics of universality" in a planetary/Marxist—not cosmopolitan/postcolonial—way. Along these lines, *A Question of Power* might be read alongside the social text of the radical ecological movements of the global South.

If we consider how the subject is put together in terms of the rhetorical conduct of the text of *A Question of Power*, we notice that long sequences of surrealist symbolism and nightmare visions are persistently interrupted by segments of realist prose descriptions of farming—tables and schemas detailing the breakdown of the selling price of commodities produced by cooperative labor. While most readings of the textual figure of Bessie Head have centered upon the construction of the race subject of colonialism, I suggest that we closely examine the story line of cooperative labor in Motabeng for the ways in which it supplies a gap and adds an excess to what Rose has termed Head's "ethics of universality." In the schematic graphs and tables following the passages of figural language describing the protagonist's mental theater is suggested another allegory of reading—antihumanist and abstract—overlooked by most critics. Head's text seems to propose that men and women are part-subjects of work.[28] And in fact, it is in the context of the voluntary work experiment that fixed presuppositions of race, class, and power relations can be reversed.

But how, and toward what felicitous end, does the emphasis on cooperative work dehumanize the subject of the story? Spivak, reading

Marx, presents an edge to the concept of the commodity of *Capital*, volumes 1 and 2, that is strikingly at odds with received platitudes of mechanical Marxism. She explains the pharmakon of the commodification of labor power in this way:

> If the worker gets beyond thinking of work as *Privatarbeit* or individual work and perceives it as a potential commodity (laborpower) of which s/he is the part-subject (since laborpower is an abstract average), s/he can begin to resist the appropriation of surplus value and turn capital toward social redistribution.
> (Spivak, *Critique*, 387)

In *A Question of Power* also, it is the narrativization of abstract, socialized labor—rather than the celebration of a race-specific working class—that is the subtext that interrupts and eventually displaces the primary narrative of the construction/breakdown of the race subject. Consider, for example, this mirror-text, which rehearses the text's central message: the critique of identity politics. This dialogue takes place between Tom and Elizabeth during a shared meal:

> Rapid economic development was his pet subject. He'd earnestly tried to impress upon Elizabeth that she ought to support, morally, Mao Tse-tung, Castro and Nyerere because they stood for rapid economic development. . . . Now he turned to Elizabeth and said: "The only people in my country who support rapid economic development are the Black Power people." . . .
> Suddenly he sprang to his feet, thrust one fist high into the air and said: "Black Power!"
> She looked up at him, alarmed: "Do black people really do that? Do they really go around sticking their fists in the air like that?"
> He looked down at her surprised: "Of course," he said. "That's the Slogan." . . .
> "I don't like exclusive brotherhoods for black people only. They wouldn't want you. You're not black." . . .
> "Just what's wrong with you?" he asked. "Why do you have to go opposite to everyone else? Why do you have to sound different?" . . .
> "Tom," she said earnestly, "once you make yourself a freak and special any bastard starts to use you. That's half of the fierce fight

in Africa. The politicians first jump on the bandwagon of past suffering." . . .

He nodded his head: "You're right about Africa," he said. "But you're wrong about America. People are literate there and they know what they're doing. They're doing the right thing."

"It seems an indignity to me to stick a fist in the air," she said quietly. "I couldn't do it. I'd feel ashamed."

"Why?"

"Because of what I see inside," she said. "Because of what I'm learning, internally." (Head, *Question*, 132–133)

The episode is a rare glimpse into an everyday encounter *in* globalization that stages the (autocritical) aid worker and aid recipient as intellectual equals and interlocutors—not subject and object of benevolence. "He was treating politics the way he treated people, a blur he embraced vaguely. He was a stupid person to argue with, if innate generosity of heart could be called stupid. He had the same idea about her" (*Question*, 132–133). Finally, however, the dedicated (leftist) developmentalist (a historical figure that we tend to overlook in contemporary discussions on globalization)[29] is moved to reconsider the impact of sloganeering politics and symbols of power. He is persuaded by Elizabeth's antidevelopment rhetoric: "'Africa isn't rising. It's up already.' . . . He turned towards her a face flaming with light. He said under his breath: 'Oh, oh, oh—That's right. Yes, that's right'" (135).

It is a frequently quoted, if problematic, passage. Some critics look on the lines "I couldn't do it. . . . Because of what I am learning, internally" as making visible the terms of internalized racialization. For others, this passage aligns Head with Njabulo Ndebele's philosophical statement calling for an aesthetics of South African literature that is "Beyond Protest." In any event, the discussion on Black Power politics that takes place between the American Peace Corps volunteer and the protagonist must also be framed by the author's contradictory insistence that *A Question of Power* is not one of her "political" books.[30] In fact, even as many editors urged her to recast her story in South Africa because there the horrors of mental disturbance might be understood in terms of racial oppression—*in terms of politics*—Head insisted that the book be set in Botswana. Of course this stance might in itself be read as challenging the hegemony of which social texts define what is political. (Rose points this out as well.) It's worthwhile noticing that Head returns to this dilemma staged in a *Question of Power* when she writes angrily of the capitalization of identity politics by the culture industry: "The biggest thing you can sell and shit on is the suffering of black people in South Africa—that's why early on I would have NOTHING to do with it."[31] Along these lines, it must not be overlooked that Head's own relationship to the Black Power movement is definitely more complicated and nuanced than that of the character Elizabeth. In her biographical writings she describes a "bit of Pan Africanism" as one of the formative influences within her life and also writes a moving tribute to Robert Sobukwe as late as 1981. But in the same volume of collected short stories, we find in "Sorrow Food" a devastating satire of a specious sloganist of pan-Africanism who now serves the interests of a virulent tribalism.

As the author stages it in *A Question of Power*, Tom and Elizabeth's is a relationship that is not a "relationship." It is intensely felt, but nonromantic. The only place where the aporias of identity politics can be crossed by them is in "irrelevant" conversations about cooperative vegetable gardening. ("Irrelevance" is, of course, a loaded term in the conceptual vocabulary of a writer who sets out to "record the irrelevant.")[32] When it comes to food production, the political economy of hunger, and ecological sanity, Tom and Elizabeth comprehend each other's ethics and politics, finding a point of communication. As the narrator puts it, "her version of agriculture was so poetic and fanciful, she was so liable to fill in her gaps of knowledge with self-invented agriculture, she so obviously amused and irritated the English manager of the farm school that here was a friend indeed" (112–113). The English farm manager looks askance at her experimental formal innovations. And yet Tom is able to enter into that secret compact with the textuality of nature. (Not incidentally, Tom is the only outsider who is able to actually hear and gauge the presence of Sello, the uninvited guest in her house.) Simply put, he shares her thoughts. When she makes a comment about ecological well-being (comforted by the orderliness of the seedbeds: "I think the vegetables like it too") he does not read this as the mad woman's projection—a desperate wish for method and order amidst chaos—but rather he hears and responds to a philosophical critique of identity politics.

The quiet coda to the heated discussion on Black Power takes place upon Elizabeth's return from the sanatorium after her breakdown and "recovery." He addresses her with *tenderness*—which according to Head's lexicon is the antonym of "power." (Recall, for example, Head's collection of short stories titled *Tales of Tenderness and Power*.)[33] The passage reads:

> "Lucrezia Borgia," he said tenderly. "Don't you love everyone? Remember what you said to me that day we first met in the vegetable garden? You said that if the garden had a big street down the middle with lots of side-streets people would come and look at everything. You said you thought the vegetables would like it too. And I thought to myself: 'What do we have here—fish or fowl? This is one hell of a girl. Ha, ha, ha, how does she know what vegetables like?' Isn't that love, not only for people but vegetables too?" (Head, *Question*, 188)

Earlier in the book the omniscient narrative voice of *A Question of Power* philosophizes, "It is impossible to become a vegetable gardener without at the same time coming into contact with the wonderful strangeness of human nature. Every man and woman is, in some way, an amateur gardener at heart and vegetables are really the central part of the daily diet" (72). In this miraculous figuration of touching from a great distance, Bessie Head echoes the words of Marx's *Early Writings*. Separated by geography and period from Marx—who went on to set an urbanist telos for thinking "industry," capital, and class—Head's critique of identitarianism begins here with the recognition of the uncanniness of nature—happened upon in the everyday rhythms of agriculture.

The "early" Marx of the economic and philosophical manuscripts observes that "the human essence of nature exists only for *social* man; for only here does nature exist for him as *a bond* with other men as his existence for others and their existence for him, as the vital element of human reality" (*Early Writings*, 349). "The human essence of nature" in Head's own writing might owe just as much to Tswana cosmography and notions of personhood as to Marx.[34] Even though she never properly learned Setswana, her apprehension of nature as continuous with bits and pieces of self-shaped interiority owes to a different mode of social semiosis than the world picture inhabited by the cosmopolitan literati (of *Drum*, for instance), for whom "the rural" represented banal simplicity. Having crossed over from one sub-Saharan country to another, Head felt that she was better authorized to represent the complexities of a "pan-Africanist" vision than some of its more revered, urbane male ideologues, writing their long-distance commentary from locations of cosmopolitan exile. But her impulse to celebrate this contradictory notion of belonging in discontinuous organicism must also be read as a willful decision to write counter to the example of her own individual experience of disconnect and ostracism. In an autocritical mood she observes to Randolph Vigne, "The critics are quite true about the writing. On the one hand, I never felt I could write about people in South Africa because they were all torn up and un-representative of any definite kind of wholeness. On the other, I find this sympathetic wholeness here but tend to reflect my own condition, which is one of unbelievable isolation."[35] In her later work (the letter is from 1966), she begins to develop her own planetary (not cosmopolitan) vision of internationalism with the African village as its locus.

WHEN RAIN CLOUDS GATHER

Poverty has a home in Africa—like a quiet second skin.
—Bessie Head, "Village People"

It is interesting to compare the discussions on agriculture, food production, and cooperative farming from *A Question of Power* (Head's third and final novel) with a similar set of discussions and monologues from her first, *When Rain Clouds Gather*, published in 1969.[36] While this first novel has been criticized for its flat characters and contrived plot devices, the male protagonist, Makhaya, certainly anticipates the richly contradictory figure of Elizabeth in *A Question of Power*. Unlike in *A Question of Power*, which is first and foremost a fictionalized biography, here the primary narrative depicts the story of agrarian labor in rural Botswana. It is mostly focalized from the point of view of Makhaya, a political refugee from South Africa who leaves the scene of politics in Johannesburg and moves to Golema Mmidi in rural Botswana to learn techniques of sustainable agriculture. In fact we know from Head's "A Note on Rain Clouds"[37] that the story of the central character of Makhaya is based on the experience of a fellow refugee living in Botswana—a Zimbabwean who refuses to enlist for military training for the national liberation struggle. The central character is also reminiscent of Head herself, if we consider that he leaves a job writing sensationalist stories for a newspaper in Johannesburg and turns to the study of farming techniques. This earlier book thus rehearses the theme of *A Question of Power*: othering-the-self in the work of agriculture.

Upon first glance, the friendship between Makhaya and the antisubject, Gilbert Balfour, a British Third World development expert, seems key to the narrativization of socialized labor—but upon closer scrutiny this relationship begins to reveal its fault lines. In contrast to Tom and Elizabeth's luminous kinship in *A Question of Power*, the friendship between the two men is a compromised one. The author writes this situation by way of a contrived plot device: a contest over a woman. (At one point Gilbert mistakenly constructs Makhaya as a competitor for the object of his affection, Dinorego's daughter, Maria.) A bigger issue arises, however, because of Gilbert's general sense of timing—and *history*. The narrator tells us, "Gilbert's mind was like a stop watch. He could abruptly break off a conversation and, ten hours later, pick it up at exactly the same point where he had left off" (77). Along these lines, he sees their work in Botswana as seamlessly continuous with the history of British Marxism: "Since poverty was so much a part of his work, Gilbert was fond of expounding on what the British Socialists and the trade union movement had done to alleviate the atrocious living and working conditions of the poor" (78). And yet when the conversation turns to Botswana "half laughing, half deep in earnest," he questions, "'Where is all this talk of democracy going to get us, Mack? . . . Only a reasonably developed country can afford the time to debate these pros and cons. What we need is a dictatorship, which says, 'Look here, Gilbert, fill in this poverty programme'" (78). In response to such statements, the characteristically silent Makhaya is prompted to speak his inner misgivings: "Makhaya [interrupts] to put forward the idea that certain types of socialism might not be suited to African development. . . . 'Why not leave this country, even Africa, to trial and error?' . . . 'This is only my opinion. I don't think I approve of dictatorships in any form'" (79). Makhaya, like Elizabeth, is skeptical of sloganeering politics—in this case of provincial (Western) Marxist pieties.

Regarding the strategic nature of Makhaya's and Gilbert's relationship, the narrator tells us:

> To Gilbert, agriculture was a vast, rambling, intricate subject. The slope of the land, even the stones that lay on that land, would spark off a thousand speculations in his mind, and there were so few good listeners in the world that Makhaya found himself trapped and almost forced to listen to long discussions on the marvels and wonders of the earth. Not that Makhaya minded. It was a welcome change to be hearing about these things. There was so much more than South Africa that he was running from, and it included everything that he felt was keeping the continent of Africa at a standstill. . . . Thus when Makhaya met Gilbert, he was almost a drowning man, and the world of facts and scientific speculation seemed so much easier to handle. Therefore Makhaya turned to agriculture for his salvation and also to Gilbert. (76–77)

Undoubtedly, their friendship is not premised upon "responsibility" in the way that Tom and Elizabeth's is. Gilbert wants a captive audience for his socialist orations. Makhaya wants to anaesthetize himself to the reality of Apartheid politics. Along these lines, it is especially interesting to consider Makhaya's rejection of the call to masculist solidarity. After all has been resolved about Maria, Gilbert quotes a verse from Kipling as emblematic of their (renewed) fraternal bond. *Seemingly* exorbitant to the discussion on agriculture and politics is this text of the British leftist quoting the imperial bard:

> "Somehow I knew this the day you stepped into Golema Mmidi," Gilbert said. "And it's just today that everything's clear to me.
> He quoted a few lines from the poem:
>
> One man in a thousand, Solomon said,
> Will stick more close than a brother.
> And it's worthwhile seeking him half your days,
> If you find him before the other.

> But [*the narrator tells us*] Makhaya had a few reservations about Mr. Kipling's sweeping statements. It was just chance that had brought him to Golema Mmidi, and it was only chance and luck that operated in his destiny. (84)

Makhaya rejects the construction of the brotherhood of man along the lines of Kipling's poetry, anticipating, perhaps, the vision of Elizabeth at the close of *A Question of Power,* whose ideas on universality are undergirded by a very different conception of the literary text and the writer's task, one that would not be at ease with Kipling's world vision. She closes the book by invoking the tradition of the All-India Progressive Writers Association, as I will discuss in the coda to this chapter.

Critics such as Ketu Katrak and Annie Gagiano overlook the conflict between the two main male characters in *When Rain Clouds Gather*, focusing instead on other parts of the story, such as the climactic suicide of the tribalist chief Matenge,[38] but I have tried to bring into relief this tension in the text because it also brings into focus one of the blind spots that Makhaya touches upon early on in the story: the marginalizing of women's working-class history. Head describes the scene in which Gilbert first arrives:

> He felt that he had stumbled on to one of the major blockages to agricultural progress in the country. The women were the traditional tillers of the earth, not the men. The women were the backbone of agriculture while the men on the whole were cattle drovers. But when it came to programmes for improved techniques in agriculture, soil conservation, the use of pesticides and fertilizers, and the production of cash crops, the lecture rooms were open to men only. . . . Why start talking about development and food production without taking into account who is really producing the food? (29)

Finally it is from Maria—excluded from the discussions on agriculture and politics—that we get an intimate view of working on the parched land of Golema Mmidi. Maria's speech consoling Makhaya after the drought-related death of Paulina's son is given in a strange, imagist language, depicting a surreal vision of an "open" subject where exteriority is interiority. If in *A Question of Power* (following Rose's phrasing) Head affirms that "[u]niversality is a part of interiority," here she figures "[n]ature as man's body without organs," in these terms: "You may see no rivers on the ground but we keep the rivers inside us. That is why all good things and all good people are called rain. Sometimes we see the rain clouds gather even though not a cloud appears in the sky. It is all in our heart" (*Rain Clouds*, 165). Gagiano finds such passages indicative of her "socializing" imagination.[39] Furthermore, we cannot help but notice that Head imparts the authorial voice to Maria, the antiheroine of the story. This is the center of the novel. It is she—not Gilbert with his "mind like a stop watch"—who knows "*when* rain clouds gather." Feminism emerges in the interstices of Head's first book.

As early as the 1980s, Ketu Katrak called for a Marxist-feminist reading of *Rain Clouds*, correcting a theoretical bias in the literary criticism of Head.[40] Her main focus is not Maria, but the characters Pauline and Mma-Millepede and the significant roles they play in bringing Makhaya to self-awareness. Admittedly this approach still constructs woman in terms of instrumentality, but Katrak's critique marks an important intervention in that it attempts to take into account the way in which Head represents the sexual division of labor alongside structures of female solidarity. While the problematic character of Maria, Gilbert's recalcitrant bride, does not enter into her discussion, she too emphasizes the saving graces of collective work and agriculture. As she puts it, "Through Paulina, Makhaya accepts human love and goodness. . . . Their love is based on the foundation of work—the agricultural project in which they form a team." Beyond simply validating the resolution of the marriage plot, however, she finds "the crux of Head's philosophical/political vision [to be the] liberat[ion] [of] the personal lives of individual women, which is crucial in any attempt to build a more just socio-political system." More recently, Anthony O'Brien extends and elaborates upon this early Marxist-feminist stance taken by Katrak—in his case, marking the links between Head's writing and other representations of the rural evoked in worker poetry and the aesthetics of South African labor feminism. He emphasizes the overlooked fact that "Bessie Head . . . was deeply formed by anarchosyndicalism in the local social action of the volunteer brigades and village co-operative movement in Serowe" (235).

My own reading, which emphasizes the importance of the labor power in Head's *A Question of Power* and *When Rain Clouds Gather*, is very much indebted to this body of critical scholarship, which, without deemphasizing the place of the unconscious in Head's text, reads the text of labor as a productive interruption—a parabasis where the text others itself. Building upon O'Brien's insights, I would suggest that ultimately Head's writings might also be supplemented by readings of poetry and drama by Nise Malange and other writers connected with the worker-writers associations based in the Natal region.[41]

If we return to *A Question of Power* by way of Head's earlier book, we notice how certain plot points in *When Rain Clouds Gather* are revisited and invested with new meaning. The othering-of-the-self in agricultural work means something immediate and pressing to the protagonist, Elizabeth: "She struggled to hold on to the morning's work, with all its humour and weird drama, but the afternoons, which were set aside for seedling work and specialities, she began to reserve for collapses" (*Question*, 161). I do not mean to suggest that working in the garden and/or the cooperative labor brigades of Motabeng village in any (simple, direct) sense *effects* Elizabeth's cure. Indeed, even toward the end of the book she must say, "I have resolved nothing" (192). But I would submit that it is in the textuality of labor networks, in changing structures of responsibility, and in the dynamism of Motabeng village that she is even briefly acquainted with the antonym of power—"tenderness."

We know that "Elizabeth was never to regain a sense of security or stability on the question of how patterns of goodness were too soft, too indefinable to counter the tumultuous roar of evil" (159). However, it is briefly but incandescently illumined for her in this scene depicting the villagers' ethics of hospitality toward "foreigners." When an international aid worker from London finds that his host family will not accept payment for food and shared space, Elizabeth is called upon to intervene. Thus she is briefly acquainted with a belief in "tenderness":

> When the woman was questioned she replied that it was kindness to a foreigner; but the story went a little deeper than that. People believe in tenderness. These belonged to a God in the sky who would do everything for the poor in some magical way. It

was quite another thing to be loved and cared for in a realistic way by other living people who came from London. These things had to be enquired into by the poor; so they opened their doors to the volunteers who wanted to live among them, so that they could comprehend a new world that had suddenly made them precious, valued. (*Question*, 159)

This is where and how the subaltern villagers encounter the international development NGOs—in shorthand, where they confront "the global." It is a touching picture that the writer paints—reversing and righting the moral economy of "donor" and "recipient" as the definitions often become fixed in developmentalist discourse. Chakravarthi Raghavan speaks to a different, but related ironic context that is the contradiction at the heart of the semantics of "donor" and "recipient" in neocolonialism when he observes in his angry foreword to *Recolonization* that "most ordinary people have heard about Aid. It is from the rich countries in the Economic North to the poor countries of the Economic South. They have never heard of 'Aid' from the South to the North."[42]

As mentioned before, I am in agreement with O'Brien when he writes, "Whether Head would or should have gone further than the radicalism of the NGO, given a wider political experience than her few years as a young adult in South Africa and among the refugees of Francistown, Batswana, and South Africa and her mature years working with Patrick Van Rensburg for community development in Serowe, I cannot say; but labeling her apolitical has always seemed bizarrely wrong" (235–236). I have tried to call attention to the places in her texts where Head imagines "the rural" as inextricably political. These segments on agricultural labor and crop growing in her books are often either overlooked, or thought of as invaluably distracting from the main narrative. (See, for example, critiques such as that of Gillian Eilersen, Head's biographer, who, reading *Rain Clouds*, finds that "the emphasis on the practical details of crop cultivation sometimes threatens to obscure the narrative entirely.")[43] But as Gayatri Chakravorty Spivak, Mahasweta Devi, Tillie Olsen, and Mulk Raj Anand have reminded us through their very different types of interventions, the space of the rural is also the forgotten predication of/for globalization.[44] The figuration of the rural and the politics of the ordinary also make up the ground of Bessie Head's ideas on universality.

CENTERING THE RURAL: *SEROWE, VILLAGE OF THE RAIN WIND*

The critique of identity politics via Head's counterintuitive narrative strategy of constructive "self-effacement" is taken to another level in the dialogic experimental form of *Serowe, Village of the Rain Wind* (1981). The later book might be understood as a perfect dialectical inversion of the storytelling pattern of *A Question of Power*. It follows as a discontinuous continuation of the narratives of farming in the previous book in that *Serowe* is loosely structured as transcripts of oral history and "irrelevant" moments of talking back by uncooperative native informants and unreliable witnesses. These sequences are supplemented on occasion by Head filling in the blanks. In terms of rhetorical conduct, here we find long sequences of documentary accounts based in reports on agricultural practices, consumers' cooperative stores, and artisanal and development project skills-training exercises, periodically interrupted by Head's subjective musings. While the book itself is put together as history writing troped as patrimony or male succession—part I constitutes "the era of Khama the Great"; part II follows under the heading: "The Era of Tshkedi Khama"; and part III is named "The Swaneng Project: Patrick Van Rensburg"—the content more often than not transcends the phrase. Some of her interviewees cannot or will not talk about the great Khama. Ramasamo Kebonang, for example, "couldn't concentrate and said all sorts of irrelevant things. . . . I decided to record the irrelevant" (67).

In most segments Head's intervention is minimal. She "handles" her subjects without leaving too many fingerprints. At times, though, boundaries become hard to discern. Whose voice is this? In perhaps a practical example of something like Foucault's archaeology of knowledge, the transcriber moves out of her own way, becoming one who writes in order "to have no face."[45] Other voices interrupt to produce the collective subject of Serowe. If in *A Question of Power* the othering of the self is projected as a cure, here the othering of the self in work projects—not incidentally, the final section is devoted entirely to the Boiteko gardens—is formalized not only in rhetorical protocols but in the very "textile" weave of the text:

It was by chance that I came to live in this village. I have lived most of my life in shattered little bits. Somehow, here, the shattered bits began to grow together. There is a sense of wovenness, a wholeness in life here; a feeling of how *strange and beautiful people can be*—just living. People do so much subsistence living here and so much mud living. . . . Women's hands build and smooth mud huts and mud courtyards and decorate the walls of the mud courtyards with intricate patterns. (x)[46]

A string of speech interferences produces moments of organicity. Metonymic part-objects compose the universal even as *women's* labor power takes center stage. Head's writing dehumanizes in the same move that it reconnects the disparate parts of dispersed individuality. Apart from the aesthetic conventions of postmodernism or philosophical interventions of poststructuralist theory, here we have an exposition of the "open text" that has implications for socialism and the "rational social": "Serowe has several arms and my book shuttles to and fro all the time, linking up to the other dwelling places of the Bamangwato tribe" (xi).

Again at the close of the book, we encounter the dialectic of the self and other. This time it is refracted through the reciprocal relationship (reminiscent in places of Walter Benjamin, perhaps) of the subjectivity of "the collector" to that of the collective.[47] Here the epigraph and opening line owe to Rupert Brooke, but the beloved objects she lists are all her "own":

These I have loved:

The hours I spent collecting together my birds, my pathways, my sunsets, and shared them, with everyone;
The small boys of this village and their homemade wire cars;
The windy nights, when the vast land mass outside my door simulates the dark roar of the ocean.
—And those mysteries: that one bird call at dawn—that single, solitary outdoor fireplace far in the bush that always captivates my eye. Who lives so far away in the middle of nowhere?
The wedding parties and beer parties of my next-door neighbors that startle with their vigour and rowdiness;

> The very old women of the village who know so well how to plough with an hoe; their friendly motherliness and insistent greetings as they pass my fence with loads of firewood or water buckets on their heads;
> My home at night and the hours I spent outside it watching the yellow glow of the candle-light through the curtains;
> The hours I spent inside it in long, solitary thought.
> These small joys were all I had, with nothing beyond them, they were indulged in over and over again, like my favourite books.
>
> (179)

Her gratitude takes the shape of a paratactic litany of thanksgiving—or to put, it more simply, a randomly ordered list. There is a lyric sweetness to this prose-poetry epilogue titled "A Poem to Serowe" that (for some critics at least) strikes a false note. No doubt Head's selective memory of harmonious collectivity is glaringly at odds with her personal experience. Even Head's most generous and accommodating readers would seem to retreat from her heroic act of transference passed off as revisionist historiography. "Ideally, *Village of the Rain Wind* should be read alongside *The Collector of Treasures*, the superb collection of short stories which is an offshoot of Head's research for the oral history," proposes Rob Nixon (115). He also notes:

> Her efforts to influence the boundaries of Serowe through historical form stress the porousness of the village's identity, its long record of accommodating migrants, refugees, and strangers. *Village of the Rain Wind* is animated by Head's desire to chart, within Serowe's (and the Bamangwato people's) history, precedents for the values she herself upholds. (115)

I do not dispute that this indeed the case. Head is a partial—in both senses of the word—historian who actively confuses desire with wish fulfillment. I would argue, however, that Head's acts of selective rememoration and re-membering must also be read against and through a practice of alternative subaltern labor history predicated in the concept of labor power and socialist ethics. The penultimate words in the text immediately preceding the epilogue are given over to labor power and the Boiteko project. The form of the graph of socialized labor (Kenosi's catalogue of prices and the breakdown of value) is here expanded into a beautifully misshapen document mirroring the critique of possessive individualism and identity politics in *A Question of Power*.

CODA: MARXISM AND (COMPARATIVE) LITERATURE

Critics have noticed the uncanny parallels between Head's philosophy of the "ordinary" and the aesthetics and politics of Njabulo Ndebele's literary-critical manifestos, but few have really focused on the significance of the closing scene in *A Question of Power*, where Elizabeth reaches for a book by the Indian writer Premchand, one of the founding members, along with Sajjad Zaheer and Mulk Raj Anand, of the Marxist-oriented All-India Progressive Writers Association (AIPWA). As the narrator describes that final scene:

> [Elizabeth] turned and picked up a book from the table beside her bed. It had waited for a whole year to be read. It was *The Gift of a Cow*, by Premchand. It was a UNESCO publication of the classic Hindi novel which exalted the poor. In their introduction to the novel they wrote that it opposed the basic trend of Indian literature, which seemed to be a literature intended only "to entertain and to satisfy our lust for the amazing" ... a literature of magic, of ghosts, of the adventures of high-born heroes and heroines. (206)

It is difficult not to read *into* that gesture of reaching out toward a different literary tradition—of responding to a distant call to solidarity. The obliterated trace of Afro-Asian unity in South Africa and the history of the promise and failings of Bandung are encrypted here. As Spivak has reminded us elsewhere: "The initial attempt in the Bandung conference (1955), to establish a third way, neither with the Eastern nor the Western bloc in the World-System, in response to the seemingly New World Order established after World War II, was not accompanied by a commensurate intellectual effort" (*Critique*, 375). But here at the close of *A Question of Power* is one such example of an effort—far distant from the boardroom meetings of UN negotiators and heads of state.

Head's part-subject of labor power is framed here in terms of questions of aesthetics and politics—in terms of problems of social justice and the literary historiography of internationalism. Proletarian writing—both as a genre and as an international social movement—facilitates other connectivities and other collectivities beyond those vouchsafed by identitarian claims and identity politics. The quotation from the UNESCO introduction cited by the narrator, in fact, corresponds to key dicta of the AIPWA manifesto:

> Indian literature, since the breakdown of classical literature, has had the fatal tendency to escape from the actualities of life. It has tried to find a refuge from reality in spiritualism and idealism. . . . We believe that the new literature of India must deal with the basic problems of existence today—the problems of hunger and poverty, social backwardness and political subjugation, *so that it may help us to understand these problems and through such understanding help us act.*

The October 1935 Hindi version appearing in the literary journal *Hans* (edited by Premchand himself) seems less constrained by the language and protocols of diplomacy employed in the *Left Review* version. The line "corresponding" to the italicized segment reads, "only then will we be able to understand these problems and the revolutionary spirit will be born in us."[48]

The narrator's criticism of "a literature intended only 'to entertain and to satisfy'" is, once again, a strange, self-estranging moment in the text. Who is speaking here—commenting on the easy entertainment value of ghosts and mysticism? It is ostensibly the narrator, providing insight into Elizabeth's voice-consciousness. But lost in a tissue of citations, the observation embedded in this nonnarrative segment resonates, also, as Head's own commentary on the "ideology of the aesthetic." (Elsewhere, as we recall, Elizabeth has already begun talking back to critics of elitist avant-garde literature and its equation of "high culture" with "incomprehensibility.")[49]

The concept of literature as "creative practice" (or, as Raymond Williams describes it, as "the struggle at the roots of the mind") is central to Head's mapping of the discursive reach of the "social." But more specifically, it is proletarian literature (where AIPWA might be considered a subset) that recasts nonbelonging as the condition of *internationalism*—not universality or elitist cosmopolitanism. If Ndebele turns to Brecht, Head broadens the focus further, turning to Premchand, even as she opens up a South–South dialogue between South Asia and sub-Saharan Africa. In the scene where Sello first enters, with all barriers transgressed, all defenses crossed, Head's protagonist is represented as "feeling global."[50] It is an *unheimlich*—uncomfortable—feeling, to be sure. But notice how *A Question of Power* ends with another scene of the protagonist reaching beyond her limits—this time crossing boundaries of national literature and the imaginary maps of literary historiography.

EPILOGUE

Working-Class Writing and the Social Imagination

> It seemed almost incidental that he was African. So vast had his inner perceptions grown over the years that he preferred an identification with mankind to an identification with a particular environment. And yet, as an African, he seemed to have made one of the most perfect statements: "I am just anyone." It was as though his soul was jigsaw; one more piece being put into place.
>
> —Bessie Head, *A Question of Power*

In David Lodge's *Nice Work*, we are made privy to the moment where the socially conscious intellectual suddenly, *fleetingly* becomes aware of the international division of labor and of her place in it as a beneficiary of the system. Lodge's heroine, a Marxist feminist scholar, acknowledges economic globalization but worries:

> What to do with the thought was another question. It was difficult to decide whether the system that produced the kettle was a miracle of ingenuity and cooperation or a colossal waste of resources, human and natural. Would we all be better off boiling our water in a pot hung over an open fire? Or was it the facility to do such things at the touch of a button that freed men, and more particularly women, from servile labor and made it possible for them to become literary critics.   (193)[1]

From her elevated position—an airplane seat, in fact—Lodge's critic acquires the literal and metaphoric distance to take in and represent the unrepresentable totality—the gendered international division of labor. Distance, removal, and disconnection appear to be the necessary preconditions for knowledge and analysis. By sleight of hand, the subdivisions of (in this case English/national) industry serve as a metonym for the general system of political economy. Whether economic globalization is ultimately good or bad for society remains an unresolved issue. Just as the thought becomes too ponderous to bear, she drops it. By the end of the novel, as we see, an all-too-tidy compromise needs to be hammered out between the interests of capital and labor (including knowledge workers), one that is reminiscent, in a way, of the condition of England novels of the 1840s. In this moment of Lodge's semiparodic, seminostalgic send up of the British working-class novel as a genre, the international division of labor viewed from a distance appears as simultaneously global *and* social—socialized labor.[2]

Considered as a heuristic device, the contrast between the aerial view vouchsafed to Lodge's literary critic and the ground-level insight afforded to Mulk Raj Anand's semiliterate coolie might also be seen as illustrating an abiding paradox of our information age. Do technological advances facilitate real connection and communication between particular working-class struggles, or do they merely enable the more efficient extraction of surplus value? Lodge's scenario from *Nice Work* might easily be updated and recast for the social media age, perhaps, with the U.S. liberal feminist literary critic, this time, pausing to consider the world opened up by the iPhone held in her hand, far removed from the struggles of Foxconn workers agitating for a reduction of hours in their working day—far removed, also, from the general nationalist furor surrounding the outsourcing of manufacturing jobs to the low-wage global South.[3]

On the one hand, the rhetoric of outsourcing continues to fragment working-class coalitional politics. The language of comparative advantage and social dumping continues to be wielded by agenda-driven factory management and trade unionists alike, attesting to the fact that we live in a paradoxical communication age of "incommunicable" social movements.[4] Fatal fires in Bangladeshi garment factories supplying cheap goods to U.S. retailers focus the global Northern consumer's attention on the disposable labor of the periphery, but only for the briefest moment, tied to the strike there or (for the duration of the media cycle covering it) the consequent boycott campaign here.⁵ Meanwhile, the construction of the U.S. worker as a casualty of offshore manufacturing also pushes further into shadow the illegal immigrant worker whose cheap labor displaces the "American" laborer from within the bounds of the nation-state.

On the other hand, the case might be made, as it has been, that it is no longer possible to conceive of national working-class struggles in isolation. The creative communication stratagems of disparate fronts of the global Occupy movement as well as messages of hope and encouragement exchanged via social media between Arab Spring revolutionaries and striking Wisconsin teachers' union members exemplify a new shape and ideological grounding for a collective social subject. Theorists of OWS (Occupy Wall Street), for example, describe emergent paradoxical meanings of social connectivity and of being-in-common that arise from the tensions and textures of "assembly movements" considered transnationally.⁶ If the sublime vision of globalization experienced by Lodge's (parodied) intellectual is a feeling of connection based in disconnection, Occupy movements somehow cathect the impossible commonality of shared class struggles *despite* geographic discontinuities and the radical particularity of the discretely different functional locations occupied.

But confronting the dilemma of global-social class relationships in just these terms still leaves undisturbed an elusive, shape-shifting keyword that remains a structural and structuring problem for "Languages of Class" as well as for working-class studies in general: *social*, a vital, though blurry, concept for working-class writing, too often banalized, sloganized, or reduced to idealized conventions.⁷ Even as Raymond Williams tracks the changing semiotics of the social, noting shifts in meaning from the value-neutral descriptive "of society" to the positively valued term pertaining to mutual cooperation from which "socialism" later derives, his last word of assessment trails off asymptotically, acknowledging "the still active sense of the social" (*Keywords*, 295). In Marx's lexicon, we find his meaning shifts from a humanist sense pertaining to association and interdependency to the posthumanist humanist *abstract* sense relating to the variable calculus of labor power, the abstract average of social labor, and the production of the possibility of mediation itself, the value form. In the peculiar

Marxian sense, socialization also involves the process of abstraction: you have to abstract to be able to see different labor as a homogeneous *social* substance. Or to phrase the problem in a different way, to rationally imagine socialized labor, then—I'll let the contradiction stand—in fact requires us to think in abstract terms: labor power (as commodity), not theories of the subject (of the worker, for example), is the basis for theories of socialism. But this rationale, which is the predication for socialism, should not be confused with a description of globalization, the breaking down of barriers to the free movement of capital.[8]

The concluding reflections of this epilogue present a supplement to the argument of the book. If class can only be understood in terms of its interrelationships, what constitutes the meaning of the social in the context of the mutual entailments and lived compromises of classes considered in a transnational frame?

The sense of the social in one established tradition of working-class writing—critical or celebratory ethnographies of working-class attitudes and *culture*—is writ large and clear, albeit in disappearing ink. This structure of feeling of the social—expressed as mutual cooperation that is categorically opposed to individualism and competitiveness—becomes sanctified as a lost ethos, the special provenance of a dying working-class culture. In Hoggart's classic *Uses of Literacy*, he speaks of a "moral capital" lost to future generations cut off from these earlier social ties and community-based modes of organization: "Among working-class people, then, how much of a decent local, personal and communal way of life remains. It remains in speech, in forms of culture (the Working-Men's Clubs, the styles of singing, the brass bands, the older types of magazine, the close group games like darts and dominoes), and in attitudes as they are expressed in everyday life" (265).

In the well-worn idiom of such an established subgenre of working-class cultural studies—we might even see Dipesh Chakrabarty's *Rethinking Working-Class History* and Aihwa Ong's groundbreaking *Spirits of Resistance and Capitalist Discipline* as aligned critical variations—the social is described as bonded by proximity, neighborliness, a spirit of community, duty-bound commitments, and local cultural struggles.[9] The preoccupation is with the immediate, proximate working-class other. But in today's era of global assembly lines, business process outsourcing, and the geographical dispersion of work, such frames of reference for meaning-making seem at an impasse with the ethical challenge at hand for working-class writing and labor organization. The very spatial *and temporal* divisions of labor are now unsettled by the expanded use of subcontracting. Ethnographies of Indian call-center workers, providing back office support and financial services across time zones, require us to rethink the language of *Languages of Class* and *Uses of Literacy*.[10] Or at the very least, the resonant titles, if not the representative historical frames of reference, of these old standard-bearers in Anglophone working-class studies might need to be rethought in light of the contemporary situation of English-speaking, American-accent trained workers pulling night shifts in India, in order to facilitate the smooth operation of the seamless business day in the United States. Viewed from the vantage point of displaced higher paid workers in the global North, these are globalization's purported winners. What ethics of mutual cooperation are imaginable across such material and ideological divides? Beginning with the decline of the American farm and the destruction of a way of life rooted in community, voluntarism, and self-reliance, Arlie Hochschild's *Outsourced Self* seeks to narrate the psychic cost to the (US) working-class subject as a result of the turn to the (global) service market to replace improvised social arrangements.[11]

As the preceding chapters have put forward, bringing "the social" into view is arguably more of a difficult proposition than representing the global (or even world literature) as "a perspective and cultural awareness."[12] Building on Raymond Williams's theses on literature, a central preoccupation of this book, my own, has been the question of how to apprehend the social as "all that is present and moving."[13] If the conjunction between world literature and distance is a given, working-class writing presumes a different relationship between the social and the personal. Its forms and figures challenge us to redraw the lines demarcating nearness from distance. A mere perspective adjustment will not suffice. Extending and elaborating upon Williams's premise, the burden of this book has been to ask what structure of feeling (if not ideology) of the working classes is imaginable across the international division of labor—across rural and industrial fronts? Which instruments, strategies, and techne manifest the social as articulations of presence?

Consider, for example, Therese Agnew's remarkable trompe-l'œil. Her *Portrait of a Textile Worker* (2005) is a 98-by-110-inch monument to the garment factory worker of the global South—the unseen, anonymous agent of economic globalization.[14] Making use of the rhetoric and sentiment of the global anti-sweatshop movement, here the artist plays with perspective to "familiarize" the Northern consumer with the unthinkable abstraction of the international division of labor. From a distance, we get a partial view, from the waist up, of a woman clothed in a sari. Prominent in the foreground is the ubiquitous Juki-brand sewing machine. The face with downcast eyes appears completely absorbed in the task at hand. There she is—performing her signature docility and dexterity. Up close, the image disintegrates into a cacophony of proper names. Made up of thirty thousand brand name labels, as Agnew explains it on her personal website, "from 20 feet away, the composition is a representational image of a remote place. As you move in closer, the illusionistic devices dissolve into labels as intimately familiar as your own clothes.... The repetition of thousands of other people cutting their labels is retained in the piece. It amplifies the presence of the woman we finally see." The artist envisions her collaborative composition as an experiment in socialized labor.

Although it runs counter to the divisive rhetoric of outsourcing, and is offered up as representational reparation to the undervalued labor of the South Asian garment factory worker, Agnew's explanation nevertheless comes off as a paradoxical gesture. Making visible the unseen garment factory worker is predicated on substituting and overwriting her labor with the "labor" of socially conscious consumers. Artistic labor, or the work of art, is substituted as a proxy for the labor of factory workers. "It amplifies the presence of the woman we finally see" is the artist's statement. Her ethical objective—circumscribed within metropolitan feminism—is to call attention to a secret history of commodity fetishism. The use of the word "amplify" reveals the desire to restore voice agency to the Third World worker in this "postindustrial" age. We are familiar with the arguments that caution against confusing the two different senses—aesthetic and political—of representation. But we also recognize this as a principled, if ideologically compromised, intervention—an effort to reveal the hidden global assembly line as both apart from us and a part of us. Agnew's collaborative text seeks to make visible the invisible diacritics of socialized labor. Her efforts, though, are restricted by her mode of address and a structure of feeling: the devalued labor of the Third World worker is brought into the foreground through an appeal to liberal guilt.[15]

The lines between nearness and distance, global and social, self and other are deconstructed in a different way in the abstract vision of labor power figured by Bessie Head. Head dramatizes both sides of the precarious equation of globalization—internationalism and schizophrenia. In *A Question of Power*, in a personal transcoding of "the social," Elizabeth's debilitating mental breakdown is figured as both a symptom and an allegory of globalization:

> It seemed as though her head simply filled out into a large horizon. It gave her a strange feeling of things being there right inside her and yet projected at the same time at a distance away from her. (22)

Globalization is unthinkably big. Class, especially in the context of the international division of labor, is ungraspably abstract, and the rules of political economy are invisible to a close-up view. In Head's multigenre novel, however, we find *all* distance is collapsed. All barriers to exchange are laid low. Voices in the head and information overload become metaphors for globalization. Her "mad" protagonist then experiences globalization as a structure of feeling. On the one hand, at a point where the personal is inseparable from the social (prior to becoming entrenched as ideology or even acquiring a fixed shape), globalization becomes a *painful* part of Elizabeth's interiority. On the other, the motif of self-estrangement repeats itself across different levels of meaning in the narrative. Estrangement from self and country also enables a counterintuitive sense of inhabiting the world—a social ethics of universality. Alienation is also the necessary precondition and predication for an other-centered world vision.

Consider this key dialogue that takes place between two agricultural cooperative workers—one a South African stateless refugee living in Botswana, and the other a Danish developmental studies project volunteer. Here the reader is thrown into the space of the future anterior. Amidst the changing dynamics of class struggle, in imagining the ethical repair work of the longue durée, the novel's protagonist (the refugee and a victim of apartheid) makes herself eccentric to her own untenable historical predicament, in order to grasp the implications of the economic contest comparatively, not competitively: "I imagine a situation in some future life . . . I imagine my face contorted with greed and hatred. I imagine myself willfully grabbing things that are not mine. And in the darkness of the soul, you will one day walk up to me and remind me of my nobility" (85). Head's counterfactual staging of the international division of labor deliberately recasts immediate, proximate, real historical race and class power relations with a view to imagining an ethics of historical materialism. Her protagonist's statement describes an uncomfortable subject position—a moment of willful disfiguring and multiple voicing, thinking ahead to excluded constituencies not yet born. It is a cautionary narrative aimed at moral victors and victims alike. My book, like Head's, considers working-class literature in a comparative frame. Or to put it another way, it charts the place in between the ideological divide separating Agnew's portrait of the international division of labor and Head's aspirational vision of the social—between description and ethics.

Although it is tempting, then, to close this book by making the usual claims that authors make for material that has been deemed obscure by one or more parts of the mainstream, or that has been overlooked, devalued, or subject to disuse, I will not do so. The formal innovations and improvisational strategies of working-class writing *have been* overlooked in the passage from realism, to modernism, to postmodernism. In a moment in the humanities devoted to all things global, transnational, traveling, migrant, border-crossing, itinerant, stateless, ephemeral, and *world literary,* working-class writing has gone *relatively* unnoticed, except within certain guises and abbreviated contexts. But working-class writing is hardly new. It should not now be deemed the repressed subaltern untheorized of postcolonial studies, or, indeed the *Lemuria,* so to speak, of world literature. This book, then, is not a recovery project—in any simple sense. Rather, it proposes that a simultaneously broader and deeper study of working-class writing compels new ways of thinking about literature, ethics, and the social imagination.

Notes

INTRODUCTION: WORLD LITERATURE OR WORKING-CLASS LITERATURE IN THE AGE OF GLOBALIZATION?

1. Mulk Raj Anand, *Coolie* (New Delhi: Penguin, 1993).

2. According to political economists and development sociologists, the rise of the globalization project corresponds with the post–World War II state-restructuring and global crisis-management efforts that led in 1944 to the founding of the Bretton Woods international financial institutions (specifically the World Bank and the IMF). The 1930s and decolonization struggles also constitute an important part of globalization's history. In the aftermath of the 1930s, the IMF and World Bank—properly speaking, the International Bank of Reconstruction and Development (IBRD)—were instituted to finance the rebuilding of war-torn Europe and to prevent another global depression. In this sense, late colonial proletarian writing (Anand's included) might be seen as anticipating globalization's debates and dilemmas. The Bretton Woods institutions were not value-neutral. Promises of aid to newly independent countries were part of an ideological agenda of containing the threat of socialism. In 1955 the Bandung Conference—which brought together heads of state, intellectuals, activists, and cultural workers from across Asia and Africa—initiated the Non-Aligned Movement (NAM) and created a framework for economic development and social justice that refused the binarism of Cold War logic and sought to navigate an alternative route for the workers of the Third World.

In most literary historiography, however, the meaning of globalization gets unmoored from its historical and economic context. Immanuel Wallerstein's "world-systems theory" model inspires literary critics who retroactively (since the term's migration from the social sciences to the humanities) see every period-genre field as, of course, contributing to globalization studies. For those literary critics who bracket its economic provenance, globalization can become synonymous with adjusting the perspective, now reframing how we undertake literary studies, moving away from literary history premised in national literature models toward comparative regionalism and formalism. In this ahistorical, decontextualized way, "globalization" becomes automatically synonymous with "transculturation": global cultural flows are the result of the breaking down of fragile, national economies. Or to put it another way, globalization becomes defined metaleptically by evidence of a sampling of its dispersed effects.

We are all familiar with the imagery used to fix globalization in the mind's eye. An incomplete list might begin (1) a world of flows (of people and information) (Appadurai); (2) a new world order predicated in the unbundling of nation-state sovereignty (Hardt and Negri and Sassen); (3) the rise of transnational corporations and the proliferation of export-processing zones; (4) the proliferation of nongovernmental organizations (NGOs); (5) renewed attention to existing transnational instruments of justice (including those of UN mandates and international law); (6) the financialization of the globe; (7) trade liberalization, where the push for poorer countries to open up their markets is accompanied by protectionism for industries in the richer ones. But, arguably, while globalization might be figured as parataxis, its history and definition should not be reduced to a list of effects. For a more detailed historical overview and theorization of debates in history and epistemology see Arjun Appadurai, ed., *Globalization* (Durham, NC: Duke University Press, 2001); David Harvey, *A Brief History of Neoliberalism* (Oxford: Oxford University Press, 2005); Philip McMichael, *Development and Social Change: A Global Perspective* (Thousand Oaks: Pine Forge Press, 1996); Chakravarthi Raghavan, *Recolonization: GATT, the Uruguay Round, and the Third World* (London: Zed Books, 1990); Saskia Sassen, *Globalization and Its Discontents* (New York: New Press, 1998); Joseph Stiglitz, *Globalization and Its Discontents* (New York: Norton, 2003), *Making Globalization Work* (New York: Norton, 2007).

3. "Empire is materializing before [his] very eyes": this is, of course, a reference to the memorable opening line of the preface to *Empire* (Michael Hardt and Antonio Negri, *Empire* [Cambridge, MA: Harvard University Press, 2000], xi). See also Sanjay Krishnan, *Reading the Global: Troubling Perspectives on Britain's Empire in Asia* (New York: Columbia University Press, 2007), 1–23. Although questions of reading globalization from below do not take center stage in his argument, Krishnan makes a persuasive case for understanding the global as an "instituted perspective."

4. In the appendix to her *Critique of Postcolonial Reason*, Spivak, elaborating upon de Man, explains irony not only as rhetorical figure but also as the basis for a cultural

politics; Gayatri Chakravorty Spivak, *A Critique of Postcolonial Reason: Toward a History of the Vanishing Present* (Cambridge, MA: Harvard University Press, 1999), 430. Also see Paul de Man, *Allegories of Reading: Figural Language in Rousseau, Nietzsche, Rilke, and Proust* (New Haven: Yale University Press, 1979), 300–301.

5. Anand's description of "Jimmie Thomas, sometime mechanic in a Lancashire mill, now for fifteen years head foreman in one of the biggest cotton mills in India" disintegrates into caricature: "Occasionally, he kicked a Coolie. But that was when he had read in the morning paper the news of a nationalist demonstration, a terrorist outrage or an attempt at seditious communist propaganda which he, as a member of the British race of India, considered to be more of a personal affront than the pursuit of an ideal of freedom on the part of the exploited. He had long since forgotten the days during which he himself had eked out a miserable existence in Lancashire" (*Coolie*, 172–173; 217).

6. Anand's nonindividuated, anonymous "Coolie" of the title must be understood as a part-subject of labor power in a very specific way. Consider, for example, that the English word derives from the Tamil word *Kuli*—the word simply for "payment" or "wage." This is a part-subject whose very name signifies the value of labor power and the capital–labor exchange relation.

7. See the epigraph to this chapter. Bessie Head, *A Question of Power* (Oxford: Heinemann, 1974). See also Bruce Robbins, *Feeling Global: Internationalism in Distress* (New York: New York University Press, 1999).

8. It is not the objective of this book to minutely catalogue these dominant literary histories. In surveying the problem of how to introduce working-class literature as a canonical category, however, we see that there have been various attempts to define working-class literature as well as attempts to read the category of the working class in relation to other established literary traditions. In fact we might say that working-class fiction as a genre has been identified with at least three different critical traditions in the American academy: (1) the "proletarian" moment in American arts and letters, corresponding to the 1930s and its immediate aftermath, the decade of literary radicalism (representative works include Tillie Olsen's *Yonnondio*; Jack Conroy's *The Disinherited*; John Dos Passos's USA trilogy; Richard Wright's *Native Son*; Agnes Smedley's *Daughter of Earth*; and Mike Gold's *Jews Without Money*); (2) the "industrial novel" of mid-nineteenth century Britain (illustrative examples would be Elizabeth Gaskell's *Mary Barton* and *North and South*; Charles Dickens's *Hard Times*; Benjamin Disraeli's *Sybil*; Charles Kingsley's *Alton Locke*; and George Eliot's *Felix Holt*); (3) working-class literature understood as a constitutive element of the realism–modernism debates (examples would be the arguments and counterarguments of Ernst Bloch, Georg Lukacs, Bertolt Brecht, Walter Benjamin, Theodor Adorno—key debates in German Marxism gathered under the heading of "aesthetics and politics").

During the debates of the 1930s in particular, there was a decisive push by theoreticians of the U.S. left to limit the category of proletarian literature to material produced by writers of working-class *origin*, in contrast to "proletarian" literature, defined as that produced by class-conscious members of the working class with a particular political agenda. Ultimately, however—even according to CPUSA-affiliated critics—proletarian literature ultimately has come to be defined broadly as literature overtly *by*, *for*, or *about* workers.

Even most so-called comparative approaches to studying the field usually establish nineteenth-century England (the industrial novel and, in a few rare instances, the chartist novel) or 1930s North America (proletarian fiction) as the standard points of departure for conceptualizing working-class literatures internationally. Gustav Klaus's well-intentioned—but perhaps misleadingly titled—*The Literature of Labor: Two Hundred Years of Working-Class Writing* is an example of this trajectory. However, his later work, coedited with Stephen Knight, calls attention to this constitutive blind spot in his earlier work. He concedes that "postindustrial" as a descriptive term "needs to be taken with some caution, as, although heavy industry and factory production of the traditional kind have indeed largely gone from Britain, they have not dematerialized, but literally gone elsewhere. They have vanished from the face of most European countries only to surface in other parts of the globe.... A lament for lost industry runs the risk of weaving a universal truth out of a local phenomenon: the world of industry and industrial fiction is wider than Eurocentric angst.... The international character of the working class remains a reality, and the nature of international working-class fictions remains a topic for future essays and collections" (*British Industrial Fictions*, ed. Gustav Klaus and Stephen Knight [Cardiff: University of Wales Press, 2000], 2). Significantly, Raymond Williams, as we know, came to consider his designation of the "industrial novel" as a misnomer, given its middle-class perspective and exclusively northern English setting. In the last chapter of *The Country and the City*, he begins to think through the ways in which "distant lands become the rural areas of industrial Britain" through export-oriented industrialization and the laboring of the colonial and neocolonial working classes.

9. See Peter Hitchcock, *Working-Class Fiction in Theory and Practice: A Reading of Alan Sillitoe* (Ann Arbor: University of Michigan Research Press, 1989), 2–3.

10. "When considering the historical development of class-specific fiction," qualifies Hitchcock, we should not overlook that writing by sympathetic bourgeois and committed socialist authors might reveal "'class effects' (pro-class cultural activity that may be the work of producers outside the class they support)" (Hitchcock, *Working-Class Fiction*, 20). To be clear, Hitchcock's work cannot be simply subsumed under the category of that of critics who insist that realism and testimonial are the best representative forms for working-class writing, although the legitimacy of working-class *origins* is here, at least (in his monograph on Sillitoe), affirmed as the defining case for working-class writing.

11. Taking "literary" and "nonliterary" *countries* as her units of measurement, Casanova assesses the relationship of aesthetics to politics in these terms: "The political

dependence of emerging literary spaces is signaled by the recourse to a functionalist aesthetic and, taking the criteria of literary modernity as a standard of measurement, the most conservative narrative, novelistic, and poetical forms. Conversely, as I have tried to show, the autonomy enjoyed by the most literary countries is marked chiefly by the depoliticization of literature: the almost complete disappearance of popular or national themes, the appearance of 'pure' writing—texts that, freed from the obligation to help to develop a particular national identity, have no social or political 'function'—and, as an aspect of this, the emergence of formal experimentation, which is to say of forms detached from political purpose and unencumbered by nonliterary conceptions of literature" (Pascale Casanova, *The World Republic of Letters* [Cambridge, MA: Harvard University Press, 2004], 197).

12. The object of my critique here is the oftentimes absorptive taxonomy of transnational modernism. In their inventory of "New Modernist studies," Mao and Walkowitz pose: "Were one seeking a single word to sum up transformations in modernist literary scholarship over the past decade or two, one could do worse than light on *expansion*" (Douglas Mao and Rebecca Walkowitz, "The New Modernist Studies," *PMLA* 123.3 [2008]: 737). But arguably, "absorption" and "recognition through assimilation" are a few words and phrases that might also have been used. The literature of labor is nowhere to be found in their overview of "New Modernist studies." Influential works in subaltern studies are completely bypassed. But furthermore, in their inventory, a classic work of internationalist anticolonial critique, such as Brent Edwards's *The Practice of Diaspora*, can be cited out of context to legitimize a project that it reframes and interrupts in crucial ways. More than an inventory, this is a sleight of hand: it becomes a magic trick with the ability to make criticism disappear—to neutralize nonconformist critical trends through selective citation. Against the neutralizing, absorptive impulses of this particular trajectory of transnational modernism, we might counterpose other works from within the canon of critical modernist studies: Cary Nelson, *Repression and Recovery* (Madison: University of Wisconsin Press, 1989); Fredric Jameson, *A Singular Modernity: Essay on the Ontology of the Present* (London: Verso, 2002); Nicholas Browne, *Utopian Generations: The Political Horizon of Twentieth-Century Literature* (Princeton: Princeton University Press, 2005). Among other more recent works that explicitly address the critical interrelationship between colonial discourse, modernization, and modernism, we might consider Krishnan, *Reading the Global*; Benjamin Conisbee Baer, "Shit Writing: Mulk Raj Anand's *Untouchable*, the Image of Gandhi, and the Progressive Writers' Association," *Modernism/Modernity* 16.3 (2009): 575–595; Kristin Bluemel, *Intermodernism: Literary Culture in Mid-Twentieth-Century Britain* (Edinburgh: Edinburgh University Press, 2009); and Michael Rubenstein, *Public Works: Infrastructure, Irish Modernism, and the Postcolonial* (Notre Dame: University of Notre Dame Press, 2010).

13. Emphasis Eagleton's; Terry Eagleton, *Literary Theory: An Introduction* (Minneapolis: University of Minnesota Press, 1983), 216. In some ways this argument can be

taken, in part, as a reprise of Terry Eagleton's—although neither the critique of the provincialism of world literature models nor a consideration of the international division of labor are his specific objects.

14. Karl Marx, "The Eighteenth Brumaire of Louis Bonaparte," *Surveys from Exile* (London: Penguin, 1992), 150.

15. In a chapter devoted to the work of literary historiographic reconstruction, and titled "The Novelists International," Michael Denning also attempts to connect proletarian writing to currents and currencies of world literature—especially to conventions and notations of magical realism. His focus here is the novel form. However, for him, arguably, the question of American exceptionalism ultimately takes center stage. I return to this point below. See Michael Denning, *Culture in the Age of Three Worlds* (London: Verso, 2004), 51–72.

16. Questions of historicism and agency are, of course, at the heart of E. P. Thompson's argument with Althusser. See Perry Anderson, *Arguments Within English Marxism* (London: Verso, 1980), 16–58.

17. Althusser's critical reading of Gramsci generates "Marxism is not a historicism" in Louis Althusser and Étienne Balibar, *Reading Capital* (New York: Verso, 1997), 119–145. I return to this formulation below.

18. On this score, I also take my bearings from Ellen Rooney's ideas on the politics and ethics of reading. As she puts it, "the heady pursuit of a 'correct' theory of ideology permits a disavowal of the elusiveness of this 'correct' political position, simultaneously affirming and denying political engagement and enabling an evasion of the absolutely unavoidable risk entailed in 'reading,' where reading is recognized as a relation among readers, a productive relation, but one that allows for no theoretical guarantee" (184). See her insightful recasting of Althusser as a theorist of reading, rather than ideology. Ellen Rooney, "Better Read Than Dead: Althusser and the Fetish of Ideology," *Yale French Studies* 88 (1995): 183–200.

19. Perry Anderson confronts the problem in these terms: "It was in the UK and USA, after all—the oldest and most powerful of capitalist states, respectively—that the most testing problems for socialist theory had always been posed, and left perforce unanswered" (Anderson, *In the Tracks of Historical Materialism* [London: Verso, 1983], 19).

20. William Empson, *Some Versions of the Pastoral* (Norfolk: New Directions, 1950), 3.

21. Gayatri Chakravorty Spivak, "From Haverstock Hill Flat to US Classroom, What's Left of Theory?," in *What's Left of Theory?*, ed. Judith Butler, John Guillory, and Kendall Thomas (New York: Routledge, 2000), 7. Here Spivak is invoking (and reframing) Foucault's formulations on "the care of the self."

22. Perry Anderson, "Internationalism: A Breviary," *New Left Review* 14 (March/April 2002): 20.

23. David Harvey, for example, warns against the ways in which this rhetorical salvo might be taken up in the service of a rootless internationalism now dubbed

cosmopolitanism. He revisits the line (in the *Manifesto*) in his compelling call to study the interrelation between geographical knowledges and the so-called cosmopolitanism revivalism: "The workers of the world (whom Marx and Engels erroneously thought of as ideal cosmopolitan subjects because they 'had no country') can still seek to unite and overthrow global bourgeois power, with its distinctive form of cosmopolitanism, though this time they too must be far more mindful of uneven geographical developments (the dialectic between socialist internationalism and geography has never functioned freely, if it has functioned at all)" (Harvey, "Cosmopolitanism and Geographical Evils," *Millennial Capitalism and the Culture of Neoliberalism*, ed. Jean Comaroff and John L. Comaroff [Durham, NC: Duke University Press, 2001], 304).

24. Karl Marx and Frederick Engels, *The Communist Manifesto* (London: Verso, 1998), 58.

25. See for example David Damrosch, *What Is World Literature?* (Princeton: Princeton University Press, 2003); Franco Moretti, "Conjectures on World Literature," *New Left Review* 1 (Jan./Feb. 2000): 54–68; Nicholas Browne, *Utopian Generations* (Princeton: Princeton University Press, 2005). Natalie Melas assesses the relationship between these theorists' visions of world literature and her own genealogy for comparative literature. Melas's specific intervention—postcolonial critique, via Said—is a nuanced defense of theories and methods that none of us can dispense with; see Natalie Melas, *All the Difference in the World: Postcoloniality and the Ends of Comparison* (Stanford: Stanford University Press, 2007).

26. Here a distinction might be drawn between David Damrosch's approach (to world literature) and that of Pascale Casanova. Casanova's main intervention calls our attention to the fact that the political economy of world literature does not correspond to mapping of power hierarchies of global politics (i.e., let's notice that the United States is not, despite its position, the leader in the "world republic of letters"). Still, as we see, her theoretical frame devolves into a selective history of Paris as the center of the global publishing industry. There is more variability in the canon of world literature proposed by David Damrosch, who turns to Goethe and his world historical moment as a frame of reference, rather than a touchstone for validating a specific European model. He would define world literature, first and foremost, as "a mode of circulation and of reading" (5). My own approach, foregrounding working-class literature as world literature, is different from this one in that it follows in the tracks of the discursive reach of world literature opened up by Marx in his later texts on class.

27. Karl Marx, "Critique of the Gotha Program," *The First International and After*, ed. David Fernbach (London: Penguin, 1992), 347.

28. Karl Marx, *Capital*, vol. 3, trans. David Fernbach (London: Penguin, 1981), 1025.

29. See Raymond Williams, *Keywords: A Vocabulary of Culture and Society* (New York: Oxford University Press, 1985), 117–120.

30. Perry Anderson, *In the Tracks of Historical Materialism* (London: Verso, 1983), 81–82.

31. Fredric Jameson, *A Singular Modernity: Essay on the Ontology of the Present* (London: Verso, 2002), 2.

32. Gayatri Chakravorty Spivak, "Translator's Preface," *Imaginary Maps*, xxv.

33. The phrasing is from John Hutnyk, who writes on Sivanadan in "The Dialectic of Here and There: Anthropology 'at Home' and British Asian Communism," *Social Identities* 11.4 (2005): 345–361.

1. COLONIALISM, RACE, AND CLASS

1. Rudyard Kipling, *Kim* (London: Penguin, 1987).

2. Mulk Raj Anand, *Conversations in Bloomsbury* (New Delhi: Oxford University Press, 1981).

3. Mulk Raj Anand, *Coolie* (New Delhi: Penguin, 1993 [1936]). Outside the scope of this intention, made public in *Conversations in Bloomsbury*, in an unpublished manuscript named "Musings on Munoo," Anand discusses conceiving the idea for *Coolie* as a reaction to the praise lavished on *Kim* by Bonamy Dobree, T.S. Eliot, and K. de B. Codrington. See Saros Cowasjee, *Coolie: An Assessment*.

4. Foreword, D. Chaman Lall, *Coolie: The Story of Labour and Capital in India* (Lahore: Oriental Publishing House, 1932). See Shaileshwar Sati Prasad's study of Anand, *The Insulted and the Injured* (Patna: Janaki Prakashan, 1997).

5. See, for example, Sara Suleri, *The Rhetoric of English India* (Chicago: University of Chicago Press, 1992); Ashis Nandy, *Intimate Enemy: Loss and Recovery of Self Under Colonialism* (Delhi: Oxford University Press, 1983); and Gayatri Chakravorty Spivak, "Resident Alien," *Relocating Postcolonialism*, ed. David Theo Goldberg and Ato Quayson (Oxford: Blackwell, 2002).

6. *The Small Hands of Slavery: Bonded Child Labor in India* (New York: Human Rights Watch, 1996).

7. Mulk Raj Anand, *Author to Critic: The Letters of Mulk Raj Anand*, ed. Saros Cowasjee (Calcutta: Writers' Workshop, 1973), 1. I return to this point later in this chapter.

8. This maneuver happens in complicated ways: See, for example, Jessica Berman, "Comparative Colonialisms: Joyce, Anand, and the Question of Engagement," *Modernism/Modernity* 13.3 (2006): 465–485. In her reading of *Coolie*, Berman writes of the "intertextual web" that connects James Joyce and Anand. But she stages the context for her argument in terms of Anand modeling himself after Joyce. Ultimately, her article becomes focused on Joyce, with an inventory of Anand's debts to modernism and the bildungsroman form tacked on. "To put it bluntly, part of what Anand is finding in Joyce, and not in Iqbal (despite the fact that Iqbal was to become [a] crucial political figure during the struggle for independence), is engagement with the self within the context of a colonial reality rather than the metaphysical world" (468). By contrast, Benjamin Conisbee Baer's recent work on colonialism and

modernism restores Anand to the historical and theoretical debates of the 1930s. Baer's work shares a focus with my own. By way of historicizing Anand's connections with the Indian Progressive Writers' Associations, he reads Anand's *Untouchable* as a representation of the subaltern. See Benjamin Conisbee Baer, "Shit Writing: Mulk Raj Anand's *Untouchable*, the Image of Gandhi, and the Progressive Writers' Association," *Modernism/Modernity* 16.3 (2009): 575–595. Kristin Blumel also has suggested an alternative to the ideological blind spots of transnational modernism—"intermodernism." Anand figures in this discourse; see Kristin Blumen, *Intermodernism: Literary Culture in Mid-Twentieth-Century Britain* (Edinburgh: Edinburgh University Press, 2009).

9. Nelson, *Repression and Recovery*, 3.

10. Dietmar Rothermund, *The Global Impact of the Great Depression, 1929–1939* (New York: Routledge, 1996).

11. See also Rothermund's *India in the Great Depression, 1929–1939* (New Delhi: Manohar, 1992), which might be supplemented by a close reading of Marx on "counteracting factors" in volume 3 of *Capital*, as well as select texts on value.

12. While I admire the meticulous scholarship and instructive theorizing of Saskia Sassen, I have often wondered at this insistent focus on the global city as the most "strategic site" in the global economy. I do not agree with the logic of "Much has been published about export processing zones, and they entail types of activity less likely to be located in cities than finance and services; hence we will not examine them in detail" (Saskia Sassen, *Cities in a World Economy* [Thousand Oaks: Pine Forge Press, 1994], 9). Of course there is a difference between 1930s global history and the history of economic globalization (the term "globalization" properly belongs to the post-1930s era of GATT, the General Agreement on Tariffs and Trade). Yet I maintain that a work such as Rothermund's *The Global Impact of the Great Depression* may contribute to an understanding of the blind spots in narratives of economic globalization. Other efforts in the same direction include Sassen's own "Toward a Feminist Analytics of the Global Economy" (first published in the *Indiana Journal of Legal Studies* 4 [1996]). See also Arturo Escobar's "Power and Visibility: Tales of Peasants, Women, and the Environment," in his *Encountering Development: The Making and Unmaking of the Third World* (Princeton: Princeton University Press, 1995), 154–211.

13. According to Saros Cowasjee, "Anand was at this time (1938) a member of the Indian Congress Party and, later, for a while, of the British Labour Party." Over the course of the decade Anand worked for the Kisan Sabha (Farmers Union) in India and also played an active part in organizing the Second All-India Progressive Writers' Conference in Calcutta. See Saros Cowasjee, *So Many Freedoms* (New Delhi: Oxford University Press, 1977), 21, 25.

14. On the "art and science of mensuration" see the education of Kim: "A boy who had passed his examination in these branches—for which, by the way there were no cram books—could, by merely marching over a country with a compass and a level and a straight eye, carry away a picture of that country which might be sold for large

sums in coined silver. . . . Here was a new craft that a man could tuck away in this head and by the look of the large wide world unfolding itself before him, it seemed that the more a man knew the better for him" (*Kim* 211).

15. The first chapter in *So Many Freedoms* deals with the problem briefly; Cowasjee draws up a list of famous names (Anand's circle of friends from the Pink Decade). But he seems to rush over the reasons Anand has been overlooked within literary historiographies of the 1930s. He does not elaborate on the consequences of Anand's staunch commitment to the Communist Party and "revolutionary defeatism" in the face of criticism from friends in the British Left.

16. Once again, Kristin Blumel's work *Intermodernism* is a notable exception.

17. Which he cofounded with Sajjad Zaheer.

18. Mulk Raj Anand, *Apology for Heroism: A Brief Autobiography of Ideas* (New Delhi: Arnold-Heinemann, 1975).

19. The July 1944 conference of forty-four financial ministers at Bretton Woods, NH, provided the opportunity to create an international banking system. It also chartered the foundation of "twin sisters," the IMF and IBRD. Some would consider this conference to mark the birth pangs of the development project. See Philip McMichael, *Democracy and Social Change* (Thousand Oaks: Pine Forge Press, 1996).

20. On the limitations of posing magical realism as the defining instance of Third World fiction see "Marginality in the Teaching Machine," in Gayatri Chakravorty Spivak, *Outside in the Teaching Machine* (New York: Routledge, 1993), 57–59.

21. This is Frantz Fanon's word from *Wretched of the Earth* (New York: Grove Press, 1968), 54.

22. Cowasjee (in a rather loose "paraphrasing" of an unpublished article by Anand), *So Many Freedoms*, 60.

23. The last two comments are made by Gustav Klaus in an otherwise attentive reading of Anand's book in his survey titled *The Literature of Labour* (New York: St. Martin's, 1985), 115, 124. See also D. Riemenschnieder's criticism that by 1938 "the all too low status of his former heroes was indeed a (technical) handicap," quoted in Margaret Berry's study *Mulk Raj Anand: The Man and the Novelist* (Amsterdam: Oriental Press, 1971), 83. Writing of Anand's *Untouchable*, Josna Rege reads the protagonist's inability to act as a by-product of the irresolution of nationalist discourse: "Like many Indian novels of its time, *Untouchable* is driven by a desire to identify with the poor of India, to rouse them to action, and to effect a social transformation in the process. Yet the nationalist discourse itself seems to dictate a strangely indirect, incomplete, circular ambit, in which action is desired and undertaken, but eventually obstructed, renounced, or deferred" (Rege, *Colonial Karma* [New York: Palgrave Macmillan, 2004], 66). I would only qualify that such a nationalist framing overlooks the conditions and constraints of class politics.

24. See Gayatri Chakravorty Spivak, *In Other Worlds: Essays in Cultural Politics*, 255.

25. In an instructive chapter in *Outside the Fold*, Gauri Viswanathan has called to our attention that in *Untouchable*, Anand conveniently leaves out any discussion of Ambedkar's contributions to Dalit politics. She makes the case that "the privileging of Gandhi as an emblem of nonpartisan feeling has, as its inverse, the demonization of Ambedkar as a purveyor of sectarian politics." In her reading of *Untouchable*, she notes that Anand makes no mention of Ambedkar at all: "Instead, the novel celebrates Gandhi as the savior of the untouchables" (220). In response to this critique of Anand I can only say that (1) I would read the episode of Gandhi as God via Marx's discussion of Bonaparte in "The Eighteenth Brumaire of Louis Bonaparte" (in his *Surveys from Exile: Political Writings*, vol. 2 [New York: Penguin, 1992]); and (2) *Coolie* is a categorically different and deliberate intervention into the politics of "class—not caste." But finally I would have to concede that this project—mine: that of a metropolitan feminist—cannot be adequately responsible to the "Dalit movement" (at this point). See Gauri Viswanathan, *Outside the Fold: Conversion, Modernity, and Belief* (Princeton: Princeton University Press, 1998).

26. See FOIL, "Those That Be in Bondage: Child Labor and IMF Strategy in India." As an example of an intervention into the question of child labor that is both outside and inside the teaching machine, see Spivak's risky concluding chapter to her *A Critique of Postcolonial Reason* (Cambridge, MA: Harvard University Press, 1999), 312–421.

27. Ellen Rooney, "Form and Contentment," *Modern Language Quarterly* 61.1 (2000): 17–40.

28. I am referring, of course, to the fact that Marx's writings on class remain unfinished.

29. Gayatri Chakravorty Spivak, "Subaltern Studies: Deconstructing Historiography," in *Selected Subaltern Studies*, ed. Ranajit Guha and Gayatri Chakravorty Spivak (New York: Oxford University Press, 1988), 16.

30. Why doesn't Anand choose to "document" these successes? Uncomplicated questions such as these are of course not useful with regard to a *literary* text, but I will refer here to Dilip Simeon's argument in *The Politics of Labour Under Late Colonialism* (New Delhi: Manohar, 1995), 341. Regarding "privileged participants in the drama of class struggle," he brings up the point that for certain nationalist literati, TISCO indexed a "Parsi industry."

31. We might say that inasmuch as this "picaresque" novel, composed to the broken rhythms of erratic coolie work, is about anything, it foregrounds the story of how some stories do not get written.

32. See Marx, "The Eighteenth Brumaire of Louis Bonaparte," 239. See also n. 42 below re the term "coolie."

33. Dipesh Chakrabarty, *Rethinking Working-Class History: Bengal, 1890–1940* (Princeton: Princeton University Press, 1989), 141.

34. Vinay Bahl, *The Making of the Indian Working Class: A Case of the Tata Iron and Steel Company, 1880–1946* (New Delhi: Sage, 1995). Her introduction is a serious,

impassioned—but in places flawed—critique of Chakrabarty's argument. See for instance comments such as these: "Chakrabarty is sacrificing the politics of liberation by denying the existence of capitalism's systematic coercion. This denial also logically removes the possibility of raising any kind of resistance to capitalism" and "[by] basing his approach on cultural particularism, Chakrabarty takes away the hope of emancipation from the working class struggle." See also her point that "these theories [newly emerging critiques of Eurocentrism in Marxism], which belong to Postmodernists and Subalternists, have no political or theoretical consequences to the existing system. However, they were able to retain the image of being a critique of the West" (21).

35. Katherine Mayo is the American writer who, in collusion with the British propaganda machine, chronicled the horrors of socially sanctioned "child abuse" and casteism in her sensationalist 1927 tract titled *Mother India*. The "proper" subject of Mayo's book is, of course, the violated girl child/child wife. Her chapter titled "Psychological Glimpses Through the Economic Lens" makes for extremely interesting reading. See Katherine Mayo, *Mother India* (London: Jonathan Cape, 1930). Also, here I employ "irony" in the sense of its minimal dictionary definition: "an ill-timed or perverse arrival of an event or circumstance that is in itself desirable."

36. See E.M. Forster, *Aspects of the Novel* (New York: Harcourt, Brace, and Co., 1927). He also proposes that the approximate center often "lies in a discussion about the art of the novel." I might add to this, drawing upon Mieke Bal's *Narratology,* that the center here is where the "embedded story" contains a suggestion as to how the text should be read. See Mieke Bal, *Narratology* (Toronto: Toronto University Press, 1985), 147.

37. See n. 13.

38. From the unpublished article, "Musings on Munoo." This article reveals that Anand's novel is the bio-graph of the friend in question, who worked in a pickle factory (as does Munoo, at one point). See also n. 3. above.

39. In an account of a conversation between Gandhi and himself, Anand recalls being asked, "Why write a novel? Why not a tract on untouchability . . . the straight book is truthful and you can reform people by saying things frankly." To which Anand replied, "Though I do want to help people, I believe in posing the question rather than answering it" (quoted in Cowasjee, *So Many Freedoms*, 42). We cannot read this statement as an easy dismissal of social responsibility when we consider Anand's continuing work as an activist and cultural worker in post-Independence India. Rather, what strikes me here is Anand's figuration of the novel form as a rhetorical question.

40. Mieke Bal's point about "focalization" is helpful to keep in mind: as she puts it, most theories of narration "do not make an explicit distinction between, on the one hand, the vision through which the elements are presented and, on the other, the identity of the voice that is verbalizing that vision. To put it more simply, they do not make a distinction between *those* who see and *those* who speak" (*Narratology*, 100–101).

41. The quotation continues: "[and] not [simply] when we have, on the one hand, a literal meaning and on the other hand, a figural meaning, but when it is impossible to decide which of the two meanings (that can be entirely incompatible) prevails" (Paul de Man, *Allegories of Reading* [New Haven: Yale University Press, 1979], 9–10).

42. With regard to the concept of "coolie" as the part-subject of labor, consider the etymology of the Tamil word *Kuli*—the word simply for "payment" or "wage." See E. Valentine Daniel, "Conclusion: The Making of a Coolie," *Journal of Peasant Studies* 19.3–4 (April/July 1992). Significantly, we must also note that there is some dispute about whether the term originated as the name of an aboriginal tribe of Gujerat.

43. Ellen Rooney, "Form and Contentment" (212).

44. In terms of the layout of the letter form, it is striking that the writer includes these overstated descriptions of "Mr. Little" in alignment with the set margins.

45. I use "supplement" to mean both "to supply a gap" and "to add an excess." Here and in the following section the reference is to "The Exorbitant. Question of Method," in Jacques Derrida, *Of Grammatology*, trans. Gayatri Chakravorty Spivak (Baltimore: Johns Hopkins University Press, 1976), 157–164.

46. Shaileshwar Sati Prasad proposes that Anand draws upon Lall for his book *Two Leaves and a Bud* as well as for *Coolie*; see *The Insulted and the Injured*.

47. Bal, *Narratology*, 71.

48. Roland Barthes, "The Death of the Author," in his *Image/Music/Text* (New York: Hill and Wang, 1977), 148.

2. POSTCOLONIAL SRI LANKA AND "BLACK STRUGGLES FOR SOCIALISM"

1. On the one hand, Michael Hardt and Antonio Negri declare *proletarian* internationalism in its "paradoxical and powerful" incarnation to be dead; see *Empire* (Cambridge, MA: Harvard University Press, 2000), 49–52. On the other hand, how to think the postcolonial/immigrant subject is foreclosed within a certain ideological cathexis of a certain school of postcolonial critique—although admittedly this bracketing off is performed in the scrupulously visible political interest of cautioning *some* who self-interestedly confuse elite and nonelite patterns of migration under the monolithizing, catchall rubric of "diaspora studies." See for example Spivak's warning: "Increasingly and metaleptically, transnationality is becoming the name of the increased migrancy of labor. To substitute this name for the change from multinational capital in the economic restructuring of the (developed/developing) globe—to re-code a change in the determination of capital as a cultural change—is a scary symptom of Cultural Studies, especially Feminist Cultural Studies" ("Diasporas Old and New: Women in the Transnational World," *Textual Practice* 10.2 [1996]: 245).

2. Ambalavaner Sivanandan, *Communities of Resistance: Writings on Black Struggles for Socialism* (London: Verso, 1990), 199–250.

3. Stuart Hall, "When Was 'The Post-colonial'? Thinking at the Limit," in *The Post-Colonial Question*, ed. Iain Chambers and Lidia Curti (London: Routledge, 1996), 242.

4. Of course, here, I am thinking of Robert Young's *Postcolonialism: An Historical Introduction* (Oxford: Blackwell, 2001).

5. See Dipesh Chakrabarty, *Provincializing Europe: Postcolonial Thought and Historical Difference* (Princeton: Princeton University Press, 2000).

6. My subheading is a pointed reordering of the key terms comprising the title of one of the hallmark anthologies on the narrative logic of race as a social formation—*"Race," Writing, and Difference*, ed. Henry Louis Gates Jr.

7. In his recent book *Conscripts of Modernity: The Tragedy of Colonial Enlightenment*, David Scott makes a case for the study of the literary genre of tragedy (versus romance) as a mode of historical emplotment for thinking anticolonial discourse in particular.

8. See the epigraph to this chapter.

9. JVP (Janatha Vimukthi Peramuna) or People's Liberation Front (in English). While at a certain juncture in Sri Lankan history the JVP might have been appropriately described as a Marxist party (in fact, this still remains the designation that it appropriates unto itself), it is now more accurately described as "nationalist socialist," if not Sinhala nationalist. Also see n. 25 in chapter 3.

10. This short story appears in *Where the Dance Is* (London: Arcadia Books, 2000), 42–64.

11. See for example this passage from Adorno's *Minima Moralia*: "Dialectical thought is an attempt to break through the coercion of logic by its own means. But since it must use these means, it is at every moment in danger of itself acquiring a coercive character: the ruse of reason would like to hold sway over the dialectic too." [*He goes on, in this same passage, to arrive at a theory of the remainder, invoking the work of Walter Benjamin*]: "Stringency and totality, the bourgeois intellectual ideals of necessity and generality, do indeed circumscribe the formula of history, but for just this reason the constitution of society finds its precipitate in those great, immovable, lordly concepts against which dialectical criticism and practice are directed. If Benjamin said that history had hitherto been written from the standpoint of the victor, and needed to be written from that of the vanquished, we might add that knowledge must indeed present the fatally rectilinear succession of victory and defeat, but should also address itself to those things which were not embraced by this dynamic, which fell by the wayside—what might be called the waste products and blind spots that have escaped the dialectic" (151).

In regard to a particular conceptualization of "rewriting as dialectical thought," I also acknowledge a debt to a formulation of Brent Hayes Edwards. In a lecture delivered in commemoration of the centennial of the publication of W.E.B. Du Bois's *The Souls of Black Folk*, Edwards elaborates an interesting reading of the cultural politics of Du Bois's postscripts and "afterthoughts" (Brent Edwards, "Late Romance," John

Hope Franklin Center, Duke University, Durham, NC, 12 November 2003). In general, the comparisons and contrasts between Sivanandan's and Du Bois's cultural politics and literary internationalism bear much further scrutiny.

12. Again we notice here that Sivanandan's invocation of "double consciousness" is not in keeping with Du Bois's sense of the term—the burden (and gift) of being able to see oneself through the eyes of others. In chapter 4 (on the Botswanan/South African refugee writer Bessie Head) I return to debates surrounding the interpretation of Du Bois's crucial concept.

13. Suvendrini Perera touches upon this point implicitly in the frame to her reflections on Sivanandan's novel. See "Unmaking the Present, Remaking Memory: Sri Lankan Stories and a Politics of Coexistence," *A World to Win: Essays in Honor of A. Sivanandan, Race and Class* 41.1/2 (July–Dec. 1999): 189–197.

14. See Gayatri Chakravorty Spivak, "Diasporas Old and New: Women in the Transnational World," *Textual Practice* 10.2 (1996): 245–269.

15. Sithaperam Nadesan, *A History of the Up-Country Tamil People* (Hatton: Nandalala, 1993), 12–13.

16. In his essay titled "Beyond Human Rights," Agamben seems to suggest that we refigure the cultural politics of human rights from the standpoint of the refugee—the paradigmatic figure of our times, as nation-states start to dissolve. As he puts it, "The refugee should be considered for what it is, namely, nothing less than a limit-concept that at once brings a radical crisis to the principles of the nation-state and clears the way for a renewal of categories that can no longer be delayed" (Giorgio Agamben, *Means Without End* [Minneapolis: University of Minnesota Press, 2000], 22–23).

17. See David Scott's "Dehistoricizing History" in *Unmaking the Nation*, ed. Pradeep Jeganathan and Qadri Ismail. This chapter on debates in Sri Lankan historiography is reprinted in his *Refashioning Futures: Criticism After Postcoloniality*.

18. The immigrant Tamils also aroused the anxiety of the national socialist JVP. During the 1970s, they proposed the "fifth column" thesis as the party line—a conspiracy theory that maintains that India was an imperial power and that "estate Tamils" (and all Tamils, for that matter) constituted a "fifth column in the service of Indian expansionism."

19. In 1834, following slave revolts in the West Indies, Britain proclaimed the abolition of slavery in its territories but continued to mine India for cheap labor. And thus imperial capitalists turned to South India to supply "the lack" of available labor in colonial Ceylon among other colonies.

20. See Ismail, *Abiding by Sri Lanka: On Peace, Place, and Postcoloniality* (Minneapolis: University of Minnesota Press, 2005), 186.

21. Those familiar with Sinhala nationalist mythology will immediately register a rethinking of the Vijaya myth.

22. Memory plays tricks on the narrator when it comes to the remembered object of life in Jaffna. Counter to the characteristic narrative logic of the novel—quite early

on we are alerted to its broken rhythm—and to verifiable historical facts, he remembers Jaffna in all its specificity as if he had "lived there all [his] life." Rajan observes, "Other memories of my school days seem so distinct, clear, separate: there are spaces between them which I cannot quite fill. But my memories of Sandilipay run on to each other, unreckoning of the time that separated my visits there, as though they had been edited for continuity. And it is not as if I had lived there all my life" (143). The narrator's timeless Jaffna is marshaled as a countermemory against competing versions of militant nationalisms and territorial claims. En route to Jaffna on the train, the narrator recalls his father's gift for making a cramped space seem bigger. In this vision of the tangled beauty of confinement, Sivanandan gives us one of the most powerful, ethical meditations of the novel: "Everything he did in that small rectangle of a compartment was so assured, deft and certain. He moved in the confines of that cubicle as though it were a house: he gave it space and breadth and dimension. It would not have surprised me one bit if a tree had sprung in our midst, or a stream or mountain, so much space there was. Perhaps space was a relationship: we had so much room because we had room for each other, and a way of belonging, perhaps to ourselves and to others" (138). The loss of Jaffna or some romantic, revisionist nostalgia for prewar rural village life and simpler, gentler times is not the defining loss of the narrative. Rather, the loss that is mourned over and over again is the death of socialist ideals, and an intangible code of ethics, and the erasure of working-class biography.

23. The reference is, of course, to Marx's "Eighteenth Brumaire of Louis Bonaparte." See *Surveys from Exile*, 2:147.

24. I am grateful to Ahilan Kadirgamar for vetting and verifying Sivanandan's English translation of this verse.

25. See Sonali Perera, "(Where) Language Acts in *When Memory Dies*," *Nethra* 4.3/4 (April–Sept. 2000): 101–107.

26. See Qadri Ismail, "Damn Good Story," *Himal* 12.8 (Aug. 1999): 22.

27. "The logic of the saga-form dictates the unsatisfying, and uncharacteristic, conclusion that our lives typically end in a tragedy that must be content with knowing tragedy's perennial nature," observes Timothy Brennan in his appraisal of *When Memory Dies*; Brennan, "Poetry and Polemic," *Race and Class* 41.1/2 (July–Dec. 1999): 23–34.

28. Vasuki Nesiah, "Monumental History and the Politics of Memory: Public Space and the Jaffna Public Library," *Lines Magazine*. http://www.lines-magazine.org/Art_Feb03/editorial_vasuki.htm (accessed Sept. 1, 2003).

3. GENDER, GENRE, AND GLOBALIZATION

1. I am referring here to Spivak's concept of "ethical singularity." Beyond codings of crisis and periods of short-term agitation, women's and feminist texts sometimes give

us alternative models for thinking working-class literature and socialist ethics. They attend to what Spivak has termed the "secret encounter" in the hidden interstices of history-making events; she defines this encounter as something that can take place only in the everyday, in the effortful striving between equals—not historian and subaltern—who are nevertheless aware that always, even within this attempt at ethical responding, some part of the message *wished to be communicated* is lost. She writes of "the slow effort of ethical responding" that is defined by other time frames than the history of revolutions. See "Translator's Preface," Mahasweta Devi, *Imaginary Maps*, trans. Spivak (New York: Routledge, 1995), xxv.

2. We might also consider the "Postface to the Second Edition of Capital," where Marx theorizes "all that is present and moving," as he rethinks the Hegelian dialectic.

3. Upon this score also see Perry Anderson, *In the Tracks of Historical Materialism* (Chicago: University of Chicago Press, 1984) and *Considerations on Western Marxism* (London: Verso, 1979).

4. Michael Denning, *The Cultural Front* (New York: Verso), 202. For the concept of formations versus institutions see Raymond Williams, *Marxism and Literature* (New York: Oxford, 1977), 115–120.

5. E. P. Thompson, *The Making of the English Working Class* (New York: Vintage, 1963), 77–101.

6. Dipesh Chakrabarty, *Rethinking Working-Class History: Bengal, 1890–1940* (Princeton: Princeton University Press, 1989).

7. This is Swasti Mitter's term. See the preface and chapter 1 of Swasti Mitter, *Common Fate, Common Bond: Women in the Global Economy* (London: Pluto, 1986), 1–24.

8. See Samir Amin, *Unequal Development* (New York: Monthly Review Press, 1976), 203–214 on the origins of extraversion. Some might say that globalization has made Amin and Mitter merely historical. On the contrary, the structures of the international division of labor that they describe persist today, even in the interstices of global finance capital.

9. We see that here the lines are opposed. There is no easy way of crossing this aporia, but difficult as it is, this structural opposition must be acknowledged.

10. Gayatri Chakravorty Spivak, *A Critique of Postcolonial Reason* (Cambridge, MA: Harvard University Press, 1999), 75.

11. While there are moments in her reading that suggest productive contradictions, Barbara Foley still classifies *Yonnondio* under the heading of a "proletarian bildungsroman," bypassing the fact that it is actually not quite a book—that the author publishes it as an uncompleted girl-child's coming of age story. I agree with Constance Coiner, on the other hand, who observes that "*Yonnondio*'s heteroglossia and the novel's four narrators represent an attempt to move beyond an individual point of view toward more collective forms" (181). To her, *Yonnondio* prefigures a postindividualistic form for novelistic discourse. See Barbara Foley, *Radical Representations* (Durham, NC: Duke University Press, 1993), 321–361. It should be noted that she quotes Coiner as a

counterexample to her own reading. See also Constance Coiner, *Better Red* (New York: Oxford University Press, 1995).

12. In "Scattered Speculations on the Question of Culture Studies," Spivak wonders, "Yet is there something particularly disqualifying about 'working-class' becoming a canonical descriptive rather than an oppositional transformative? [*She observes that*] certainly the basic argument of Jonathan Rée's *Proletarian Philosophers* would seem to suggest so" (*Outside in the Teaching Machine* 273).

13. Tillie Olsen, *Yonnondio: From the Thirties* (New York: Delta, 1974). A brief summary follows. *Yonnondio* tracks the various dislocations of the working-class Holbrook family as they move from region to region in search of work. They start out in a small mining town in Wyoming, move to a farm in South Dakota, and then finally end up living and working among the packing houses of an (unnamed) city. The narrative, we notice, shifts in focalization from the girl-child/subject of the story, Mazie, to the mother, Anna, to—on occasion—the father, Jim. A crucial subplot of the story involves the breakdown and recovery of the working-class mother. The staging of her "recovery" complicates the text in productive ways.

14. See Raymond Williams's chapter on "Structures of Feeling" in *Marxism*, 128.

15. V. N. Vološinov, *Marxism and the Philosophy of Language* (Cambridge, MA: Harvard University Press, 1973), 140.

16. Tillie Olsen, *Tell Me a Riddle* (New York: Delta, 1956), 1–12, 63–116.

17. In August 2001 a militant nationalist organization naming itself the Sinhala Commission recommended to the ruling government that as a means of righting British colonial wrongs, it take measures to retroactively deny citizenship to the descendents of Indian-origin Tamil workers, imported as indentured labor to serve on the coffee and tea plantations of the colonial period—a scandalous use of the epistemology of postcolonialism in the service of Sinhala nationalism.

18. Certainly the framing of such questions of subjectivity and representation is not without complications. Perhaps it also remains to be asked whose "interest" staking a claim for such a subject—one that figures "unity-in-dispersal"—serves? If Spivak's admonition addressed to French poststructuralist thinkers in "Can the Subaltern Speak?" was not to monolithize the working class, even in the avowed interest of theorizing a coalitional politics, it is a caution that must be heeded by Marxist-feminist literary critics even as they reach to articulate the terms of a feminist class politics across the new international division of labor, in the shadow of economisms like comparative advantage—or what has been called the NGOization of feminism.

19. Eagleton describes a concept of (British) working-class writing that portends the interrogation of "ruling definitions of literature" in the concluding section of *Literary Theory*: "The fourth and final area is that of the strongly emergent movement of working-class writing. Silenced for generations, taught to regard literature as a coterie activity beyond their grasp, working people over the past decade in Britain have been

actively organizing to find their own literary styles and voices. The worker-writers' movement is almost unknown to academia, and has not been exactly encouraged by the cultural organs of the state; but is one sign of a significant break from the dominant relations of literary production. Community and cooperative publishing enterprises are associated projects, concerned not simply with a literature wedded to alternative social values, but with one which challenges and changes the existing social relations between writers, publishers, readers, and other literary workers. It is because such ventures interrogate the ruling *definitions* of literature that they cannot so easily be incorporated by a literary institution quite happy to welcome *Sons and Lovers*, and even, from time to time, Robert Tressel" (216). I am grateful to Peter Hitchcock for calling this passage to my attention.

20. This again underscores the fact that *Dabindu* represents a heterogeneous, dynamic collectivity, rather than a synchronous collective class subject. I am indebted to Kumudini Samuel for drawing my attention to the point that the changing volunteer editors of the periodical (who are not identified or credited within the later editions) are affiliated with a range of different feminist and human rights groups in Sri Lanka. I am also grateful to her for her insights into the unwritten history of ideological battles and left-party politics (such as those of the RMP/Revolutionary Marxist Party) associated with the convening of the initial organizational group. I am also indebted to Kumari Jayawardena, Fara Haniffa, Sepali Kottegoda, and Ranjith Perera for energizing conversations—especially for their responses to a version of this paper discussed at the Social Scientists' Association, Colombo, Sri Lanka, on 16 June 2005.

21. See also Rosa's "Strategies of Organisation and Resistance: Women Workers in Sri Lankan Free Trade Zones" in "Capital & Class," 27–35.

22. It is a matter of record that some of *Dabindu*'s worker education projects were funded by the Canadian International Development Agency (CIDA) during the 1998–2000 period. However, I find it particularly interesting to note that commemorative histories and "self-representations" of *Dabindu* tend to omit the specific details of the group's transformation into an NGO; consider, for example, H. I. Samanmalie's "The Birth of *Dabindu*" (more on this presently). For now I wonder if we can read this omission symptomatically. Many theorists of globalization have commented on the structural limitations of the "NGOization of feminism." Others have celebrated global NGO culture as the rise of international civil society. However, bracketing the polarizing debates for a moment, we do well to bear in mind the complex prehistories of different NGOs such as *Dabindu*. We might question, for example, what brought these groups together before they became NGOs. What existing structures are NGOs built upon? For more commentary on NGOs and left politics see Deborah Mindry's "Non-governmental Organizations, 'Grassroots,' and the Politics of Virtue." Michael Hardt and Antonio Negri share a slightly different critical viewpoint, even as they characterize NGOs as Empire's "instruments of moral intervention" (35–38). By contrast, for an illuminating reading of the categorical demonizing of NGOs—especially as this stance

relates to the contemporary political scene in Sri Lanka—see Kumari Jayawardena's "The NGO Bogey" published in *Pravada* (n.d.).

23. "Motherland is in the tiger's mouth. Wake up, all ye Sinhalese!"

24. The direct translation would be "(drops of) sweat." For a brief history of the founding of *Dabindu* refer to the sixteenth commemorative issue of the paper. H. I Samanmalie, "The Birth of *Dabindu*," *Dabindu* 16.1 (Sept. 2000): 2–3. All translations from the Sinhala are my own, but I am extremely grateful to Professor Victor Hapuarachchi, formerly of Colombo and Kelaniya universities, for taking the time to review my work.

25. The JVP (Janatha Vimukthi Peramuna; in English, "People's Liberation Front") needs to be distinguished from the Trotskyite old left parties in Sri Lanka. The JVP, it has been argued, once was the voice of the Sinhala-educated unemployed. It is now, since the 1970s insurgency, perhaps better defined as a pseudo-Marxist party in the service of Sinhala nationalism. It continues to be routinely and *incorrectly* described as "Marxist" in newspapers. For a more nuanced reading of this complex phenomenon (which cannot possibly be contained within a footnote), see the chapter on "The JVP and the Ethnic Question" in Kumari Jayawardena's *Ethnic and Class Conflict in Sri Lanka*. For a general historical overview of Sri Lankan Marxist parties, see also Robert Kearney's "The Marxist Parties of Ceylon," in *Radical Politics in South Asia*, ed. Paul R. Brass and Marcus F. Franda (Cambridge, MA: MIT Press, 1973), 401–439.

26. Actually, the direct translation of this title would be "Women's Creative Production/Making." It is worthwhile pointing this out, taking into consideration also the general project of feminism within which these worker-activists were engaged. For the native speaker, it is impossible also, not to hear the phrasing "building of women" in "stri nirmana." I am grateful to Gayatri Chakravorty Spivak for always listening with "a translator's ear for difference." It should also be noted here that the *Stri nirmana* booklet is the collaborative effort of certain *Dabindu* writers and feminist activists of the Women's Education and Research Center in Kandana.

27. Organizing Committee, "Preface," *Stri nirmana* (Ja Ela: Dabindu Collective, 1988).

28. Anonymous, "Apatada nidahasak natha," *Dabindu* 13.6 (Feb. 1998): 1.

29. See "Mulu bara janathava matha" (The entire weight lies upon the people), *Dabindu* 13.3 (Nov. 1997): 1. A pinstripe-suited, seven-headed G7 monster rides upon the shoulders of the World Bank—personified as riding the "common man"—while sticking a sharp stick (labeled in English "condition-alities") into his rear end. The man is shown sweating in his attempt to grab the money bag (labeled $) that the WB dangles just out of his reach. (It seems particularly interesting that here *Dabindu* represents "The People" in neocolonialism in terms of a sarong-clad man. See also Anonymous, "The Question of Child-Workers in Bangladesh," *Dabindu* 13.3 (Nov. 1997): 2, and 8; and Anonymous, "Bangladeshi Women's Rights," *Dabindu* 12.10 (July 1997): 2.

30. Sandya Hewamanne and James Brow, "If They Allow Us We Will Fight," *Pravada* 6.11 (2001): 22.

31. See, for instance, Deepika Thrima Vitana, "Chintanaya nidahas nam" (Thinking freedom), *Dabindu* (June 1994): 4; Charuni Gamage, "Nonimi ginna" (The unstoppable fire), *Dabindu* 10.12 (March 1994): 6; Deniyaye Arosha, "Mavu kusin nova mihi kusin SiriLaka upan viru daruvane . . ." (O heroic children born not of mother's womb, but of the earth of Mother Lanka . . .), *Dabindu* (April/May 1998): 6; D. W. Vijayalatha, "Vathu kamkaru striya" (The tea plantation worker-woman), Swarna P. Galappaththi, "Vathu kamkaru striya" (The tea plantation worker-woman), *Stri nirmana* (Ja Ela: Dabindu Collective, 1988), 27, 37; A. C. Perera, "Padada pathum" (Vagabond wishes), *Dabindu* (June 1994): 5; S. Udayalata Menike, "Mai Dinaya" (May Day), *Dabindu* (April 2000): 6.

32. The word "garment" here is shorthand for "garment industry." It would properly be *aghalum karmanthaya*, but here the colloquial term is rendered from English into phonetic Sinhala. It is important to consider the "universality" of this lexicalization across South and Southeast Asia, where "garment" always "means" garment industry or garment factory, lexicalized into the mother tongue.

33. These ellipses occur in the poem.

34. See the proposal advocating decentralization and devolution. Sri Lankan Branch, Committee for Democracy and Justice in Sri Lanka, "Let's Defeat the Call for War and Push for a Parliamentary Solution," *Dabindu* (Sept./Oct. 1995): 3.

35. Deepika Thrima Vitana, "Chintanaya nidahas nam" (Unthinking freedom), *Dabindu* (June 1994): 4.

36. The direct translation would actually involve a subjunctive mood construction: "if . . . were": "If there were freedom of the act-of-thinking."

37. Although in Olsen's case the narrative also contains a critique of the ameliorative structures of civil society. Consider for example the episode in which Emily is sent to the convalescent home.

38. K. G. Jayasundera Manike's "Jivithaya" (Life) is also quoted in its entirety in Rosa's "The Conditions and Organisational Activities of Women in Free Trade Zones: Malaysia, Phillipines, and Sri Lanka, 1970–1990," as well as in *A Review of Free Trade Zones in Sri Lanka*, ed. Sunila Abeyesekera, trans. Punyani Gunaratne (Ja Ela: Dabindu Collective, 1997).

39. Davies, Tony. "Unfinished Business: Realism and Working-Class Writing," in *The British Working-Class Novel in the Twentieth Century*, ed. Jeremy Hawthorne (London: Edward Arnold, 1984), 125.

40. I am thinking here of a piece of cultural anthropology where the author, through a painstaking analysis of the language of presidential speeches, reports, and interviews with factory bosses, finds the free-trade-zone women workers to be unwittingly complicit with a nationalist development agenda. It is over and against the ideological construction of "woman" in these official texts of historiography that I attempt to read the literature of these factory workers in an attempt to approach how woman as subject for history is imagined. See Caitrin Lynch's "The 'Good Girls'

of Sri Lankan Modernity: Moral Orders of Nationalism and Capitalism," *Identities* 6.1 (1999): 55–89.

41. Somalatha, "Kalapayen vathukarayata" (From zone to plantation), *Dabindu* 13.1 (Sept. 1997): 8–9.

42. This phrasing, of course, calls to mind Fredric Jameson's *Postmodernism; or, The Cultural Logic of Late Capitalism*. I would argue that such a systematization (of "dominant" cultural logic) is only possible by bracketing other residual aesthetic practices and ideologies of form such as those discussed here. Throughout it has been my objective to show that the calculus changes if we consider heterogeneous examples of working-class literature from across the gendered international division of labor. Also see Spivak's crucial last chapter on "Culture" in *A Critique of Postcolonial Reason* (312–421).

43. It is true that Hardt and Negri do not use the term "proletarian" as a contemporary descriptor of working-class relations in the new international division of labor. As they put it, "the proletariat is not what it used to be, but that does not mean it has vanished. It means, rather, that we are faced once again with the analytical task of understanding the new composition of the proletariat as a class" (*Empire*, 52). And yet, they don't consider the feminization of labor or the history of social movements of the global South as having an impact on their analysis and our collective endeavor in any pressing way. Elsewhere in *Empire* they maintain that ethico-political agency has shifted from the proletarian collective subject to "the poor." See for instance the lyrical passage that postulates that "once again in postmodernity emerges in the blinding light of clear day the multitude, the common name of the poor. It comes out fully in the open because in postmodernity the subjugated has absorbed the exploited. In other words, the poor, every poor person, the multitude of poor people, have eaten up and digested the multitude of proletarians. By that fact itself the poor have become productive" (158). Furthermore, according to Hardt and Negri, the signs of life that register proletarian solidarity are those that are intelligible as world historical "events": "The fact that the cycle as the specific form of the assemblage of struggles has vanished, however, does not simply open up to an abyss. On the contrary, we can recognize powerful events on the world scene that reveal the trace of the multitude's refusal of explanation and that signal a new kind of proletarian solidarity and militancy" (54).

44. Consider, for example, Annanya Bhattacharjee, Ashim Roy, V. Chandra et al., "A New Path for Indian Labor? International Solidarity in the Age of Outsourcing?" The Cornell Global Labor institute convened this forum on Nov. 30, 2004, bringing union members of the New Trade Union Initiative in India together with a coalition of U.S. unionized workers (affiliated with Jobs with Justice) to discuss prospects for dialogue, solidarity, and effective compromises on a global scale.

45. Some readers might point to the fact that these names are rather decidedly ethnically marked. My point is that Olsen does not feel the need (as Ibarro does in

her plea) to qualify that these workers are "American-born" and *therefore* entitled to consideration.

46. I am thinking here, for example, of Gloria Anzaldúa's amazing poem "*Cihuatlyotl*, Woman Alone" as one of the many works that negotiate the complex figuration of an individual/collective Chicana subject in different ways.

47. Mahasweta Devi, *Dust on the Road: The Activist Writings of Mahasweta Devi*, ed. Maitreya Ghatak (Calcutta: Seagull Books, 2000), 211.

48. Perry Anderson, *In the Tracks of Historical Materialism* (Chicago: University of Chicago Press, 1984), 82–83.

49. E. P. Thompson, *The Poverty of Theory* (London: Merlin, 1978), 235.

50. Gayatri Chakravorty Spivak, "From Haverstock Hill Flat to US Classroom, What's Left of Theory?"

51. See Spivak's foreword to *Other Asias* (Oxford: Blackwell, 2008), 2.

52. Devi, *Dust on the Road*, 89.

53. See, for example, the appendix to Spivak's *A Critique of Postcolonial Reason* (423–431), where she relates the concepts of allegory, irony, and parabasis to ethical practice as well as to the political interpretation of narrative.

54. Partha Chatterjee, *The Present History of West Bengal* (New Delhi: Oxford, 1997), 94.

55. The specific critic is not named by Spivak, who brings up this criticism in her "Translator's Preface," *Imaginary Maps*, xxvi.

56. The reference is to Fredric Jameson, *The Political Unconscious* (Ithaca: Cornell University Press, 1981), 127.

57. See Spivak's translation: "and her face, in sleep within the depths of this *fairy tale ravine*, looks most fulfilled" (Devi, *Fairytale*, 104; emphasis mine).

58. Cynthia Enloe, "Women Textile Workers in the Militarization of Southeast Asia," in *Women, Men, and the International Division of Labor* (Albany: State University of New York Press, 1983), 409.

59. An internationalism that also struggles to remain alive in grassroots organizations such as the Sinhala-Tamil rural women's front, and in fora like Rural Women (*Gami Kantha*), a newspaper dedicated to foreign domestic workers.

60. Karl Marx, *Capital*, vol. 3 (London: Penguin, 1981), 959. Emphasis mine.

4. SOCIALIZED LABOR AND THE CRITIQUE OF IDENTITY POLITICS IN BESSIE HEAD'S *A QUESTION OF POWER*

1. Bessie Head, *A Woman Alone*, ed. Craig Mackenzie (Oxford: Heinemann, 1990).

2. My understanding of the "practice of diaspora" owes much to Brent Hayes Edwards's study *The Practice of Diaspora: Literature, Translation, and the Rise of Black Internationalism*, which illuminates with exacting precision the historical agency of

literature as creative practice even as it expands the provenance of the Harlem Renaissance beyond Anglophone texts and authors. Edwards's exemplary case is black periodical cultures and the dialogism inherent in traditions of black internationalism.

3. Rob Nixon calls attention to how the designation "colored" emerges through the layered negations of state speech: "The population Registration Act of 1950, for example, defined a 'colored' as someone 'who in appearance is obviously not White or Indian and who is not a member of an aboriginal race or African tribe'" (Nixon, *Homelands, Harlem, and Hollywood* [New York: Routledge, 1994], 104).

4. Most biographies begin with the dramatic disclosure of Head's place of birth—Fort Napier Mental Hospital, Pietermaritzburg, South Africa. Her mother, Bessie Amelia Emery, struggled with mental illness for the greater part of her adult life and had been institutionalized by her family before. And yet, too often, key facts of the story are omitted or reordered to produce the most sensationalist (colonial and or anticolonial) retelling of the origins story. Certain versions conjure Bessie Amelia Emery as a defiant transgressor of the Immorality Act. Some have her incarcerated in an asylum as a *result* of her actions. Head's father drops out of calculus entirely.

5. He goes so far as to suggest that Head in effect exploits a privileged subject position: "Ironically enough, this feeling [of exclusion] is less pronounced in South Africa, where the colored writer enjoys the psychological support of what has become a large national minority" (Lewis Nkosi, *Tasks and Masks* [Essex: Longman, 1981], 101).

6. Ernest Allen Jr. gives us an itinerary of the many creative mistranslations that W.E.B. Du Bois's concept of "double consciousness" undergoes. His section devoted to sociologists' pathologizing readings of the "dualism of the soul" and "schizoid twoness" of the mulatto is subtitled "a mini-history of a misconception." See Ernest Allen Jr., "Du Boisian Double Consciousness: The Unsustainable Argument," *Massachusetts Review* 43.2 (2002): 217–253. His overall argument elaborates a shift in meaning in Du Bois's own lexicon between the publication dates of "Strivings of the Negro People" and "Conservation of the Races." I am grateful to Donna Murch for calling this article to my attention. As a side note—certainly an "exorbitant supplement"—perhaps, panning outward to the political and rhetorical ploys of the 2008 U.S. presidential election, we might consider representations (including self-representations) of Barack Obama's "conciliatory politics" via reductivist readings of his "biracialism."

7. Nixon, *Homelands, Harlem, and Hollywood*, 112.

8. Anthony O'Brien, *Against Normalization* (Durham, NC: Duke University Press, 2001), 235–236.

9. See Gayatri Chakravorty Spivak, "Diasporas Old and New: Women in the Transnational World," *Textual Practice* 10.2 (1996): 257–258.

10. "History is a process without a subject," Althusser tells us, and leaves it at that. Bessie Head's work interrogates identity (and the *individual* subject) in the interest of making way for the historical agency of other collectivities.

11. See n. 18.

12. I am thinking here of Freud's essay on "The Uncanny," in *Standard Edition of the Complete Psychological Works*, trans. James Strachey et al. (London: Hogarth Press, 1961–), 17:217–252.

13. See Thomas Keenan, *Fables of Responsibility: Aberrations and Predicaments in Ethics and Politics* (Stanford: Stanford University Press, 1997), 122.

14. My chapter 3 contains an elaboration of the ethico-political figure of speech interferences via the reading of Olsen's *Yonnondio*.

15. "The analysis that I am undertaking is psychological. In spite of this it is apparent to me that the effective disalienation of the black man entails an immediate recognition of social and economic realities. If there is an inferiority complex, it is the outcome of a double process:—primarily, economic;—subsequently, the internalization—or, better, the epidermalization—of this inferiority" (Fanon, *Black Skin, White Masks*, 11).

16. Mahmood Mamdani, *When Victims Become Killers: Colonialism, Nativism, and the Genocide in Rwanda* (Princeton: Princeton University Press, 2001).

17. While there are some poststructuralist readings of Marx that at least approach the question of Marx's counterintuitive "humanism" via the question of abstract labor, most Marxist scholars of critical race theory as well as subaltern studies construe the concept of abstract labor as a problematic stumbling block rather than a productive contradiction. Upon this score, see, for example, Lisa Lowe, *Immigrant Acts: On Asian American Cultural Politics*, 154–173, especially 170. Dipesh Chakrabarty approaches the question slightly differently. He begins with the following premise: "Abstract labor may thus be read as an account of how the logic of capital sublates into itself the differences of history" (655). But questioning his own line of thinking, he then goes on to show how Marx's own thoughts may be made to resist an idea central to Marx's critique of capital—that "the logic of capital sublates differences into itself." See Chakrabarty, "Universalism and Belonging in the Logic of Capital" in *Public Culture*. The difference between Chakrabarty and Spivak is that Spivak would make a case for the potential for an enabling, or just, use of abstraction in Marx: "His analysis must use the same method that makes the object of his analysis an evil: abstracting out individual heterogeneity into a quantitative measure of homogeneous labour so that calculation may be possible" (Gayatri Chakravorty Spivak, "Speculations on Reading Marx After Reading Derrida," in *Post-structuralism and the Question of History*, ed. Derek Attridge et al. [Cambridge: Cambridge University Press, 1987], 30–62). Also see Keenan, "The Point Is to (Ex)change It: Reading 'Capital,' Rhetorically," in *Fables of Responsibility*.

18. Some find abstract labor's quintessential expression/realization in "computational thinking"—the hallmark of the information age. See, for example, Hardt and Negri's readings of labor power and abstract labor. Theirs is a revisionary project that admittedly set out to question "old notion(s) . . . common to classical and Marxian political economics." However, I would distinguish Bessie Head's stagings of labor power and her own processes of "defetishizing the concrete" (illustrated as they are in

working-class narratives of food production and agriculture) from Hardt and Negri's axioms. Their revisions pose abstract labor as a phase leading up to the contemporary period of immaterial labor: "In previous periods, however, the tools [for abstraction] generally were related in a relatively inflexible way to certain groups of tasks; different tools corresponded to different activities.... The computer proposes itself, in contrast, as the universal tool, or rather as the central tool, through which all activities might pass. Through the computerization of production, then, labor tends toward the position of abstract labor" (*Empire*, 292). In Hardt and Negri's lexicon it is immaterial labor—abstract labor gets subsumed under this general rubric—that "seems to provide a potential for a kind of spontaneous and elementary communism" (294). For a diametrically opposed reading of the structural and structuring power relations of computational thinking see David Golumbia, *The Cultural Logic of Computation* (Cambridge, MA: Harvard University Press, 2009).

19. "Hauntopology" builds on Derrida's concept of "ontopology": "(By *ontopology* we mean an axiomatics linking indissociably the ontological value of present-being [*on*] to its *situation*, to the stable and presentable determination of a locality, the *topos* of territory, native soil, city, body in general)" (Jacques Derrida, *Specters of Marx: The State of the Debt, the Work of Mourning, and the New International* [New York: Routledge, 1994], 82).

20. "This militancy makes resistance into counterpower and makes rebellion into love" (*Empire*, 413). The turn to love in Head's *A Question of Power* recalls but also perhaps *revises* Hardt and Negri's concluding theme. At the close of *Empire*, they propose that the future of a radically resignified communist militancy might find an emblematic figure in Saint Francis of Assisi. On the other hand, John McClure's insightful reading of this moment poses a challenge to secular thinkers like Hardt and Negri. He calls our attention to what is overlooked in certain grounding ethical assumptions of postsocialist alternatives. See *Partial Faiths: Postsecular Fiction in the Age of Pynchon and Morrison* (Athens: University of Georgia Press, 2007), 23. McClure lists *A Question of Power* as a postcolonial example of "postsecular fiction." Figures representing a vague, untethered, ahistorical, "partial" Buddhism (along with bits and pieces of Christianity, Islam, Hinduism, and Greek mythology) recur in *A Question of Power*—even as they are ultimately dispelled and displaced by the credo of literary internationalism. I return to this point in the coda to this chapter.

21. Jacqueline Rose, "On the 'Universality' of Madness: Bessie Head's *A Question of Power*," *Critical Inquiry* 20 (1994): 415.

22. See Alfred Sohn-Rethel, *Intellectual and Manual Labour: A Critique of Epistemology* (Atlantic Highlands, NJ: Humanities Press, 1978), and Slavoj Žižek, *The Sublime Object of Ideology* (London: Verso, 1989), 19.

23. The subheading is also a play on "capitalism and schizophrenia"; see Deleuze and Guattari, *Anti-Oedipus: Capitalism and Schizophrenia* (Minneapolis: University of Minnesota Press, 1983).

24. See for example Njabulo Ndebele, *Rediscovery of the Ordinary* (Johannesburg: COSAW, 1991), 37–57, and Kelwyn Sole, "'The Deep Thoughts the One in Need Falls Into': Quotidian Experience and the Perspectives of Poetry in Postliberation South Africa" in *Postcolonial Studies and Beyond* (Durham, NC: Duke University Press, 2005), 182–205.

25. Sanders reads Keenan's *Fables of Responsibility* against and through the politics of South African history in "Reading Lessons," *Diacritics* 29.3 (1999): 3–20.

26. Nixon, *Homelands, Harlem, and Hollywood*, 112–117.

27. Translation modified. "The universality of man manifests itself in practice in that universality which makes the whole of nature his *inorganic* [*unorganisch*] body" (Karl Marx, *Early Writings* [London: Penguin, 1974], 328). See Gayatri Chakravorty Spivak, *A Critique of Postcolonial Reason*, 76, n. 101: "Since Nature is exactly not 'inorganic,' there can be no doubt that *unorganisch* means 'without organs.'"

28. Admittedly, Head has a complicated relationship with organized feminism.

29. See for example Arturo Escobar, who historicizes the concept of "development" from the 1950s to the 1970s but also asks us to consider it as discourse: "Even those who opposed the prevailing capitalist strategies were obliged to couch their critique in terms of the need for development, through concepts such as 'another development,' 'participatory development,' 'socialist development' and the like" (Arturo Escobar, *Encountering Development* [Princeton: Princeton University Press, 1995], 5).

30. In "Notes from a Quiet Backwater II" Head qualifies the scope of her "earlier work," including her three novels. "Having defined the personal, my work became more social and outward-looking" (Bessie Head, *A Woman Alone*, 78).

31. Quoted in Gillian Eilersen, *Thunder Behind Her Ears* (Portsmouth, NH: Heinemann, 1995), 268.

32. "I decided to record the irrelevant" (Bessie Head, *Serowe, Village of the Rain Wind* [London: Heinemann, 1981], 67).

33. Bessie Head, *Tales of Tenderness and Power* (Johannesburg: Donker, 1989).

34. My thinking here is indebted to Julie Livingston. See her brilliant study of an ethics of care charted against and through concepts of Tswana physiology and personhood: Julie Livingston, *Debility and the Moral Imagination in Botswana* (Bloomington: Indiana University Press, 2005).

35. Bessie Head, *A Gesture of Belonging: Letters from Bessie Head, 1965–1979*, ed. Randolph Vigne (London: Heinemann, 1991), 27.

36. Bessie Head, *When Rain Clouds Gather* (Oxford: Heinemann, 1969).

37. See Bessie Head, *A Woman Alone*, 72–73.

38. Ketu H. Katrak, "From Pauline to Dikeledi: The Philosophical and Political Vision of Bessie Head's Protagonists," *Ba Shiru* 12.2 (1985): 26–35; Annie Gagiano, *Achebe, Head, Marechera: On Power and Change in Africa* (Boulder: Lynne Rienner, 2000).

39. See Gagiano, *Achebe*, 136.

40. Katrak, "From Pauline to Dikeledi."

41. I hope to continue with this work in an extended study based on this chapter. For now I have had to bracket this comparative reading. See also O'Brien, *Against Normalization*, 176–214. I am grateful to Rob Nixon for suggesting Anthony O'Brien's work to me.

42. He is of course, speaking of wealth flowing from primary producers to industrialized countries. See Chakravarthi Raghavan, *Recolonization* (London: Zed Books, 1990), 21. See also Deborah Mindry, "Nongovernmental Organizations, 'Grassroots,' and the Politics of Virtue," *Signs: Journal of Women in Culture and Society* 26.4 (2001): 1188–1211.

43. Eilersen, *Thunder Behind Her Ears*, 96.

44. See the section titled "Rural/Indigenous" in Spivak, "From Haverstock Hill Flat to US Classroom."

45. "'What, do you imagine that I would take so much trouble and so much pleasure in writing, do you think that I would keep so persistently to my task, if I were not preparing—with a rather shaky hand—a labyrinth into which I can venture, in which I can move my discourse, opening up underground passages, forcing it to go far from itself, finding overhangs that reduce and deform its itinerary, in which I can lose myself and appear at last to eyes that I will never have to meet again. I am no doubt not the only one who writes in order to have no face. Do not ask who I am and do not ask me to remain the same: leave it to our bureaucrats and our police to see that our papers are in order. At least spare us their morality when we write'" (Michel Foucault, *The Archaeology of Knowledge and the Discourse on Language* [New York: Pantheon Books, 1972], 17).

46. Emphasis mine. Livingston proposes that "the notion of building is an important concept in Tswana personhood" (15). Head's concepts of building/erasing as well as the part-objects of women's cooperative voluntary labor might also be read against and through the critical ethnographer/historian's commentary: "[*building or self-making, she observes,*] is the primary means through which the promise of liberal individualism (manifest in education, entrepreneurship, wage work) can be harnessed to the making of social selves."

47. "[S]ome people become attached to leaflets and prospectuses, others to handwriting facsimiles or typewritten copies of unobtainable books; and certainly periodicals can form the prismatic fringes of a library," considers Benjamin. And yet the subjectivity of the collector seems to overwrite the subjectivity of the collection in Benjamin's case. Whereas in Head's, the subjectivity of the collective/collection takes precedence. Bessie Head would have had a lot to say Walter Benjamin. She, like him, was an ephemerist. A sustained consideration of this comparison might lead us to think about two very different ideological underpinnings of post-Marxist scholarship—demarcated as "postcolonial" versus Frankfurt School. See Walter Benjamin, *Illuminations* (New York: Shocken Books), 66.

48. Quoted in Carlo Coppola, ed., *Marxist Influences and South Asian Literature* (Delhi: Chanakya, 1988), 11. Here I am indebted to Coppola's translation of the *Hans* version.

49. See, for example, this instructive moment in the text where the character Camilla comments patronizingly to Elizabeth: "In our country culture has become so complex, this complexity is reflected in our literature. It takes a certain level of education to understand our novelists. The ordinary man cannot understand them.... And she reeled off a list of authors, smiling smugly. It never occurred to her that those authors had ceased to be of any value whatsoever to their society—or was it really true that an extreme height of culture and the incomprehensible went hand in hand?" (79).

50. The reference is to Bruce Robbins, *Feeling Global: Internationalism in Distress* (New York: New York University Press, 1999).

EPILOGUE: WORKING-CLASS WRITING AND THE SOCIAL IMAGINATION

1. David Lodge, *Nice Work* (London: Secker and Warburg, 1988).

2. See Bruce Robbins's insightful reading of this moment in Lodge's novel in which he calls our attention to how the discursive construction of an "international popular" generally falls short of international solidarity or action. Bruce Robbins, "The Sweatshop Sublime," *PMLA* 117.1 (2002): 84–97.

3. Joel Johnson, "1 Million Workers. 90 Million iPhones. 17 Suicides. Who's to Blame?" *Wired* 28 (Feb. 2011); Web version 15 March 2011.

4. As Hardt and Negri put it, "in other words, (potential) revolutionaries in other parts of the world did not hear of the events in Beijing, Nablus, Los Angeles, Chiapas, Paris, or Seoul and immediately recognize them as their own struggles. Furthermore, these struggles not only fail to communicate to other contexts but also lack even a local communication, and thus often have a very brief duration where they are born, burning out in a flash. This is certainly one of the central and most urgent political paradoxes of our time: in our much celebrated age of communication, *struggles have become all but incommunicable*" (*Empire*, 54). Writing in 2000, their call was to understand the global implications of local strikes and uprisings whose specific meanings could not be translated into different contexts.

5. "Fatal Fire in Bangladesh Highlights the Dangers Facing Garment Workers," *New York Times*, 26 Nov. 2012: A4.

6. "There is an interesting paradox in the name *assembly movement*. No doubt we are speaking of a movement that spans a great geopolitical range, even if this expanse is discontinuous. A product less of contagion than of resonance, the occupation of public spaces by protesters signifies a broader phenomenon that has global dimensions in the assembly of its differential particularities. *Movement* thus refers to this process of resonance, the way that distinct events merging from their social-historical ground

come to recognize themselves in one another without evading their particularity" (Stathis Gourgouris, "Assembly Movements and the Deregulation of the Political," *PMLA* 127.4 [2012]: 1004).

7. The reference is to a classic title in working-class studies: Gareth Stedman Jones, *Languages of Class: Studies in English Working-Class History, 1832–1982* (Cambridge: Cambridge University Press, 1983).

8. Étienne Balibar's recent work on the "disjunctive synthesis" of the social in Marx is a painstaking elaboration of the problems and possibilities. I am grateful to him for finding some time to answer my questions following his address, "Marx's Two Discoveries: A Disjunctive Synthesis and Its Current Relevance" (keynote speech, "World of Capital: Conditions, Meanings, Situations" conference, Columbia University, New York, 29 April 2011).

9. But not all countries and cities are valued equally for projects of historical recovery or as case studies for epistemology. Similar philosophical worldviews, when arising from different spaces in the international division of labor, pose a problem for debates in Western Marxism. That is to say, the semantics of the social as rooted in the illiberal bases of shared responsibility and duty are more often than not dismissed as backward, feudal, or *precapitalist*. Chakrabarty's *Rethinking Working-Class History*, however, ultimately asks us to consider an ethics of responsibility, rather than equal rights, constitutionalism, and historical precedent as a foundation for socialist class politics. Both Hoggart's and Chakrabarty's are risky investments in culture. But reading them together allows us to pose a question: What does it mean to speak of (a) working-class culture in a global and unequal world without resorting to narrative hierarchies of cultural relativism and historical difference?

10. See for instance, Shehzad Nadeem, *Dead Ringers: How Outsourcing Is Changing the Way Indians Understand Themselves* (Princeton: Princeton University Press, 2011).

11. Arlie Russell Hochschild, *The Outsourced Self: Intimate Life in Market Times* (New York: Metropolitan Books, 2012).

12. This is an argument for the ethical recuperation of world literature. The phrase in quotation marks is from David Damrosch. But the call for "distant reading" comes from Franco Morretti. To gain a comprehensive understanding of the world we are told we must dispense with our penchant for close reading. Systemic thinking of the sort proposed by Moretti, then, calls for a species of "distant reading . . . where distance is a condition of knowledge." Distance, here, translates into a worldview that is a priori against the optics of national historiography. As a process and method, distant reading privileges the vantage point of social history over *literary* close reading. But "distance," in Moretti's vision, is also counterposed as the antonym to a discursive assemblage of loosely related opposed meanings—among them, "local," "rooted," "personal." Lodge's feminist critic, perhaps, models this distant reader of the world-as-a-global system—"one and unequal," but a system nonetheless.

13. As should be clear by now, my understanding of the uses of the literary is deeply indebted to the thinking of Raymond Williams. The beautiful turn of phrase that lends itself to my theme is his way of describing the ephemerality of history and "the social" as receding presence, sometimes glimpsed at in literature through figures at the edge of semantic availability. See Raymond Williams, *Marxism and Literature*, 128.

14. Terese Agnew, "Portrait of a Textile Worker: Art Quilt Project by Terese Agnew," accessed at http://www.tardart.com/html/ptw.php on 2 Feb. 2010. This representation of the iconic South Asian figure is based on a snapshot of a Bangladeshi garment factory worker. Agnew's mixed-media portrait is based on a 2002 photograph taken by Charles Kernaghan, the director of the National Labor Committee, on an undercover visit to a factory in Bangladesh. I am grateful to Richard Miller for calling my attention to this artist's work and for gifting me the poster version.

15. Ethel Brooks's analysis of the symbolic economy of transnational protest recalls us to the limitations of boycott politics: "Everyday forms of violence in garment producing sites and communities along with everyday battles to organize women working in garment factories throughout the world, are marginalized when they cannot be represented or sold to a consuming Northern audience" (Brooks, "Ideal Sweatshop? Gender and Transnational Protest," in *Sweatshop USA*, ed. Daniel Bender and Richard Greenwald [New York: Routledge, 2003], 283).

Bibliography

Adorno, Theodor. *Minima Moralia: Reflections on a Damaged Life*. Trans. E. F. N. Jephcott. New York: Verso, 2005.
Agamben, Giorgio. *Means Without End: Notes on Politics*. Trans. Vincenzo Binetti and Cesare Casarino. Minneapolis: University of Minnesota Press, 2000.
Allen, Ernest, Jr. "Du Boisian Double Consciousness: The Unsustainable Argument." *Massachusetts Review* 43.2 (2002): 217–253.
Althusser, Louis, and Étienne Balibar. *Reading Capital*. New York: Verso, 1997.
Amin, Samir. *Unequal Development*. New York: Monthly Review Press, 1976.
Anand, Mulk Raj. *Apology for Heroism: A Brief Autobiography of Ideas*. New Delhi: Arnold-Heinemann, 1975.
———. *Author to Critic: The Letters of Mulk Raj Anand*. Ed. Saros Cowasjee. Calcutta: Writers' Workshop, 1973.
———. *Conversations in Bloomsbury*. New Delhi: Arnold-Heinemann, 1981.
———. *Coolie*. New Delhi: Penguin, 1993.
———. *Two Leaves and a Bud*. New Delhi: Arnold, 1994.
Anderson, Perry. *Considerations on Western Marxism*. London: Verso, 1979.
———. "Internationalism: A Breviary." *New Left Review* 14 (March/April 2002).
———. *In the Tracks of Historical Materialism*. Chicago: University of Chicago Press, 1984.
Appadurai, Arjun, ed. *Globalization*. Durham, NC: Duke University Press, 2001.
———. *Modernity at Large*. Minneapolis: University of Minnesota Press, 1996.

Baer, Benjamin Conisbee. "Shit Writing: Mulk Raj Anand's *Untouchable*, the Image of Gandhi, and the Progressive Writers' Association." *Modernism/Modernity* 16.3 (2009): 575–595.

Bahl, Vinay. *The Making of the Indian Working Class: A Case of the Tata Iron and Steel Company, 1880–1946.* New Delhi: Sage, 1995.

Bal, Mieke. *Narratology*. Toronto: University of Toronto Press, 1985.

Balibar, Étienne. "In Search of the Proletariat: The Notion of Class Politics in Marx." *Masses, Classes, Ideas: Studies on Politics and Philosophy Before and After Marx*, 125–149. Routledge: New York, 1994.

"Bangladeshi Women's Rights." *Dabindu* 12.10 (July 1997): 2.

Barthes, Roland. "The Death of the Author." *Image/Music/Text*, 142–148. New York: Hill and Wang, 1977.

Benjamin, Walter. *Illuminations*. New York: Shocken.

Berman, Jessica. "Comparative Colonialisms: Joyce, Anand, and the Question of Engagement." *Modernism/Modernity* 13.3 (2006): 465–485.

Berry, Margaret. *Mulk Raj Anand: The Man and the Novelist*. Amsterdam: Oriental Press, 1971.

Blumen, Kristin. *Intermodernism: Literary Culture in Mid-Twentieth-Century Britain*. Edinburgh: Edinburgh University Press, 2009.

Bremen, Jan, and E. Valentine Daniel. "Conclusion: The Making of a Coolie." Ed. E. Valentine Daniel, Henry Bernstein, and Tom Brass. *Journal of Peasant Studies* 19.3–4 (1992): 268–295.

Brennan, Timothy. "Poetry and Polemic." In *A World to Win: Essays in Honor of A. Sivanandan. Race and Class* 41.1/2 (July–Dec. 1999): 23–34.

Brooks, Ethel. "The Ideal Sweatshop? Gender and Transnational Protest." In *Sweatshop USA: The American Sweatshop in Historical and Global Perspective*, ed. Daniel Bender and Richard Greenwald, 265–286. New York: Routledge, 2003.

Browne, Nicholas. *Utopian Generations: The Political Horizon of Twentieth-Century Literature*. Princeton: Princeton University Press, 2005.

Cabral, Amilcar. "Identity and Dignity in the Context of the National Liberation Struggle." *Return to the Source: Selected Speeches by Amilcar Cabral*, 57–69. Ed. African Information Service. New York: Monthly Review Press, 1973.

Casanova, Pascale. *The World Republic of Letters*. Cambridge, MA: Harvard University Press, 2004.

Chakrabarty, Dipesh. *Provincializing Europe: Postcolonial Thought and Historical Difference*. Princeton: Princeton University Press, 2000.

———. *Rethinking Working-Class History: Bengal, 1890–1940*. Princeton: Princeton University Press, 1989.

———. "Universalism and Belonging in the Logic of Capital." *Public Culture* 12.3 (Fall 2000): 653–678.

Chatterjee, Partha. *The Present History of West Bengal*. New Delhi: Oxford University Press, 1998.
Cixous, Hélène. "The Laugh of the Medusa." In *French Feminism Revisited*, ed. Kelly Oliver, 257–275. Lanham: Rowman and Littlefield, 2000.
Coiner, Constance. *Better Red: The Writing and Resistance of Tillie Olsen and Meridel Le Sueur*. New York: Oxford University Press, 1995.
Cowasjee, Saros. *Coolie: An Assessment*. New Delhi: Oxford University Press, 1976.
———. *So Many Freedoms*. New Delhi: Oxford University Press, 1977.
Dabindu Collective. "Preface." *Stri nirmana*. Ja Ela: Dabindu Collective, 1988.
Damrosch, David. *What Is World Literature?* Princeton: Princeton University Press, 2003.
Davies, Tony. "Unfinished Business: Realism and Working-Class Writing." In *The British Working-Class Novel in the Twentieth Century*, ed. Jeremy Hawthorne, 125–136. London: Edward Arnold, 1984.
Davis, Angela. "Interview with Lisa Lowe." In *The Politics of Culture in the Shadow of Capital*, ed. Lisa Lowe and David Lloyd, 303–323. Durham, NC: Duke University Press, 1997.
De Man, Paul. *Allegories of Reading: Figural Language in Rousseau, Nietzsche, Rilke, and Proust*. New Haven: Yale University Press, 1979.
Deniyaye, Arosha. "Mavu kusin nova mihi kusin SiriLaka upan viru daruvane . . ." (O heroic children born not of mother's womb, but of the earth of Mother Lanka . . .). *Dabindu* 13.8 (April/May 1998): 6.
Denning, Michael. *The Cultural Front: The Laboring of American Culture in the Twentieth Century*. New York: Verso, 1996.
———. *Culture in the Age of Three Worlds*. London: Verso, 2004.
Derrida, Jacques. "The Exorbitant. Question of Method." *Of Grammatology*, 157–164. Trans. Gayatri Spivak. Baltimore: Johns Hopkins University Press, 1974.
———. *Specters of Marx: The State of the Debt, the Work of Mourning, and the New International*. New York: Routledge, 1994.
Devi, Mahasweta. "Douloti the Bountiful." *Imaginary Maps*, 19–93. Trans. Gayatri Spivak. New York: Routledge, 1995.
———. *Dust on the Road: The Activist Writings of Mahasweta Devi*. Ed. Maitreya Ghatak. Calcutta: Seagull, 2000.
———. "The Fairy Tale of Mohanpur." *Old Women*, 73–104. Trans. Gayatri Spivak. Calcutta: Seagull, 1999.
———. "Pterodactyl, Puran Sahay, and Pirtha." *Imaginary Maps*, 95–196. Trans. Gayatri Spivak. New York: Routledge, 1995.
Dhaliwal, Amarpal. "Responses." *Socialist Review* 23.3 (1994): 81–99.
Dhammika Padmini. "Kandurelle kandulu binduva" (Tear drops from the hills). *Dabindu* 13.11 (Aug. 1998): 6; *Dabindu* 14.9 (May 1999): 6.

Du Bois, W.E.B. *The Souls of Black Folk*. New York: Signet, 1995.

Eagleton, Terry. *Literary Theory: An Introduction*. Minneapolis: University of Minnesota Press, 1983.

Edwards, Brent. *The Practice of Diaspora: Literature, Translation, and the Rise of Black Internationalism*. Cambridge, MA: Harvard University Press, 2003.

Eilersen, Gillian. *Bessie Head: Thunder Behind Her Ears*. Portsmouth, NH: Heinemann, 1996.

Empson, William. *Some Versions of the Pastoral*. Norfolk: New Directions, 1950.

Enloe, Cynthia. "Women Textile Workers in the Militarization of Southeast Asia." In *Women, Men, and the International Division of Labor*, ed. June Nash and María Patricia Fernández-Kelly, 407–425. Albany: State University of New York Press, 1983.

"The Entire Weight Lies Upon the People." *Dabindu* 13.3 (Nov. 1997): 1.

Escobar, Arturo. *Encountering Development: The Making and Unmaking of the Third World*. Princeton: Princeton University Press, 1995.

Fanon, Frantz. *Black Skin, White Masks*. New York: Grove Press, 1967.

———. *Wretched of the Earth*. New York: Grove Press, 1968.

FOIL. "Those That Be in Bondage: Child Labor and IMF Strategy in India." Fall 1996. http://www.proxsa.org/economy/labor/chldlbr.html. Accessed 11 May 2013.

Foley, Barbara. *Radical Representations*. Durham, NC: Duke University Press, 1993.

Forster, E.M. *Aspects of the Novel*. New York: Harcourt, Brace, and Co., 1927.

"For Us, There Is No Freedom." *Dabindu* 13.6 (Feb. 1998): 1.

Gagiano, Annie. *Achebe, Head, Marechera: On Power and Change in Africa*. Boulder: Lynne Rienner, 2000.

Galappaththi, Swarna P. "Vathu kamkaru striya" (The tea plantation worker-woman). In *Stri nirmana*, 37. Ja Ela: Dabindu Collective, 1988.

Gamage, Charuni. "Nonimi ginna" (The unstoppable fire). *Dabindu* 10.12 (March 1994): 6.

Gates, Henry Louis, Jr., ed. *"Race," Writing, and Difference*. Chicago: University of Chicago Press, 1985.

Golumbia, David. *The Cultural Logic of Computation*. Cambridge, MA: Harvard University Press, 2009.

Gourgouris, Stathis. "Assembly Movements and the Deregulation of the Political." *PMLA* 127.4 (2012): 1001–1005.

Guha, Ranajit. "The Prose of Counter-Insurgency." In *Selected Subaltern Studies*, ed. Ranajit Guha and Gayatri Chakravorty Spivak, 45–88. New York: Oxford University Press, 1988.

Hall, Stuart. "When Was 'The Post-colonial'? Thinking at the Limit." In *The Post-Colonial Question: Common Skies, Different Horizons*, ed. Iain Chambers and Lidia Curti, 242–261. London: Routledge, 1996.

Hardt, Michael, and Antonio Negri. *Empire*. Cambridge, MA: Harvard University Press, 2000.

Harvey, David. *A Brief History of Neoliberalism*. Oxford: Oxford University Press, 2005.
———. "Cosmopolitanism and the Banality of Geographical Evils." In *Millenial Capitalism and the Culture of Neoliberalism*, ed. Jean Comaroff and John L. Comaroff, 271–310. Durham, NC: Duke University Press, 2001.
Hasuna (Letter). *Dabindu* 15.12 (Aug. 2000): 7.
Head, Bessie. *A Question of Power*. Oxford: Heinemann, 1974.
———. *A Woman Alone*. Ed. Craig Mackenzie. Oxford: Heinemann, 1990.
———. *The Collector of Treasures and Other Botswana Village Tales*. Oxford: Heinemann, 1977.
———. *Serowe: Village of the Rain Wind*. Oxford: Heinemann, 1981.
———. *Tales of Tenderness and Power*. Johannesburg: Donker, 1989.
———. *When Rain Clouds Gather*. Oxford: Heinemann, 1969.
Hewamanne, Sandya, and James Brow. "If They Allow Us We Will Fight." *Pravada* 6.11 (2001): 22.
Hitchcock, Peter. *Working-Class Fiction in Theory and Practice: A Reading of Alan Sillitoe*. Ann Arbor: University of Michigan Research Press, 1989.
Hochschild, Arlie Russell. *The Outsourced Self: Intimate Life in Market Times*. New York: Metropolitan Books, 2012.
Hoggart, Richard. *The Uses of Literacy: Aspects of Working-Class Life, with Special References to Publications and Entertainments*. London: Chatto and Windus, 1957.
Ibarro, Felipe. Letter. *New Masses* 10.2 (Jan. 9, 1934): 22.
Ismail, Qadri. *Abiding by Sri Lanka: On Peace, Place, and Postcoloniality*. Minneapolis: University of Minnesota Press, 2005.
Jameson, Fredric. *The Political Unconscious*. Ithaca: Cornell University Press, 1981.
———. *A Singular Modernity: Essay on the Ontology of the Present*. London: Verso, 2002.
Jayasundera, Menike, K. G. "Jivithaya" (Menike's Sorrows). Trans. Punyani Gunaratna. In *A Review of Free Trade Zones in Sri Lanka*, ed. Sunila Abeyesekera, 18–19. Ja Ela: Dabindu Collective, 1997.
Jayawardena, Visakha Kumari. "The NGO Bogey." *Pravada* (n.d.): 10–11.
———. *The Rise of the Labor Movement in Ceylon*. Durham, NC: Duke University Press, 1972.
Katrak, Ketu. "From Pauline to Dikeledi: The Philosophical and Political Vision of Bessie Head's Protagonists." *Ba Shiru* 12.2 (1985): 26–35.
Kearney, Robert. "The Marxist Parties of Ceylon." In *Radical Politics in South Asia*, ed. Paul R. Brass and Marcus F. Franda, 401–439. Cambridge, MA: MIT Press, 1973.
Keenan, Thomas. *Fables of Responsibility: Aberrations and Predicaments in Ethics and Politics*. Stanford: Stanford University Press, 1997.
Kipling, Rudyard. *Kim*. London: Penguin, 1987.
Klaus, Gustav. *The Literature of Labour: Two Hundred Years of Working-Class Writing*. New York: St. Martin's, 1985.
Klaus, Gustav, and Stephen Knight, eds. *British Industrial Fictions*. Cardiff: University of Wales Press, 2000.

Krishnan, Sanjay. *Reading the Global: Troubling Perspectives on Britain's Empire in Asia.* New York: Columbia University Press, 2007.

Kristeva, Julia. "Women's Time." In *French Feminism Reader*, ed. Kelly Oliver, 181–200. Lanham: Rowman and Littlefield, 2000.

Lall, D. Chaman. *Coolie: The Story of Labor and Capital in India.* Lahore: Oriental Publishing House, 1932.

Linkon, Sherry Lee, and Bill Mullen, eds. *Radical Revisions: Rereading 1930s Culture.* Chicago: University of Illinois Press, 1996.

Livingston, Julie. *Debility and the Moral Imagination in Botswana.* Bloomington: Indiana University Press, 2005.

Lodge, David. *Nice Work.* London: Secker and Warburg, 1988.

Lowe, Lisa. *Immigrant Acts: On Asian American Cultural Politics.* Durham, NC: Duke University Press, 1996.

Lynch, Caitrin. "The 'Good Girls' of Sri Lankan Modernity: Moral Orders of Nationalism and Capitalism." *Identities* 6.1 (1999): 55–89.

Mamdani, Mahmood. *When Victims Become Killers: Colonialism, Nativism, and the Genocide in Rwanda.* Princeton: Princeton University Press, 2001.

Mao, Douglas, and Rebecca Walkowitz. "The New Modernist Studies." *PMLA* 123.3 (2008): 737–748.

Marx, Karl. *Capital Volume I.* New York: Penguin, 1990.

———. *Capital Volume II.* New York: Penguin, 1992.

———. *Capital Volume III.* Trans. David Fernbach. New York: Penguin, 1981.

———. *Early Writings.* London: Penguin, 1974.

———. *The First International and After.* London: Penguin, 1992.

———. *Surveys from Exile.* New York: Penguin, 1992.

Marx, Karl, and Friedrich Engels. *The Communist Manifesto.* London: Verso, 1998.

Mayo, Katherine. *Mother India.* London: Jonathan Cape, 1930.

McClure, John. *Partial Faiths: Postsecular Fiction in the Age of Pynchon and Morrison.* Athens: University of Georgia Press, 2007.

McMichael, Philip. *Development and Social Change: A Global Perspective.* Thousand Oaks: Pine Forge Press, 1996.

Melas, Natalie. *All the Difference in the World: Postcoloniality and the Ends of Comparison.* Stanford: Stanford University Press, 2007.

Mindry, Deborah. "Nongovernmental Organizations, 'Grassroots,' and the Politics of Virtue." *Signs: Journal of Women in Culture and Society* 26.4 (2001): 1188–1211.

Mitter, Swasti. *Common Fate, Common Bond: Women in the Global Economy.* London: Pluto, 1986.

Moretti, Franco. "Conjectures on World Literature." *New Left Review* 1 (Jan./Feb. 2000): 54–68.

Murphy, James. *The Proletarian Moment.* Chicago: University of Illinois Press, 1991.

Nadeem, Shehzad. *Dead Ringers: How Outsourcing Is Changing the Way Indians Understand Themselves*. Princeton: Princeton University Press, 2011.

Nadesan, Sithaperam. *A History of the Up-Country Tamil People*. Hatton: Nandalala, 1993.

Nandy, Ashis. *Intimate Enemy: Loss and Recovery of Self Under Colonialism*. Delhi: Oxford University Press, 1983.

Nash, June, and María Patricia Fernández-Kelly, eds. *Women, Men, and the International Division of Labor*. Albany: State University of New York Press, 1983.

Ndebele, Njabulo. *Rediscovery of the Ordinary: Essays on South African Literature and Culture*. Johannesburg: COSAW, 1991.

Nelson, Cary. *Repression and Recovery: Modern American Poetry and the Politics of Cultural Memory, 1910–1945*. Madison: University of Wisconsin Press, 1989.

Nesiah, Vasuki. "Monumental History and the Politics of Memory: Public Space and the Jaffna Public Library." *Lines Magazine*. http://www.lines-magazine.org/Art_Feb03/editorial_vasuki.htm.

Nixon, Rob. *Homelands, Harlem, and Hollywood: South African Culture and the World Beyond*. New York: Routledge, 1994.

Nkosi, Lewis. *Tasks and Masks: Themes and Styles of African Literature*. Essex: Longman, 1981.

O'Brien, Anthony. *Against Normalization: Writing Radical Democracy in South Africa*. Durham, NC: Duke University Press, 2001.

Oliver, Kelly, ed. *French Feminism Reader*. Lanham: Rowman and Littlefield, 2000.

Olsen, Tillie. "Requa." *Hard Choices: An Iowa Review Reader*, 7–39. Ed. David Hamilton. Iowa City: University of Iowa Press, 1996.

———. *Tell Me A Riddle*. New York: Delta, 1956.

———. *Yonnondio: From the Thirties*. New York: Delta, 1974.

Ong, Aihwa. *Spirits of Resistance and Capitalist Discipline: Factory Women in Malaysia*. Albany: State University of New York Press, 1987.

Perera, A. C. "Padada pathum" (Vagabond wishes). *Dabindu* 10.15 (June 1994): 5.

Perera, Sonali. "(Where) Language Acts in *When Memory Dies*." *Nethra* 4.3/4 (April–Sept. 2000): 101–107.

Perera, Suvendrini. "Unmaking the Present, Remaking Memory: Sri Lankan Stories and a Politics of Coexistence." In *A World to Win: Essays in Honor of A. Sivanandan*. *Race and Class* 41.1/2 (July–Dec. 1999): 189–197.

Prakash, Gyan. *Bonded Histories: Genealogies of Labor Servitude in Colonial India*. Cambridge: Cambridge University Press, 1990.

Prasad, Shaileshwar Sati. *The Insulted and the Injured*. Patna: Janaki Prakashan, 1997.

"The Question of Child-Workers in Bangladesh." *Dabindu* 13.3 (Nov. 1997): 2, 8.

Rabinowitz, Paula. *Labor and Desire*. Chapel Hill: University of North Carolina Press, 1991.

Raghavan, Chakravarthi. *Recolonization: GATT, the Uruguay Round, and the Third World.* London: Zed Books, 1990.

Rée, Jonathan. *Proletarian Philosophers.* Oxford: Clarendon Press, 1984.

Rege, Josna. *Colonial Karma: Self, Action, and Nation in the Indian English Novel.* New York: Palgrave Macmillan, 2004.

Robbins, Bruce. *Feeling Global: Internationalism in Distress.* New York: New York University Press, 1999.

——. "The Sweatshop Sublime." *PMLA* 117.1 (2002): 84–97.

Rooney, Ellen. "Better Read Than Dead: Althusser and the Fetish of Ideology." *Yale French Studies* 88 (1995): 183–200.

——. "Form and Contentment." *Modern Language Quarterly* 61.1 (2000): 17–40.

Rosa, Kumudhini. "The Conditions and Organisational Activities of Women in Free Trade Zones: Malaysia, Philippines, and Sri Lanka, 1970–1990." In *Dignity and Daily Bread,* ed. Sheila Rowbotham and Swasti Mitter, 73–99. London: Routledge, 1994.

——. "Strategies of Organisation and Resistance: Women Workers in Sri Lankan Free Trade Zones." *Capital and Class* 45 (1991): 27–35.

Rose, Jacqueline. "On the 'Universality' of Madness: Bessie Head's *A Question of Power.*" *Critical Inquiry* 20 (1994): 401–418.

Rothermund, Dietmar. *The Global Impact of the Great Depression, 1929–1939.* New York: Routledge, 1996.

——. *India in the Great Depression, 1929–1939.* New Delhi: Manohar, 1992.

Samanmalie, H. I. "The Birth of *Dabindu.*" *Dabindu* 16.1 (Sept. 2000): 2–3.

Sassen, Saskia. *Cities in a World Economy.* Thousand Oaks: Pine Forge Press, 1994.

——. "Toward a Feminist Analytics of the Global Economy." *Indiana Journal of Legal Studies* 4 (1996): 7–41.

——. *Globalization and Its Discontents.* New York: New Press, 1998.

Scott, David. *Conscripts of Modernity: The Tragedy of Colonial Enlightenment.* Durham, NC: Duke University Press, 2004.

——. "Dehistoricising History." In *Unmaking the Nation: The Politics of Identity and History in Modern Sri Lanka,* ed. Pradeep Jeganathan and Qadri Ismail, 10–24. Colombo: Social Scientists' Association, 1995.

Simeon, Dilip. *The Politics of Labour Under Late Colonialism.* New Delhi: Manohar, 1995.

Sivanandan, Ambalavener. *Communities of Resistance: Writings on Black Struggles for Socialism.* London: Verso, 1990.

——. *A Different Hunger.* London: Pluto Press, 1982.

——. *When Memory Dies.* New Delhi: Penguin, 1998.

——. *Where the Dance Is.* London: Arcadia, 2000.

Smethhurst, James Edward. *The New Red Negro: The Literary Left and African American Poetry, 1930–1946.* New York: Oxford University Press, 1999.

Sohn-Rethel, Alfred. *Intellectual and Manual Labour: A Critique of Epistemology.* Atlantic Highlands, NJ: Humanities Press, 1978.

Somalatha. "Kalapayen Vathukarayata" (From zone to plantation). *Dabindu* 13.1 (Sept. 1997): 8–9.
Spivak, Gayatri Chakravorty. "Breast-Giver: For Author, Reader, Teacher, Subaltern, Historian . . ." In *Breast Stories*, ed. Mahasweta Devi, 76–137. Calcutta: Seagull, 1997.
———. "Can the Subaltern Speak?" In *Marxism and the Interpretation of Culture*, ed. Cary Nelson and Lawrence Grossberg, 271–313. Urbana: University of Illinois Press, 1988.
———. *A Critique of Postcolonial Reason: Toward a History of the Vanishing Present*. Cambridge, MA: Harvard University Press, 1999.
———. "Feminism in Decolonization." *Differences* 3.3 (1991): 139–170.
———. "From Haverstock Hill Flat to U.S. Classroom, What's Left of Theory?" In *What's Left of Theory?*, ed. Judith Butler, John Guillory, and Kendall Thomas, 1–39. New York: Routledge, 2000.
———. "Marginality in the Teaching Machine." *Outside in the Teaching Machine*, 57–59. New York: Routledge, 1993.
———. "Resident Alien." In *Relocating Postcolonialism*, ed David Theo Goldberg and Ato Quayson, 47–65. Oxford: Blackwell, 2002.
———. "Speculations on Reading Marx After Reading Derrida." In *Post-structuralism and the Question of History*, ed. Derek Attridge et al., 30–62. Cambridge: Cambridge University Press, 1987.
———. "Subaltern Studies: Deconstructing Historiography." *Selected Subaltern Studies*. Ed. Ranajit Guha and Gayatri Chakravorty Spivak. New York: Oxford University Press, 1988.
———. "Translator's Preface." Mahasweta Devi, *Imaginary Maps*. Trans. Spivak. New York: Routledge, 1995.
Stiglitz, Joseph. *Globalization and Its Discontents*. New York: Norton, 2003.
———. *Making Globalization Work*. New York: Norton, 2007.
S. Udayalata Menike. "Mai Dinaya" (May Day). *Dabindu* 15.8 (April 2000): 6.
Suleri, Sara. *The Rhetoric of English India*. Chicago: University of Chicago Press, 1992.
Thompson, E. P. *The Making of the English Working Class*. New York: Vintage, 1963.
Tressel, Robert. *The Ragged Trousered Philanthropists*. London, 1971.
Vijayalatha, D. W. "Vathu kamkaru striya" (The tea plantation worker-woman). In *Stri nirmana*, 27. Ja Ela: Dabindu Collective, 1988.
Viswanathan, Gauri. *Outside the Fold: Conversion, Modernity, and Belief*. Princeton: Princeton University Press, 1998.
Vitana, Deepika Thrima. "Chintanaya nidahas nam" (Thinking freedom). *Dabindu* 10.15 (June 1994): 4.
Vološinov, V. N. *Marxism and the Philosophy of Language*. Cambridge, MA: Harvard University Press, 1973.
Wald, Alan. *Writing from the Left: New Essays on Radical Culture and Politics*. New York: Verso, 1994.

Weerakoon, R. *The Evolution of Labour Law in Sri Lanka: Tea Plantation to Free Trade Zone*. Colombo: Ceylon Federation of Labour, 1986.

Williams, Patrick. "Kim and Orientalism." In *Colonial Discourse and Post-Colonial Theory*, ed. Patrick Williams and Laura Chrisman, 480–487. New York: Columbia University Press, 1994.

Williams, Raymond. *The Country and the City*. New York: Oxford University Press, 1973.

——. *Keywords: A Vocabulary of Culture and Society*. New York: Oxford University Press, 1985.

——. *Marxism and Literature*. New York: Oxford University Press, 1977.

Žižek, Slavoj. *The Sublime Object of Ideology*. London: Verso, 1989.

Index

abstract labor, 127–28, 134, 145, 170, 197–98n18. *See also* labor power
abstraction, 108–9, 127–28, 156; political utility of, 133; power and, 131–32, 155; socialized labor and, 133–34, 147–48; the social and, 166–67
Adorno, Theodor, 186n9
aesthetics, 9–10, 176–77n11; politics and, 7, 9, 34, 76, 79–80, 83, 96, 114–15, 161
Afro-Asian unity, 161
Agamben, Giorgio, 62, 187n16
agency, 77, 100
Agnew, Therese, 169–70, 203n12
agrarian movements, 31, 117
Allegories of Reading (de Man), 60–61
Allen, Ernest, Jr., 196n6
All-India Progressive Writers Association (AIPWA), 154, 161–63, 180–81n8
Anand, Mulk Raj, 14, 23–24, 157; deauthorizing moments in, 7–8; ideological viewpoint, 33, 34; internationalism, 33–34, 180–81n8, 181nn13, 15; irony in, 7–8; as modernist, 29; overlooked in scholarship, 24, 32–33, 180–81n8, 181n15; on writing historical fiction, 39; *Works: Apology for Heroism: A Brief Autobiography of Ideas*, 33; *Author to Critic*, 32–33; *Conversations in Bloomsbury*, 27–28; *Two Leaves and a Bud*, 31, 32; *Untouchable* (Anand), 32, 35, 182nn23, 25. *See also Coolie*
Anderson, Perry, 14, 19, 103, 112, 178n19
Andi ("The Fairy Tale of Mohanpur"), 116–20
anticolonial historiography, 37, 44, 49
anticolonial writing, 4, 24, 33
anti-essentialism, 76, 78, 81, 82, 84, 128
antihumanism, 113, 124, 127, 134, 140, 146

antinationalism, 16, 29
Apology for Heroism: A Brief Autobiography of Ideas (Anand), 33
aporia, ethical, 2, 11, 40, 42
Arab Spring, 166
archetypes, 9, 10, 78–79, 125
"Articles on India and China" (Marx), 18–19
assembly movement, 166, 201–2n6
audience, 2, 139
authors, working-class origins, 9, 176n10
authorship, 85; collaborative form, 11–12, 16, 89, 93–95
autocritique/self-criticism, 20, 25, 60, 92–93, 106, 151; Marx on, 8–9, 22, 100, 101

Badiou, Alain, 19, 20
Baer, Benjamin Conisbee, 180–81n8
Bahl, Vinay, 37, 183n34
Bal, Mieke, 45, 184n40
Bandung conference (1955), 161, 173n2
Barrack-Room Ballads (Kipling), 27
Barthes, Roland, 34
Bechuanaland, 26, 122
Benjamin, Walter, 115, 124, 159, 186n11
Berger, John, 56
Berman, Jessica, 180n8
bildungsroman, 81, 86, 92
black, as political color, 48
black British cultural studies, 24–25, 50
Black Power politics, 147–48
Black Skin, White Masks (Fanon), 131, 197n15
black socialism, 48, 49–50, 53
Blumel, Kristin, 181n8
Boiteko (voluntary cooperative labor), 127, 145
Bose, Asoke, 101–2
bourgeoisie, rise of world literature and, 15–16

Brandt Commission, 97
Brecht, Bertolt, 139, 140
Brennan, Timothy, 56, 188n27
Bretton Woods conference (1944), 173n2, 182n19
Britain, 24; black British cultural studies, 24–25, 50; black struggles in, 51, 52, 74; industrial revolution, 49, 79; Marx's focus on, 108; Notting Hill riots, 51, 52; politically charged worker categories, 48; three-class system debunked, 17–18; trade unionist socialism, 2, 25, 28–29, 52
British Marxism, 9
Brooke, Rupert, 159
Brooks, Ethel, 203n15
Brow, James, 90
building, concept of, 200n46

Cabral, Amilcar, 54, 69
Campaign Against Racial Discrimination (CARD), 73–74
"Can the Subaltern Speak?" (Spivak), 40, 110, 190n18
Capital (Marx), 1, 27, 100, 108, 121; "Classes," 17, 23; "Trinity Formula," 17–18, 133
capitalism, defective modes, 110–11
capitalist modernity, 28
capital-logic, 107–8, 120
cartographies of labor, 5, 6, 17, 24, 26, 63, 66; gender and, 95, 98
Casanova, Pascale, 5, 176–77n11, 179n26
caste system, 32, 35, 182n24; class compared with, 35–36
cause, 37
center of story, 6, 71, 117, 129, 155, 184n35; *Coolie*, 38–40; *When Memory Dies*, 57, 61
Ceylon Citizenship Act (No. 18), 63

Chakrabarty, Dipesh, 37, 43, 50, 65, 79, 167, 183n34, 202n9
Chatterjee, Partha, 117
Chicana protest poetry, 99
Chicana women factory workers, 96–99
child laborers, 1–2, 4, 183n26, 184n35; caste system, 32
child-protagonist, 1–2, 24
Children (Pledging of Labor) Act, 29
China, strikes, 2–3
"Chintanaya nidahas nam" (Thinking freedom) (Vitana), 91–93
class: as abstract, 170; as anti-essentialist category, 49; caste system compared with, 35–36; collective identity and, 94; counterintuitive making/unmaking of, 38; Eurocentric, masculinist analytics of, 49; intranational differences, 96; limited meanings of, 8; Marx's rethinking of, 17–18; provisionality of, 10–11; structural and structuring aspects of, 10, 16, 33, 116, 166, 198n18
class struggle, 3, 5, 7, 11; anticolonial nationalism vs., 24, 29; two-sided version, 17
Coiner, Constance, 189n11
collaborative form, 11–12, 16, 89, 93–95
collective identity, 33, 143
collectivity, 60, 64, 124, 141, 143, 160, 191n20; modes of, 18–19, 111, 121; women's, 25, 116
colonial counterdiscourse, 30
colonialism: late/1930s, 2, 24; race subject of, 145–46
coming-of-age stories, 29, 37, 189n11
Committee for Democracy and Justice in Sri Lanka, 91
The Communist Manifesto (Marx and Engels), 15–17, 44, 69

commodity, 108, 130–35, 144, 147; value composition, 133–34
communalism, 47, 54
Communist Party India (CPI), 101
Communist Party of India (Marxist-Leninist) (CPI-ML), 117
Communities of Resistance: Writings on Black Struggles for Socialism (Sivanandan), 47, 50, 53, 54, 55, 61
comparative frame, 3–6, 11, 17, 107, 171; feminist, 80; tradition and, 14
comparative literature, 4, 24, 160–63, 176n8
Conversations in Bloomsbury (Anand), 27–28
Coolie (Anand), 1–4, 14, 23–24, 27–46; authorial figure in, 38–39, 40; boardroom discussion scene, 38, 42–43; center of book, 38–40; child kidnapping theme, 2, 34, 36, 38–40, 41; class and caste in, 35–36; classifications of, 30; consensus-breaking episodes, 28–29; as corrective to *Kim*, 24, 27, 32, 37, 43; failed strike episode, 2, 34, 36, 41; failings, 34–36; fatalism, attributed to Indian working class, 2, 24, 35, 37; interruptions in, 29, 40–41; Jimmie Thomas character, 3, 175n5; as literary representation of the subaltern, 30; Munoo overhears Congress, 38–39; plot, 24; rhetorical conduct of, 30; short time scene, 41–42; silences in, 38, 40–41, 45, 46; trade union plot elements, 34–35. *See also* Anand, Mulk Raj
coolie, as term, 175n6, 185n42
Coolie: The Story of Labor and Capital in India (Lall), 28, 43–46
Coomaraswamy, Radhika, 65
cooperative labor, 127, 145–46, 200n46

cosmopolitanism, 14–16, 59, 126–27, 151, 163, 178–79n23
The Country and the City (Williams), 47, 52, 98, 176n8
Cowasjee, Saros, 32–33, 181nn13, 15
crisis management efforts, 2, 42, 93, 119, 173n2
Critique of Postcolonial Reason: Toward a History of the Vanishing Present (Spivak), 79, 112, 174–75n4, 199n27
"Critique of the Gotha Program" (Marx), 17
cultural dominant/dominance, 10, 29
cultural politics, 23, 186n11; antinationalist, 34; of class struggle, 25, 54, 105–6; of literature, 105–6, 109; of working-class studies, 78–79
cultural relativism, 34, 107
cultural studies, 167–68, 185n1

Dabindu Collective, 6, 25, 77, 81–82, 84–85, 87–95, 101, 121; anonymous epistolary novel (Hasuna), 94; collective subject, 85, 99, 191n20; early goals, 88–89; heterogeneity of narrative forms, 90–91, 93–95; JVP uprising, 88, 91; as NGO, 86, 88, 191n22; proscribed as antigovernment, 88; serialized form, 100; studies of, 89–90; *writings:* "Apatada nidahasak natha" (For us, there is no freedom), 89; "Chintanaya nidahas nam" (Thinking freedom) (Vitana), 91–93; "From zone to plantation" ("Kalapayen vathukarayata"), 94–95; "Mai Dinaya"/May Day (Menike), 92–93; "Vagrant wishes/Padada pathum" (Perera), 90–91. *See also* Sri Lanka
Damrosch, David, 179n26
Davies, Tony, 93
de Man, Paul, 60–61

deauthorization, 7–8, 59
"Dehistoricizing History" (Scott), 65
denationalization, 5, 15
Denning, Michael, 16, 78
destinerrance, 121, 124
development: food politics, 22–23, 157; unequal, 14, 16
developmentalist, as character, 144, 148, 152
developmentalist logic, 19, 22–23, 76, 88, 173n2, 182n19, 191n22, 193n40; Devi's works and, 110–11, 113, 120; Head's work and, 138–39, 142–44, 152–54, 156–58, 170; historicization of, 199n29
Devi, Mahasweta, 6, 22–23, 25, 75, 77, 100–121; historical materialism in, 100, 102–3, 106, 111–12, 114–15; journalistic writing, 115–16; leftism critiqued, 102–3, 107, 116–18; repeated interruptions in, 100–101, 105, 116, 121; Spivak and, 101, 104, 108–14, 110, 117, 120, 121; structure in works of, 105; thesis on the philosophy of history, 115–16; unfinished texts, 101; voice-consciousness in, 108, 116; *Works: Agnigarbha*, 117; "Douloti the Bountiful," 117; *Dust on the Road*, 105, 115–16; "The Fairy Tale of Mohanpur," 25, 103, 116–20; *Imaginary Maps*, 111; *Mother of 1084*, 117; "Pterodactyl, Puran Sahay, and Pirtha," 101, 104–5
dialectic, 186n9; of the everyday, 54, 106, 139; as felt sensibility, 60, 62, 67, 68–69; of race and class, 48–49, 58–62; as revolutionary, 100
dialectical revisionism, 56, 62, 106
diaspora, 123–24, 127; practice of, 123, 177n12, 195n2; question of, 60, 61, 62, 63
diaspora studies, 185n1

"Diasporas Old and New" (Spivak), 127
didactic intrusions, 2
difference without hierarchy, 109, 110
A Different Hunger (Sivanandan), 73
distance and proximity, 30, 70, 129, 168–70
dominant ideology/narratives, 4, 7, 10, 13, 18, 20, 33–34, 175n8; of Sri Lanka, 61, 91
double consciousness, 60, 125, 129, 187n12, 196n6
Drum, 123, 125
Du Bois, W. E. B., 125, 186n11, 187n12, 196n6
Dust on the Road (Devi), 105, 115–16

Eagleton, Terry, 6, 85, 190–91n19
East Bengal (Bangladesh), 101
economic historiography, 31–32
Edwards, Brent, 177n12, 186n11, 195n2
Eilersen, Gillian, 157
Eliot, T. S., 28, 43
Elizabeth (*A Question of Power*), 128–37
embourgeoisement, 71
Empire (Hardt and Negri), 11–12, 15, 23, 96, 110, 127, 174n3, 185n1, 194n43, 197–98n18, 201n4
Empson, William, 11
Engels, Friedrich, 17, 18
Enloe, Cynthia, 120
epochal analysis, 13–14
equality, 109–10
erasure, 124, 188
Escobar, Arturo, 199n29
essentialism, feminist, 81
ethical singularity, 21–22, 75, 111–13; secret encounter, 111–12, 121, 188–89n1
ethical universal, 52
ethico-political agendas, 6, 19–21, 26, 75, 77, 194n43; in *Dabindu* works, 121; in Devi's work, 99, 113, 121; in Head's work, 132, 139; in Olsen's work, 99, 121; oversimplification as strategy, 99
ethics, 3–4; of historical materialism, 10–11, 14, 25, 76, 171; as intuitions, 20; love and, 22–23, 110–11, 113; responsibility-based, 20, 110–11, 118–19; return of as regression, 19; socialist, 5, 48–49, 108–11; supplementation and, 22, 113; task-oriented ethical work, 20, 21–22, 105, 113; of universality, 131, 136–37, 145–46, 170; working-class writing and, 9, 12, 19–23
Ethnicity and Social Change (Social Scientists Association), 65, 66
Eurocentrism, 120
everyday, 4, 5, 19, 71, 93, 148; back-and-forth movements of, 62, 70, 93; dialectic as, 54, 106, 139; ethical singularity and, 111–13
exile, concept of, 55, 60–61, 60–62, 70, 141
exiles, literary, 26, 64–65, 126, 151
extraverted economies, 79

Facets of Ethnicity, 65
"The Fairy Tale of Mohanpur" (Devi), 25, 103, 116–20; "unreliable" narrator, 117–18
Fanon, Frantz, 131, 197n15
fatalism, attributed to Indian working class, 2, 24, 35, 37
feminism: 1930s overlooked, 80; 1970s U.S., 86; NGOization of, 190n1, 191n22; practices of ethical responsibility, 118–19; recovery of lost subject, 81
feminist critiques, 20, 49; of individualism, 5, 99, 101; rethinking of working-class literature, 82–87
feminist proletarian texts, 25

feminist working-class studies, 99
feminization of labor, 84–85, 90, 155, 194n43
figures, 9, 10
focalization, 118, 119–20, 184n40
FOIL (Forum of Indian Leftists), 35, 183n26
Foley, Barbara, 189n11
food politics, 22, 45–46; famine in India, 45–46; sustainable farming, 122, 123, 144–45; wheat economy, 1–2, 31–32, 45–46
"Forgotten Mornings" (Thomas), 54
form: collaborative, 11–12, 16, 89, 93–95; as effect of reading, 36; ideology and, 56, 57–58; sociologies of, 5, 82, 138, 144; working-class literature as literary, 9–10; working-class literature as serial interrupted, 7–14, 16, 100, 124. See also interrupted form
Forster, E. M., 39, 184n36
Foucault, Michel, 40, 110–11, 158, 200n45
Free Trade Zones (FTZ) (Sri Lanka), 86, 87–88; exempt from laws and regulations, 88
freeborn Englishman figure, 11, 78–79
free-trade-zone workers, 25
Freud, Sigmund, 138
"From zone to plantation" ("Kalapayen vathukarayata"), 94–95
future anterior, 110, 121, 138, 170–71

Gagiano, Annie, 154, 155
garment, as term, 91, 193n32
GCEC (Greater Colombo Economic Commission), 87
gender, 25, 77, 118–20; collective subject and, 118–19; ethical responsibility and, 112, 118–19; globalization and, 77–82; responsibility-based ethics, 111–13, 118–19

gendered: binary oppositions in working-class literature, 80–81
genres, 77, 79–82; correspondence poetry, 97; literary radicalism, 116–17; mixed-genre texts, 26; period-genre category, 8; South African protest literature, 139–40; testimonial, 93; transnational, 4–5; working-class literature as canonical genre, 16, 20–21, 82–83, 175–76n8
Ghostwriting (Spivak), 128
The Gift of a Cow (Premchand), 161
Gilbert (*When Rain Clouds Gather*), 152–54
global, the, 8, 14
The Global Impact of the Great Depression (Rothermund), 31–32, 44
globalization, 1–3, 107; abstraction and, 128; defined, 167, 173–74n2; feminist negotiations within, 86, 99; feminization of labor, 84–85, 90, 155, 164–65, 194n43; gender issues, 77–82, 86; imagery of, 174n2; as international division of labor, 3, 6; metropolitan immigrants, 124, 125–26; as structure of feeling, 170; as term, 181n12
Gobindo ("The Fairy Tale of Mohanpur"), 116, 118–20
Gourgouris, Stathis, 201–2n6
Gramsci, Antonio, 6, 101, 102
grand narratives, 10, 23, 75
Great Depression, 31
Guha, Ranajit, 37
Gunasinghe, Newton, 65

Hall, Stuart, 50, 73
Hans, 162
Hardt, Michael, 11–12, 15, 23, 110, 127, 174n3, 185n1, 194n43, 201n4
Harvey, David, 178–79n23
hauntopology, 135, 198n19

Head, Bessie, 3–4, 6, 22–23, 26, 34, 122–63; agricultural reform model, 127; background, 122–23; biographical lensing of, 124–25, 196n4; critique of identity politics in, 26, 129–30, 134, 145, 147, 149, 158, 161–62; deauthorizing moments in, 7–8; ethics of universality, 131, 136–37, 145–46, 170; ironic moments in, 7–8; irrelevance, concept of, 140, 149, 158; letters, 123; as organic intellectual, 126; philosophy of socialist ethics, 125; as political philosopher, 126–27; selective memory, 160–61; as stateless person, 123, 125–26; Works: "A Note on Rain Clouds," 152; *The Collector of Treasures*, 160; *Living on an Horizon*, 124; "A Poem to Serowe," 160; *Serowe, Village of the Rain Wind*, 122, 126, 158–61; "Sorrow Food," 149; *Tales of Tenderness and Power*, 150; "Village People," 151; *When Rain Clouds Gather*, 151–57; *A Woman Alone*, 123, 132. See also *A Question of Power* (Head)

Hegelian totality, 7

Hewamanne, Sandya, 90

Heyzer, Noeleen, 127

historical materialism: autocritical ethics of, 25, 114–15; in Devi's works, 100, 102–3, 106, 111–12, 114–15; ethics absent from, 19; ethics of, 10–11, 14, 25, 76, 112, 171; love as common name for an ethics of, 23

historicism: critique of, 54, 57, 60, 64–65, 75, 116, 120; feminist views, 120; humanism and, 9, 76, 103–4, 127; as ideology of history, 18, 103; Marxism is not a historicism, 10, 18, 76, 102–3, 114; value-form, 108

historicist histories, 54, 57, 61

history: dehistoricizing, 62–66; dialectical revisionist, 56, 62, 106; nationalist, 25, 38, 52, 57, 61, 64, 79, 87, 182n23; revisionist, 54–55, 64, 70–71, 103–4, 106, 160, 197–98n18

Hitchcock, Peter, 5, 176n10

Hochschild, Arlie, 168

Hoggart, Richard, 167

Hopkins, Gerard Manley, 72

humanism, 20, 53, 64; critique of, 137, 140; historicism and, 9, 76, 103–4, 127; of Marx, 114, 127, 134, 150, 197n17; universality and, 26, 127, 136, 141, 144–45

hybridity, 125, 140

"I Stand Here Ironing" (Olsen), 7, 84, 93

"I Want You Women Up North to Know" (Olsen), 79, 95–99

Ibarro, Felipe, 97, 98

ideal constructions, 78–79

identity, collective, 33

identity politics, 3, 8; critique of, 26, 147–48, 149–50; critique of in Devi's work, 25; critique of in Head's work, 26, 129–30, 134, 145, 147, 149, 158, 161–62; critique of in Olsen's work, 98–99; distance and proximity, 129; irrelevance and, 149

ideological blind spots, 19, 101, 125, 154, 176n8, 181nn8, 12, 186n11; Anand's work and, 24, 28–29, 32–33, 49; in Marxism, 101, 125; in modernism, 30; Sivanandan's work and, 64–65

ideologies: comparative, 5; form and, 56, 57–58

Imaginary Maps (Devi), 111

immaterial labor, 127–28

immigration: metropolitan migration, 124–26; political vs. economic, 59–60. *See also* stateless workers/refugees

immigration studies, 47–48
imperialist-as-boy, 29
improvisatory practices, 5, 12–13
In Other Worlds (Spivak), 1
indentured labor, 28, 32, 57, 66, 190n17
India: 1930s resistance, 44–45; famine, 45–46; left tradition, 103; postcolonial state, 104–5. *See also* West Bengal
Indian Congress Party, 39
individualism, 108–10; feminist critique of, 5, 99, 101
industrial novel, 175–76n8
industrial revolution, 8, 49, 79
information age, 197–98n18
Institute of Race Relations (IRR), 73
intangible forms, 130–32
interiority, 26, 129–31, 136–37, 142–45, 154–55, 170; self-shaped, 150–51
international, as unstable category, 16–17
International Bank of Reconstruction and Development (IBRD), 173n2
international credit system, 31, 87, 173n2
international cultural imaginary, 117
international division of labor, 3, 6, 49, 189n8; feminization of, 84–85, 90, 120–21, 155, 164–65, 194n43; intellectuals and, 164–65; outsourcing, 165–66; racialization of, 52; women's texts, 77. *See also* labor
International Monetary Fund, 87–88, 173n2
International Women's Day, 89
International Workingmen's Association, 79
internationalism, 3; 1930s, 29; antinationalism and, 15; literary, 4–5, 14–15, 24, 80, 97, 132, 162, 198n20; as masculine province, 79; as normative, 14–15; partial form, 7; planetary, 113, 146, 151; proletarian, 11–12, 96;

proletarian writing as practice of, 29; reading, 58–62; schizophrenia and, 130, 137, 143–44, 170; self-interest, 96, 97; as structure of feeling, 58, 60; as transference, 58
interrupted form, 3, 4, 6, 18; in Devi's works, 100–101, 105, 116, 121; in *A Question of Power*, 26; working-class literature as, 7–14, 16, 100, 124. *See also* form
interruptions, 7, 25, 100–101, 124; structural and structuring aspects of class, 10, 16, 33, 116, 166, 198n18; time and, 105–6
irony, 7–8, 116, 120, 184n35
Ismail, Qadri, 66, 71

Jameson, Fredric, 19, 72, 106, 138, 194n42
Janatha Vimukthi Peramuna (JVP), 88, 91, 186n9, 187n18, 192n25
Jayawardena, Kumari, 65
journalism, 104, 107, 112

Katrak, Ketu, 154, 155
Keenan, Thomas, 130
Keywords (Williams), 19
Kim (Kipling): *Coolie* as corrective to, 24, 27, 32, 37, 43; "Great Game," 24, 29
Kipling, Rudyard, 24, 27–28, 43, 153–54
Klaus, Gustav, 34, 35, 176n8, 182n23
Knight, Stephen, 176n8
Kristeva, Julia, 120

labor: cartographies of, 5, 6, 24, 26, 63, 66, 95, 98; feminization of, 84–85, 90, 155, 194n43; immaterial, 127–28; indentured, 28, 32, 57, 66, 190n17. *See also* abstract labor; child laborers; international division of labor; socialized labor

Labor and Desire (Rabinowitz), 80–81
labor power, 126, 134, 160–61; as abstraction, 145, 170; commodification of, 146–47; part-subject of, 40, 114, 131, 138–39, 141–42, 144, 146–47, 162, 175n6, 185n42; race and, 146–47; of women, 159; work as, 134. *See also* power
labor theory of value, 128
Lall, Diwan Chaman, 28, 43–46
Lefebvre, Henri, 140
left cultural imperialism, 52
Left Review, 162
left-wing party politics, 6, 25, 49, 57, 77; in Devi's works, 102–3, 107, 116–18; Head repudiates, 122
Liberation Tigers of Tamil Eelam (LTTE), 53, 54
linguistic turn, 55–56
literariness, 9, 36, 76
literary criticism, Marxist, 55–56
literary internationalism, 4–5, 14–15, 24, 80, 97, 132, 162, 198n20
literary radicalism, 116–17, 175n8; as genre, 117; traditions of, 6–7; in West Bengal, 116–17; *Yonnondio* as, 81, 99
literary rewriting, 53–55
literature: as antihistoricist, 76; comparative, 4, 24, 160–63, 176n8; denationalized, 5, 15; depoliticization of, 5; Marxism of, 68–69; ruling definitions, 6, 85, 190n19; as supplement, 28, 36, 42, 46, 50, 66, 84; turn to by socialist writers, 49; working-class writing interrogates ruling definitions of, 6; writing race and class and, 52–55. *See also* working-class literature
The Literature of Labor (Klaus), 34
Livingston, Julie, 200n46
Lodge, David, 164–65, 203n12

loss, 112, 188n22
love, 135–36, 138, 141, 145, 150, 155; ethics and, 22–23, 110–11, 113

"Mai Dinaya"/May Day (Menike), 92–93
Makhaya (*When Rain Clouds Gather*), 151–57
The Making of the Indian Working Class (Bahl), 37
Maria (*When Rain Clouds Gather*), 154–55
Marx, Karl, 1; abstraction, view of, 132–34; class, rethinking of, 17–18; concept metaphors, 130; on development, 27; ethics of, 18, 19; future anterior, 110, 121, 138, 170–71; humanist vs. antihumanist, 114, 127, 134, 150, 166, 197n17; on proletarian revolutions, 100, 124; rational social, concept of, 23, 133–34, 137, 167; on self-criticism, 8–9, 100, 101; spectral social, concept of, 127, 130, 133, 134; as theorist of literary internationalism, 14–15; totality, view of, 76; world literature, view of, 14–17; *Works*: "Articles on India and China," 18–19; *Capital*, 1, 17–18, 27, 100, 108, 121, 133; *The Communist Manifesto*, 15–17, 69; "Critique of the Gotha Program," 17; *Early Writings:* 150; "Eighteenth Brumaire," 110
Marxism, 4; abstraction in, 132–33; ethics absent from, 112, 114; Eurocentric, 18, 48–49, 134; ideological blind spots, 101, 125; Indian, 79, 117; literary criticism, 55–56; of literature, 68–69; not a historicism, 10, 18, 76, 102–3, 114; in *A Question of Power*, 127, 130, 144–45; Sri Lankan, 65; women as agents of, 79
Marxism and Literature (Williams), 10, 13, 76, 78

Marxism and the Philosophy of Language (Volosinov), 83
Mayo, Katherine, 38–39, 184n35
McClure, John, 198n20
Meena (*When Memory Dies*), 53, 57, 62–63
Melas, Natalie, 179n25
memory: reading and, 69–70
Menike, K. G. Jayasundera, 93
Menike, S. Udyalata, 92–93
metropolitan migration, 124–26
modernism, 5, 29–30, 52, 81, 177n12, 181n8
modernist studies, 24, 29, 177n12
moral capital, 167
Morretti, Franco, 202–3n12
multitude, 11–12, 137, 194n43
Munoo (*Coolie*), 1–2, 24, 35, 38–39, 45
"Myths Without Conscience: Tamil and Sinhalese Nationalist Writings of the 1980s" (Coomaraswamy), 65

Nadesan, Sithaperam, 61–62, 63, 66
narrative: structuralist analysis, 37
national proletariat, 11–12
national working class, 3
nationalist history/historiography, 25, 38, 52, 57, 61, 63, 66, 79, 87, 121, 182n23
nature, 146, 150–51, 155
Naxalbari (village), 8, 117
Naxalism, 117
Naxalite revolt, 77, 116–17, 119
Ndebele, Njabulo, 139–40, 148
Negri, Antonio, 11–12, 15, 23, 96, 110, 127, 174n3, 185n1, 194n43, 197–98n18, 201n4
Nekola, Charlotte, 97–98
Nelson, Cary, 30
neocolonial countries, 79
Nesiah, Vasuki, 73

New African, 123, 124
New Statesman, 123
New World Order, 161
NGO culture, 103, 105
Nice Work (Lodge), 164–65, 203n12
Nixon, Rob, 126, 146, 160, 196n3
Nkosi, Lewis, 125
Non-Aligned Movement (NAM), 173n2
nongovernmental organizations (NGOs), 23, 25, 26, 81, 86, 88, 103, 105
North–South divide, 97, 98

O'Brien, Anthony, 126–27, 146, 155, 156, 157
Occupy movements, 30, 166
official discourse: constructedness of, 37–38
Olsen, Tillie, 6, 7, 14, 75, 77, 81–82, 100–101, 121, 157; deliberate incompleteness in, 20–21; representational strategy, 83–84; socialist ethics, 98–99; voice-consciousness of characters, 83, 98; *Works:* "I Stand Here Ironing," 7, 84, 93; "I Want You Women Up North to Know," 79, 95–99; "Tell Me a Riddle," 84. *See also Yonnondio: From the Thirties* (Olsen)
"On the Universality of Madness" (Rose), 144–45
Ong, Aihwa, 167
organic intellectual, 55, 57, 61, 81
origin myths, 66, 67
Outsourced Self (Hochschild), 168
outsourcing, 165–66, 168, 170

PAC (Pan-Africanist Congress), 122
parabasis, 11, 116, 142, 156
parataxis, 105, 107, 142, 175n2
Partisan Review, 99
Paulina (*When Rain Clouds Gather*), 155
Perera, Suvendrini, 187n13

periphery, 3, 10, 24, 51–52, 165–66; in Anand's writing, 31–32, 39–40, 43–44
philosophy of history, 115–16
planetary internationalism, 113, 146, 151
The Political Unconscious (Jameson), 138
Politics of Modernism (Williams), 125
Portrait of a Textile Worker (Agnew), 169–70, 203n12
postcolonial scholarship: critique, 115–16, 179n25
postcolonial state, 104–5
postcolonial studies, 18–19, 24, 29, 47–48, 50, 114; neutralizing impulse of, 71
postindividualist form, 20
postindustrial age, 11–12, 79, 169, 176n8
poststructuralist theory, 37–38, 55–56, 64, 101, 110, 138, 140, 159
poverty, 114–15, 156–57, 161, 194n43
power: abstraction and, 131–32, 155; alternative systems, 37; tenderness as antonym of, 156–57. *See also* labor power
power relations, 3–4
"precapitalist" space, 109
Premchand, Munshi, 161, 163
Present History of West Bengal (Chatterjee), 117
progress, ideology of, 9, 51, 103–4, 109, 111
Progressive Writers Association, 33–34
proletarian: abstract meaning, 100; as male, 25
proletarian writing. *see* working-class literature
proletarianization, partial, 18
proletariat: historical task, 100; national, 11–12
"The Prose of Counter Insurgency" (Guha), 37
protest, transnational, 203n15

provincialization, 14–15, 50, 55, 65
psychoanalysis, 26, 131, 136, 144
"Pterodactyl, Puran Sahay, and Pirtha" (Devi), 22–23, 25, 101, 104–15; progress, ideology of, 104–5; rodent and rhododendron meditation, 107–10; value, question of, 108–10
Punjab, 31
Puran Sahay ("Pterodactyl, Puran Shay, and Pirha"), 104–11, 113–15

A Question of Power (Head), 3–4, 6, 22–23, 25, 122–51, 156; belonging, concept of, 140, 141, 151, 163; blurring of boundaries in, 130, 135, 137, 158; Botswana setting, 148–49; "breakdown," signification of, 129–31, 136, 143–44; center of novel, 129; closing scene, 160–63; dialectical approach, 127; dialectical dyads in, 127, 138; form of, 6; future anterior in, 110, 121, 138, 170–71; ghost story in, 127, 128–30; horizon, trope of, 129; interiority and exteriority in, 26, 129–31, 136–37, 142–45, 150–51, 154–55, 170; Marxist concerns in, 127, 130, 144–45; othering of self, 142, 152, 156, 158; paradoxical notions of universality and humanism, 127, 136, 141, 144; plot summary, 142–44; race, class, and intangible forms in, 128–37; self-estrangement in, 130, 134–35, 137–41, 143, 162, 170; as surrealist-realist, 3, 26, 129, 133, 140, 144, 146; text as split subject, 128–29; textual figure of Bessie Head, 146; voice-consciousness in, 141–42, 162

Rabinowitz, Paula, 80–81
race: abstraction and, 131–32; changing terms of international division of labor, 131–32; labor power and,

race (continued)
146–47; racialization, 51, 52; racism as structural, 52, 100; subject of colonialism, 145–46
Race and Class, 24, 53
Rajan (*When Memory Dies*), 57, 59
rational social, 23, 133–34, 137, 159, 167
reading, 11, 14, 178n18; allegories of, 34, 60–61; back-and-forth movement, 62, 70; distant, 202–3n12; form as effect of, 36, 41; mode of, 68; narratological meaning, 67, 73; proletarian writing, 34–43; reading internationalism, 58–62; reading-as-translation, 69–70
Reading Capital (Althusser), 76–77, 103–4
realism, 5, 9, 16, 52, 56, 176n10; gender and, 80–81, 83, 90, 93, 96, 115–16
recognition, as assimilation, 94
recovery projects, 24
The Rediscovery of the Ordinary (Ndebele), 139–40
Refashioning Futures (Scott), 64
referential reading-moment, 60–61
Rege, Josna, 182n23
relationships: "love" and ethics, 22–23, 110–11, 113; unlikely friendships, 26, 145–46
repetition, 102, 104–5, 113
representation, 10, 169, 170; effacement and, 40, 61; figural, 137; literary, 130–33, 139; of subaltern, 30, 40, 181n8; systems of, 38
representational strategy, 83, 115–16
resistance: in 1930s India, 44–45; coded as disorganization, 37; commodification of, 99; to development, 111; feminist models, 80; to formalization, 7
resistant collectivities, 109
responsibility, 109, 111–12
responsibility-based ethics, 20, 111–13, 118–19, 145

Rethinking Working-Class History: Bengal, 1890–1940 (Chakrabarty), 37, 43, 79, 109, 167, 202n9
revisionist history, 54–55, 64, 70–71, 103–4, 106, 160, 197–98n18; dialectical, 56, 62, 106
revolution, 2–3, 8, 71
revolutionary conjuncture, 79–80, 93, 112, 121
rhetorical questions, 39–40, 41
Riemenschneider, D., 182n23
Rooney, Ellen, 36, 178n18
Rosa, Kumudhini, 86
Rose, Jacqueline, 136–37, 141, 144–45, 149, 154–55
Rothermund, Dietmar, 31–32, 44, 181n12
rumor, 2, 34, 37, 41
rural transnationalism, 126, 146, 157
rural-centered approach, 31–32, 125–27

Sahadevan (*When Memory Dies*), 57
Salih, Tayeb, 126
Samuel, Kumudini, 86
Sanders, Mark, 140–41
Sanji (*When Memory Dies*), 57, 59, 66
Sassen, Saskia, 181n12
schizophrenia, internationalism and, 130, 137, 143–44, 170
Scott, David, 64, 65–66, 186n7
Season of Migration to the North (Salih), 126
self, othering of, 142, 152, 156, 158–59
self-constitution as literature, 72
self-estrangement, 130, 134–35, 137–41, 143, 162, 170
self-interest, 20, 34–35, 48, 99; as collective interest, 12; internationalism and, 96, 97; love beyond reason and, 23; national worker vs. foreign worker, 48
Sen, Amartya, 46

serial interrupted form, 7–14, 16, 100, 124
Serowe (Botswana), 122–23
Serowe, Village of the Rain Wind (Head), 122, 126, 158–61
silences, 38, 40–41, 45, 46
Simeon, Dilip, 183n29
singularity. *see* ethical singularity
Sinhala Commission, 66, 84, 95, 190n17
Sirima-Shastri Pact (1964), 63–64
Sivanandan, Ambalavaner, 6, 23–25, 47–74; doubling in works of, 25, 48, 50, 55, 59–60, 67, 70; interview, 1990s, 50–51; as librarian, 73–74; move to England, 50–51; political journalism, 25, 49–50, 52–53; schools of readership, 50; structural connection between exploitation in Britain and Sri Lanka, 51–52; turn to literature, 49–50, 53–54, 67–73; Works: "Casualties of Imperialism," 51–52; *Communities of Resistance*, 47, 50, 53, 54, 55, 61; *A Different Hunger*, 73; "The Man Who Loved the Dialectic," 54; "Marxism and Literature," 53; "Sri Lanka: A Case Study," 52–53, 54, 66, 67–68. See also *When Memory Dies*
sloganeering politics, 58, 60, 76–77, 95, 102, 118, 123, 131, 139–40, 147–49, 153
So Many Freedoms (Cowasjee), 32–33
Sobukwe, Robert, 149
social, the: as all that is present and moving, 83, 168, 189n2; formal relationship with, 36; global incommensurable with, 8, 14; Marx's view, 6, 17, 134; as term, 166–67; two senses of, 134–35; in *When Memory Dies*, 58–59
social media, 166
Social Scientists Association, 65
socialism: black, 48; nonrevolutionary, 92–93; as path to liberation, 53, 67, 68; as process of liberation, 53
socialist ethics, 5, 48–49; individualism critiqued, 108–9; Spivak's view, 110–11
socialized labor, 126–27; abstraction and, 133–34, 147–48; cooperative, 127; as spectralized labor, 127, 130, 133, 134; universality and, 144–45
sociologies of form, 5, 82, 138, 144
Sohn-Rethel, Alfred, 137
Sole, Kelwyn, 140
South, the, 98
South Africa, 34, 122; apartheid, 22, 26, 34, 139–41, 153, 171; protest literature, 139–40, 148; *ubuntu*, 140–41
space management, 32
speech interferences, 2, 9, 21; in Devi's works, 105, 120; in Head's work, 131, 159; in Olsen's work, 82–83, 86
Spirits of Resistance and Capitalist Discipline (Ong), 167
Spivak, Gayatri Chakravorty, 36, 75, 101, 104, 134, 157, 161; on cultural studies, 185n1; Devi and, 101, 104, 108–14, 110, 117, 120, 121; as Devi's translator, 110, 111, 114; ethical singularity, 21–22, 75, 188–89n1; Marx, reading of, 110–11, 134, 146–47; pharmakonic, concept of, 108; on political movements, 21–22, 112; on working-class canon, 190n12; Works: "Can the Subaltern Speak?", 40, 110, 190n17; *Critique of Postcolonial Reason*, 79, 112, 174–75n4, 199n27; "Diasporas Old and New," 127; *Ghostwriting*, 128; *Other Worlds*, 120
Sri Lanka, 6, 14, 24–25, 47–74; 1958 riots, 51, 52, 58; activist scholarship, 65–66; anticolonial working-class

Sri Lanka (*continued*)
    movements, 65, 88; Black July (July 1983), 52, 70; burning of Jaffna public library, 73–74; crisis imagery, 87; dehistoricizing history, 62–66; fifty years of freedom, 89; Free Trade Zones (FTZ) (Sri Lanka), 86, 87–88; free-trade-zone workers, 84–86, 87–88; independence from Britain, 63, 94; Indian immigrant labor in, 61–62; leftist political culture ignored, 51; multinational corporations, 90–91; postcolonial theory, 64; provincializing, 50–52; stateless workers, 48. *See also* Dabindu collective
"Sri Lanka: A Case Study" (Sivanandan), 52–53, 54, 66, 67–68
Star Garments (Sri Lanka), 93
stateless workers/refugees, 142; as antisubjects, 60; forced migration, 61–62, 63, 66; Head as, 123; immigrant and national, 48; Indian-origin Tamil laborers, 59, 61–64, 94, 187n18; noncitizens, 64, 66, 73, 94, 190n17; repatriation to India, 57, 63–64; Sri Lanka benefits by, 61–62; writers, 3, 123, 125–26. *See also* immigration
Stri nirmana (Women's writing), 89
strikes, India, 2–3; in *Coolie*, 34–35; TISCO (Tata Iron and Steel Company), 36–37
"structures of feeling," 3, 11, 12, 22, 58, 167–70
subaltern: literary representation of, 30, 40; post-Independence, 59; romanticizing of, 106, 117, 118, 121; rumor and discourse, 41; women workers, 25
subaltern studies, 24, 37–38, 106
Subaltern Studies collective, 37

subject: bourgeois, 138; decentered, 8, 82, 135, 138–40, 152; feminist, 77; individual as, 60, 90; multinational corporation as, 90–91; nonsubject, 59, 80–81; part-subject, 40, 114, 131, 138–39, 141–42, 144, 146–47, 162, 175n6, 185n42; race and, 145–46; rational, 80–81; rejection of individual as, 80–81; text as split, 85, 128–29; theorized by Sivanandan, 48
subject, collective, 21, 25, 99, 109, 115, 138, 158; Dabindu collective, 85, 191n20; gendered, 118–19; social media and, 166
subjectivity: nonindividual, 81–82, 86; of system, 114–15
supplementation, 13, 20–22, 99, 101, 104, 185n45; ethics and, 22, 113; literature as, 28, 36, 42, 46, 50, 66, 84; to Marx, 101, 104, 113–14; in *When Memory Dies*, 66, 76; in *Yonnondio*, 84
surplus value, 28, 133–34, 147, 165
sustainable farming, 122, 123, 144–45
Swaneng project, 122

Tales of Tenderness and Power (Head), 150
task-oriented ethical work, 20, 21–22, 105, 113
Tasks and Masks (Nkosi), 125
"Tell Me a Riddle" (Olsen), 84
tenderness, 156–57
testimony, 5, 9, 39, 93, 176n10; fiction vs., 39, 43; in Lall's work, 43–44
textual space, 36–37
Third World literature: said to be national allegory, 34
Thomas, Dylan, 54, 72
Thomas, Jimmie (*Coolie*), 3, 42, 175n5
Thompson, E. P., 11, 78, 109
time, 104–6, 113, 121

TISCO (Tata Iron and Steel Company), 36–37
Tom *(A Question of Power)*, 147–48
totality, 76, 186n11
trade unionist socialism, 18, 93, 165; British, 2, 25, 28–29, 52; in *Coolie*, 2, 34, 36, 37–38, 41; in Devi's works, 111, 116, 118
tradition, 13–14
transference, 58, 70
Transition, 123
transnational corporations, 2–3
transnational modernism, 24, 29, 177n12, 181n8
TRC (Truth and Reconciliation Commission), 140–41
Two Leaves and a Bud (Anand), 31, 32
2008 financial crisis, 29–30

ubuntu, 140–41
United National Party (UNP) (Sri Lanka), 88
United Nations, 33, 90
United Nations High Commission for Refugees (UNHCR), 64
universality, 53; ethics of, 131, 136–37, 145–46, 170; in Head's work, 130; humanism and, 26, 127, 136, 141, 144–45; interiority and, 136–37; socialized labor and, 144–45; unlikely friendships, 26, 145–46
Untouchable (Anand), 24, 32, 35, 182nn23, 25
Uses of Literacy (Hoggart), 167
use-values, 10, 130, 132–33

valorization, 110, 134–35
value, 108–11
Van Rensburg, Patrick, 127, 157
Vigne, Randolphe, 151
Vijaya/Vijayan *(When Memory Dies)*, 54, 57, 64–65, 68–70, 72–73

visual metaphors, 118
Viswanathan, Gauri, 182n25
Vitana, Deepika Thrima, 91–92
voice-consciousness: in *Dabindu* works, 95; in Devi's works, 108, 116; in Olsen's works, 83, 98; in *A Question of Power*, 141–42, 162
Volosinov, V. N., 83

Wallerstein, Immanuel, 174n2
West Bengal, 100–101, 104; genre commemorating Naxalite movement, 116–17; literary radicalism in, 116–17
wheat economy, 1–2, 31–32, 45–46
When Memory Dies (Sivanandan), 23–25, 47–74; center, lack of, 57, 61; counters dominant narrative, 61; dehistoricizing history, 62–67; dialectic of race and class, 58–62; didactic intrusions, 67–68; epigraphs, 72; final scene, 67–68; literary rewriting in, 53–55, 56, 66; narrative chronology, 58–59; narrative sequencing, 66–67; narrator as reader, 62; opening scene, 58–60, 62; political writings incorporated into, 53; postcolonial scholarship, 50; prefatory pages, 51; reading internationalism, 58–62; reading scenes in, 68–69, 72; reading-as-translation, 69–70; saga form, 56, 58, 188n27; telling history in, 55–58, 61; three sequential parts, 58
When Rain Clouds Gather (Head), 151–57
Williams, Raymond, 10, 76, 83–84, 125; *The Country and the City* (Williams), 47, 52, 98, 176n8; on formations, not institutions, 13–14, 78; on literature as creative practice, 162; semiotics of the social, 166; "structures of feeling," 3, 11, 12, 22, 58, 167–70; on subjectivity, 82

Women, Men, and the International Division of Labor (Nash and Kelly), 120
women workers: Chicana factory workers, 96–99; free-trade-zone workers, 69, 84; as new proletariat, 79; as subalterns, 25; as subjects for history, 85
women working-class writers: critique of subject, 81–82
"Women's Time" (Kristeva), 120
worker-writers associations, 156, 190n19
Working Women of Southeast Asia (Heyzer), 127
working-class coalitional politics, 112, 165–66, 190n18
working-class culture, 167
working-class literature: absence of common language, 96–97; Anand's considered nationalist writing, 32–34; collaborative form, 11–12, 16, 89, 93–95; comparative frame, 3–6, 11, 17; as counterglobalist movement, 33; critique of colonial counterdiscourse, 30; discursive unity, 5–6; ethics and, 19–23; feminist rethinking of, 82–87; as formation, 13–14; gendered binary oppositions, 80–81; improvisatory practices, 12–13; international alliances, 33–34; literariness of, 76; as literary form, 9–10; literature as supplement, 28, 36, 42, 46, 50, 66, 84; as male, metropolitan, and revolutionary, 9, 79, 80–81; metropolitan migrant as staple of, 125–26; as non-static, 77–78; overlooked, 34, 49, 171; potentiality of, 10–11; proletarian novel, U.S. 1930s, 28, 31–34, 175–76n8; provincialization of, 14; questions of canonicity, 16, 20–21, 82–83, 175–76n8; reading, 34–43; recuperation of, 29–30; rural-based, 125–27; as serial interrupted form, 7–14, 16, 100, 124; as social formation, 4, 29; speech interferences, 21, 83; Sri Lankan traditions, 86–87; as transnational genre, 4–5; as world literature, 6, 14–19. *See also* literature
World Bank, 87, 173n2
world literature, 168, 179n26, 202n12; bourgeoisie and rise of, 15–16; as corollary to economic processes, 15–16; working-class literature vs., 6, 14–19
world republic of letters, 5, 16, 179n26
world-systems theory, 2, 174n2
writing, historical fiction vs. history, 39–40

Yonnondio: From the Thirties (Olsen), 20–21, 25, 189n11; autoreferential passages, 83; epigraph, 85; interruptions in, 75, 95; misconstrued as bildungsroman, 81; plot summary, 190n13; representational strategy, 83–84; speech interference in, 82–83, 86, 105; text as split subject, 85
Young, Robert, 50

Zaheer, Sajjad, 161, 182n17
Žižek, Slavoj, 133, 137

GPSR Authorized Representative: Easy Access System Europe, Mustamäe tee 50, 10621 Tallinn, Estonia, gpsr.requests@easproject.com

www.ingramcontent.com/pod-product-compliance
Lightning Source LLC
Chambersburg PA
CBHW021401290426
44108CB00010B/334